T0148703

# INDIAN ECONOMY'S GREATEST CRISIS

# INDIAN ECONOMY'S GREATEST CRISIS

Impact of the CORONAVIRUS
and the ROAD AHEAD

# ARUN KUMAR

PORTFOLIO
PENGUIN

An imprint of Penguin Random House

# PORTFOLIO

USA | Canada | UK | Ireland | Australia
New Zealand | India | South Africa | China

Portfolio is part of the Penguin Random House group of companies
whose addresses can be found at global.penguinrandomhouse.com

Published by Penguin Random House India Pvt. Ltd
7th Floor, Infinity Tower C, DLF Cyber City,
Gurgaon 122 002, Haryana, India

First published in Portfolio by Penguin Random House India 2020

Copyright © Arun Kumar 2020

All rights reserved

10 9 8 7 6 5 4 3 2

The views and opinions expressed in this book are the author's own and the
facts are as reported by him which have been verified to the extent possible,
and the publishers are not in any way liable for the same.

ISBN 9780670094554

Typeset in Adobe Garamond Pro by Manipal Technologies Limited, Manipal
Printed at Replika Press Pvt. Ltd, India

www.penguin.co.in

*To my nephew Anish, his wife Jean,*
*my niece Anjani, who are all doctors,*
*and to all the doctors who are today front-line warriors*
*in the fight against the pandemic afflicting the world*

# Contents

*Preface*                                                                                      ix

  I.   Introduction
      Corona: An Invisible Enemy Has Caught Us by Our Throats        1

  II.  Nuts and Bolts of the Pandemic: Disease, Health and Lockdown   19

 III.  Modern-Day Economy: Why the Lockdown Hits Hard                   52

 IV.  Lockdown and After: Understanding the Macroeconomic Aspects       74

  V.  The Indian Economy's Performance                               97

 VI.  What Should the Government Do?                                    139

VII.  Conclusion
      Unfair Polity: Its High Cost and Lessons for the Future       178

*Epilogue: Post-Script: Uncertainty Persists*                                                 201
*Acknowledgements*                                                                            211
*Annexures*                                                                                   213
*Tables*                                                                                      241
*Graphs*                                                                                      253
*Bibliography*                                                                                271

# Preface

The COVID-19-induced crisis in India reminds one of the turmoil brought on in November 2016 by demonetization of high-denomination currency notes. The entire society—farmers, workers, businesses, middle class and the rich—faced an unprecedented crisis and, now, once again, there is a repeat of the same turmoil, but with even greater force.

The difference is that India is not alone in facing such a crisis—there is a global calamity brought on by a pandemic of serious proportions. The situation is worse than what was faced during the Second World War, which ended seventy-five years back. Life has turned topsy-turvy since February 2020, when the disease spread its tentacles across the globe. Countries that could bring down the number of cases of infection did relax their strict lockdowns, but experts have been warning nations not to be complacent, since the virus is still around. Partial lockdowns have had to be reimposed in many parts of the world. The worry of a second wave of attack as the winter approaches is turning out to be a reality in much of Europe and the US.

Even though a lot has been learnt about the virus in the past eight months, it does not amount to much and new findings keep emerging every week. Thus, there is huge uncertainty and anxiety. People have been obtaining information on the latest developments via social media and TV channels. The shape of our lives in January and February seems like a distant memory, since everyone is coping with a wholly new situation.

The daily life of citizens has been severely impacted—children not able to go to school and studying from home; people not able to go to work or losing their jobs; people not able to pay their respects to the departed; and families not able to cremate their loved ones. Visits to friends and relatives have become rare. The Olympics have been postponed, and cricket and basketball are being played in empty stadiums. Monkeys outside temples are going hungry because worshippers have stopped visiting. Courts are functioning minimally and justice is being delayed. TV debates are taking place with guests sitting in their homes rather than in the studio. The list of the new normal is long and society is trying to adjust to it.

I realized in the middle of January that the crisis in Wuhan, China, was likely to have a global impact, since it is an important part of the global supply chain. I flagged the issue at a semi-official discussion with some top economists of the country in the third week of January. Since then, in my writings, I have mentioned the likely impact of the spread of the disease.

From late February, it was clear that the disease had spread and was going to affect all countries of the world sooner rather than later. I started asking organizers of meetings to which I was invited to not book my tickets, since the disease was likely to spread across the country. What Gandhi said in his book *Hind Swaraj* about the railways enabling faster travel and hence a quicker spread of a pandemic, holds true with even greater force these days with air travel. Instead of the disease spreading in a few days across a country, it can now spread across continents in just a matter of hours.

I started writing and speaking in panel discussions on TV on the pandemic's economic impact from early March and have been talking about the imperatives to deal with the pandemic and its fallout.

But due to a lack of holistic thinking and possibly apathy, policymakers did not anticipate the nature of the crisis and my suggestions were initially brushed aside as impractical. However, over time, many of my recommendations have been taken up by them. But some key ideas have not been implemented or when executed, carried out in a half-hearted manner, so that they did not have the desired impact.

Manish Kumar from Penguin Random House India first requested me to write a book in April 2020 and I agreed to do so. My motivation in writing this book has been to explain my ideas in a more detailed and holistic manner to help generate an informed public debate. In spite of many friends arguing that the government needlessly panicked and that the lockdown was unnecessary, I have argued in its favour, along with the plea that success of a lockdown requires that the imperatives spelt out in this book are implemented.

Writing a book when the situation is fast changing is challenging, since data keeps changing. However, since the focus of the book is more on the economic aspects, the task was relatively simpler, since the theoretical aspects of what was likely to happen in the economy were clear. For ease of reading, certain complex economic ideas have been explained in simple terms and also briefly repeated across chapters and sections. How readers will react to this remains to be seen—will they be annoyed or be appreciative?

Most of the experts were behind the curve and when the economy had shut down, they were still talking of a marginal decline in the economy's rate of growth. This was a repeat of the mistake they had committed during the global financial crisis of 2007–09. In my interaction with some of them, it became apparent that they were not factoring in the catastrophic impact on the vast unorganized sector in India. This is not new. It was the same during demonetization. Our quarterly GDP data, which is what we usually discuss in public, does not factor in the impact on much of the unorganized sector and, therefore, overstates the growth of the economy.

In fact, a bare perusal of the official document giving the data for growth in the economy during the period of the lockdown makes it clear that little data was available for that period. The document itself mentions that the data is likely to be revised.

India has turned out to be the worst-impacted major economy of the world, with its rate of growth falling the most in the period from April to June. This is a reflection of the severe lockdown and its impact on the large unorganized sector.

It has been clear from the beginning that while all sections will be hit by the lockdown and the pandemic, the unorganized sector of the economy and the marginalized sections will be hit the hardest and that they need to be taken care of. The suddenness with which the lockdown was imposed created an unprecedented crisis, just as the sudden imposition of the misconceived demonetization had done in 2016—only much worse.

The abiding image of this crisis will be the millions of destitute walking down the streets of cities and highways, with children in tow and their belongings on their backs. The veil that had hidden their miserable living conditions for many of the upper-class citizens was lifted. Civil-society organizations and individuals came forward to help, but this was not enough. Perhaps these images and experiences will arouse many citizens out of their comfort zones and make them rethink inequality and environmental destruction. This could be a step towards deeper social change in due course of time. This book, by presenting a holistic view of the situation, attempts to help this process.

I have been arguing that the Indian economy is in a depression due to the lockdown. Only essential production, which is less than 25 per cent of the GDP, is feasible during one. Once the lockdown is relaxed or lifted, recovery will be slow and the depression will continue for some time. This will lead to a resource shortage to tackle the crisis. I have argued since mid-March that what is needed now is a survival package for small businesses, agriculture and workers.

I have argued that the situation is worse than in a war, with both supply and demand collapsing during the lockdown and global trade faltering. It is not the usual business cycle, which can be tackled by fiscal and monetary policies.

It is clear that markets have failed and cannot on their own lift the economy back to its earlier levels. Massive government intervention is called for, but that has not been forthcoming. This has prolonged the economic crisis in India. In contrast, governments of many countries have implemented big relief packages, and that has helped them avoid the severe downturn that India has faced. The Indian government has largely pushed through policy changes that were on its agenda since 2014, which will only deliver over the long term, without helping increase demand in the short run. I have argued that this is like not dousing the fire when the house is burning and, instead, focusing on setting up fire stations for dealing with future fires.

The most important lesson that the pandemic has taught us is that we are a collective and we will sink or swim together. The disease has to be tackled globally, and for all; the disease recognizes no borders or classes—the poorest, the richest and the most powerful are equally vulnerable. For the sake of the collective, people have to exercise caution—wear masks, maintain hygiene and keep physical distance. These are not matters of individual choice.

The importance of science and scientific approach has been underlined; dogmas and superstitions have no place in dealing with this disease. There is also a need for much more research. New viruses have been afflicting humankind every few years and society has to be prepared to deal with them quickly. The greater concern for humans may not be a meteor that may decimate life on this planet but a tiny new virus. Clearly, education has to be strengthened so that people develop a more scientific understanding of life—ignorance is not bliss. Education needs to inculcate critical thinking and develop new socially relevant knowledge.

The old way of thinking will not resolve the problems being faced today. There is a new normal now and the situation, even when the virus has been brought under control, will be quite different from what prevailed in January 2020. So there is a need to rethink our basic premises about how we should run society. We need to focus entirely on the long-term welfare of the collective by eschewing any kind of divisiveness in society or that which creates alienation among the people.

Arun Kumar
20 November 2020
Gurugram, Haryana

# I

# Introduction

## Corona: An Invisible Enemy
## Has Caught Us by Our Throats

The COVID-19 (coronavirus 2019) pandemic, has been a continuing saga since January 2020, when China, after much initial denial, announced it to the world. Except for the continent of Antarctica, it has spread to all countries in the world. The present situation is unprecedented because nothing like this has been experienced by the current generation. Nations have been taken by surprise and people have been left bewildered as they found themselves ill-equipped to deal with this unusual situation.

I remember my mother telling me about the plague epidemic in western Uttar Pradesh in the 1930s, when she was still a child. Half her family perished—father, brother and uncles—and towards the end, it was even difficult to find people to cremate the bodies. The surviving members of the family were reduced to penury—working at other people's homes and getting buttermilk from their landlord to survive. During the current coronavirus pandemic, there have been cases in India where family members have even refused to come forward to claim the bodies of their loved ones. In some countries, the television has aired images of mass graves, some being dug up in the hundreds in advance. Clearly, an epidemic is not just a health emergency but also an economic and social challenge of huge proportions that needs analysis.

## A Virus Little Known

As children, one used to hear one's grandmother say that an ant could be more powerful than an elephant. She would explain that the ant could enter the brain of the elephant via the trunk and kill it. We used to be awestruck. But fast forward to today, the human race has been laid low by a tiny virus—125 nanometres across, which is 15 million times smaller than a human being. It highlights that even as we try to venture to Mars, there are mysteries in nature that we have not even begun to understand.

The behaviour of this virus has been unpredictable, since it has shown different patterns in different countries and at different times. No wonder, then, that there is such uncertainty and fear among people. News of the global rising death toll and hospitalization of people with severe illness due to the virus, along with having well-known people such as Donald Trump and Amit Shah, or those close to us contracting the disease, has led to much despair.

It is the SARS-CoV-2 virus that results in COVID-19. A virus is different from a bacteria and, often, there is no protective medicine against it. Vaccines are developed to enable the body to build immunity against it but this takes time. Given the present crisis and the urgency, more than a hundred groups across the world are trying to develop a safe vaccine against this virus. The Oxford Group, the Wuhan Group, Pfizer and Moderna are the most advanced in their development work on the vaccine. However, developing a vaccine is not a cakewalk.

As we know, no vaccine has been found for HIV in the past thirty-five years, so one needs to be circumspect. Various medicines are being researched and the efficacy of some existing antiviral medicines, such as remdesivir, are being tried out. In India, the antimalarial drug hydroxychloroquine is being given both as a prophylactic to prevent the disease and also as a medicine to cure it, but the World Health Organization (WHO) is not convinced that it helps.

It was initially hoped that heat would kill the virus and stem the spread of the disease, but even in the intense Indian heat, the virus spread fast. Initially, only a few children contracted the disease and it was thought that they had some form of immunity to it, but in New York City, children were found to be increasingly affected. It was also believed that the young would only be mildly impacted due to their stronger immunity, but many have also died, though proportionately less than the elderly. So scientists are still trying to get a handle on the disease and have much to discover about it.

Viral attacks are nothing new. H1N1, Ebola, SARS, MERS, Zika and Nipah viruses have emerged over the past two decades. Fortunately, the SARS-CoV-2 virus does not cause as many deaths as, say, Ebola, so what is so special about it? It is much more virulent than the other viruses and has spread rapidly across the globe. Scientists are still not certain about its origins but the most accepted theory is that it started from a wet market in Wuhan in the Hubei province in China in December 2019. Newer theories suggest that it started in August 2019. Some suggest that it had reached Europe in November or December itself. Quickly, the disease reached all parts of the globe affecting 213 countries and territories. By 20 October 2020, about 40 million people had been infected and about 1 million had died.

The virus is transmitted from one infected person to another. This can occur due to close proximity with an infected person, touching a surface that has been infected or even via the air in close proximity to an infected person. A lot of infected persons are asymptomatic and do not show symptoms of the disease. However, they can and, in many cases, do infect others. When one cannot trace the source of the spread of the disease, it is called 'community transmission', which is difficult to control. There is speculation on whether it can spread via the shoes of nurses working in a hospital's COVID-19 ward. How the disease is spread and what the best way is to protect oneself is still unclear as new hypotheses have emerged from time to time since January 2020.

## *Lockdown to Check the Spread of Disease*

To slow the spread of the virus, since no medicine or vaccine is available, the movement of people has to be stopped so that a physical distance can be maintained among them. That requires a 'lockdown' of the population. It was brutal in many ways but it was successful in stemming the spread of the virus in Wuhan city and the larger Hubei province. China managed to contain it, but by then it had already spread to other countries and they had to try and replicate what China did but with mixed results (Graph 01 gives the picture of the five worst-affected countries), given the differences in the systems of different countries.

A lockdown is not a solution to the problem but it does slow the spread of the disease so that the medical systems can cope with it and prevent them from getting overwhelmed. Further, it gives much-needed time to ramp up medical facilities to try and cater to the rising number of cases. In some countries it did overwhelm the medical facilities, like in Italy and Spain, but in New York City, which saw the biggest outbreak in the world, the lockdown gave the system a chance to cope with the disease.

India went into lockdown suddenly on 25 March 2020. The country went into a state of panic, but it should have been anticipated since there was a partial lockdown from around 15 March. Subsequently, from 14 April, lockdown was relaxed in stages and there has been an official 'unlock' since 1 June (See Annexure 01). But all this took place when cases of infection were rising dramatically and medical systems were breaking down in major metropolitan cities in India.

So, unlike in most advanced countries, India relaxed the lockdown when the spread of the disease had not yet been checked. It needs to be noted that even in countries where the lockdown was relaxed after the disease had been controlled, there had been a resurgence (like in Spain, China, Singapore and South Korea) and there was danger of a second wave of the spread of the disease. So if the disease was going to spread anyway, was the lockdown necessary? The logic of what was done and what needed to be done needs to be understood.

## Impact of the Lockdown

During a lockdown, because few are allowed to move, production largely stops, except for essentials and some services. Most workers lose work and their incomes. Businesses lose revenue, since sales do not take place, and start running into losses. The government's revenue collection plummets while it needs to spend more to support the newly impoverished workers. The situation is worse than a war—and, in this case, far worse than the global financial crisis of 2007–09. This is because supply dries up as production declines and demand evaporates as the incomes of the vast majority of people plummet. Such a twin challenge has never been faced by countries simultaneously and in such a short time. Modern-day economies have never faced such a situation with growth plummeting (Graph 02). Policymakers have found it difficult to deal with the crisis.

A friend called me up on 25 March and asked me about how an economy works during a lockdown. He wondered how production would happen when factories and offices were shut. My short answer was that the economy had largely come to a halt and growth had plummeted (Graph 03). So how would people survive? Especially in India, where a sizeable part of the population are daily-wage earners, whose lives and daily necessities are dependent on their daily toil. They don't have enough savings to buy essentials even for a week.

So during the lockdown, survival became a challenge for them. They quickly fell below the poverty line.

The sections that were slightly better off had savings, which they used to hoard essentials to see them through the period of the lockdown—and this was the case globally. There were pictures of shelves emptied out in supermarkets. But if production had stopped, how were these items being continuously supplied? Would supplies run out soon? If so, there could be a breakdown of society.

The poor in India, who largely migrate from villages to cities for work, live in rather uncivilized conditions, since they are not paid a living wage. They live in crowded conditions, sometimes ten in a room, with people sleeping in shifts. How were they expected to practise physical distancing—a more appropriate term than social distancing—which was so necessary to keep infection at bay? They have common toilets, and that is another potential source of the spread of disease. Clean water is hardly available, so washing hands several times a day is difficult. Since they cannot stock up on essentials, they have to go out looking for food and supplies, and in that they have to come in contact with others.

So the lockdown was very difficult for poor workers. Vast numbers started to migrate to their villages in pitiful conditions, carrying their children and luggage without access to water or food, walking or cycling thousands of kilometres or getting into crowded trucks or trains, which took them home via circuitous routes. They got beaten up by the police, cheated by transporters and extorted by officials. No wonder that in India disaster is called the 'third crop', in which those in power make money. Migrants moved to their villages largely untested, since India lacked the testing capacity needed. This led to the spread of the disease to rural and semi-rural areas too. Because these areas lack medical facilities, there was concern about the disease spreading uncontrollably.

Even in several urban agglomerations, such as Delhi and Mumbai, which have a developed medical system, there was a breakdown of medical infrastructure, with patients running from pillar to post for treatment. The number of deaths and the number of infection cases were not correctly reported in many parts of the country. Above all, due to lack of adequate testing, the full extent of the spread of the disease could not be gauged.

In India, Kerala was the first state to report COVID-19 cases, among those returning from China and West Asia. However, thanks to its well-developed healthcare systems, a literate citizenry and an aware population, it managed to check the spread of the disease quickly. It was considered a global case study in how to tackle the disease in spite of the resurgence starting August due to big crowds gathering on the occasion of the major festival Onam and the political demonstrations that took place. Again, it is a lesson in what the public has to do to keep the disease in check. Namely, there can be no lowering of one's guard—physical distancing has to be maintained, masks have to be used in public places and hands have to be washed regularly.

## Unlocking the Economy Prematurely

Businesses, except those producing essentials, incurred huge losses during the lockdown. Their revenues dried up while they had to continue to incur fixed costs and pay interest charges on borrowing. The government announced a moratorium on interest payments but the interest continued to accrue. So the moratorium only postponed the day of reckoning. Many businesses were already facing problems before the pandemic due to the slowing economy (See graphs 04 and 05), and their troubles only mounted. They wanted to start producing immediately to generate revenue.

Industry associations, such as CII, argued that there was a trade-off between 'life and livelihood'. They stated that without work and income, workers would die anyway. It was said that deaths due to COVID-19 were not so many, but without wages many more would die of hunger. But this argument is flawed because there does not need to be a trade-off. If one protects life today, livelihood is feasible when the pandemic is over. If in the process of reopening businesses, many die, they can never be returned.

Graph 01 shows how the US opened up prematurely, without many parts of the country having tamed the disease. So there was a spurt in cases in early June. Spain and Britain succeeded in taming the disease and then started opening up, and, as the graph shows, their cases went down. Brazil never went for a lockdown and its cases rose alarmingly. India opened up without taming the disease and, in June, as 'Unlock 1', the first phase of opening up, (Annexure 01) was initiated, there was a surge in the number of cases. The lesson is clear—the disease is deadly and there should not be any premature opening up. There is no option but to implement a lockdown properly. But why couldn't India do it? Further, why does anyone have to die of hunger when the country has a huge surplus of foodstock? In April, there was a stock of 75 million tonnes of foodgrain and rabi was a bumper harvest, which resulted in even larger foodstock. There were reports of vegetables and fruits rotting in fields due to lack of demand. All this could have been distributed to the poor and the newly unemployed, and there would not have been hunger in India. So what went wrong?

Work could have been provided to those migrating to villages via the Mahatma Gandhi National Rural Employment Guarantee Scheme (MGNREGS), and a similar scheme could have been started in urban areas. This would have provided incomes to those who had lost their jobs, so they would not starve. Thus, if the government wanted, there could have been both employment and food for the unemployed. This is no doubt a herculean task, but the situation is worse than a war and the government needed to mobilize like in a war by focusing on just this task. Why was this not done?

However, due to pressure from businesses for ending the lockdown, the country eased its lockdown without first controlling the spread of the disease. This premature opening up led to the disease spreading rapidly across the country. In this sense, the lockdown failed in India. But the question arises: What should have been done for the lockdown to be a success in a developing economy such as India, with a lot of poverty?

The government neither anticipated what needed to be done, nor effectively implemented policies. The time afforded by the lockdown to put things in place was not properly utilized. Testing and contact tracing have been vastly inadequate, with India at the bottom of the list of countries for testing per million of the population (Graph 06). India has also lagged behind in ramping up medical facilities and making sure protective equipment, masks and ventilators are readily available.

Opening up requires testing and contact tracing, so those infected can be quickly isolated to prevent the spread of the disease. Without this, businesses and factories will find it difficult to restart with any degree of certainty, thus defeating the purpose of opening up the economy. If the disease spreads rapidly in the winter months, as is usually the case with such viruses, another lockdown may become necessary, and that would be much more painful. Chennai, which had to go through another lockdown period, is a case in point.

There has been a lingering doubt among citizens that the government deliberately did not do what was needed to make the lockdown a success. If workers find work in rural areas, they may not return to factories and offices in the cities, leading to a shortage of workers and making restarting production difficult. No wonder, then, that the additional allocation to MGNREGS was wholly inadequate. But what was not anticipated was that without demand, production would anyway not go back to the pre-pandemic levels and returning workers would not get work— and their crisis would continue.

All this indicates that the leadership has a poor understanding of the situation. This is compounded by very weak governance in the country. There has been so much confusion in policy and even worse, poor implementation. Different states followed different policies, leading to confusion, such as in the case of migrants. One state announced the availability of transport at its borders while the other closed its borders, leading to chaos and tremendous hardship for the migrants. The courts intervened sporadically but the highest court of the land initially refused to act in the matter (PTI, 2020c). Fortunately, from early June, this changed—perhaps due to the moral pressure of seeing the conditions of the poor in the country— and orders were issued. But, by then, millions had already suffered and many had died. What does this indicate about the political economy of the country?

## The Economic Impact

Is there something about the modern-day economy that makes it more prone to disruption during a lockdown? Empty roads, closed markets, a decline in consumption of diesel and electricity by around 30 per cent, a drastic fall in air- and water-pollution levels, all suggest that economic activity had largely come to a halt during the lockdown. This was not only true of India but in a large number of countries, affecting global production and trade (Graph 02). Supplies are needed to continue production but with the cessation of transport and trade, supply chains were disrupted. Raw materials did not reach producers and the final product could not reach consumers.

Supply chains are now global and, once disrupted, may be difficult to restore soon. China, in the last two decades, had become the most important hub in the global manufacturing supply chain and that was disrupted when COVID-19 started to spread. According to the World Trade Organization (WTO, 2020), global trade can fall by 12–30 per cent in 2020–21—that was only the best guess.

Before the pandemic struck, the global economy was challenged, with major economies slowing down, such as China and India, or at a standstill, such as Germany and Japan. The trade war initiated by the United States, its sanctions on Iran and Venezuela, fighting in several countries in West Asia, etc., were destabilizing the world economy.

The Indian economy was laid low by policy-induced shocks of demonetization, the Goods and Services Tax (GST) and digitization.

The banking crisis brought on by large non-performing assets (NPAs) added to the problem. The rate of growth of the Indian economy had officially plummeted to 3.1 per cent in Q4 of 2019–20 from 8.1 per cent eight quarters back in Q4 of 2017–18 (See Table 01 and Graph 05). Actually, this is an overestimate, since it does not take into account the unorganized sectors of the economy, which have been declining. If they are included separately in the calculations, it will be seen that the economy was already in recession (Kumar, 2019c).

Thus, any recovery from the pandemic-induced crisis also has to contend with the pre-existing problems in the Indian economy. There was a demand shortage due to the extreme inequality in the economy and the impact of the shocks mentioned above on the unorganized sectors (Kumar, 2018 and 2019a). Now the pandemic has hit this same unorganized sector hard and it is finding it tough to revive. It employs 94 per cent of the workforce and a large fraction of them lost employment and incomes. Naturally, then, demand shortage becomes severe.

Agriculture was immediately impacted due to the decline in demand for food. Prices in rural markets collapsed as a result. Fruits and vegetables were reported to be rotting in the fields, since it was not profitable to harvest and bring them to the cities, where the prices had risen due to shortages. Thus, both the rural producers and the urban consumers suffered.

Work also stopped in the organized sector of the economy. Immediately, contract labour was laid off. Even though the government asked businesses to not fire workers or cut their wages, most businesses could not afford not to, since they were also incurring losses and these would only increase if the workers were paid their salaries. In many cases, it was reported that workers were told to resign; if not, they would be fired.

All manner of businesses got impacted—retailers, wholesalers, auto companies, white goods manufacturers, airlines, airports, construction, entertainment business, etc. Many services that require close contact with customers also closed down, such as restaurants, hotels, transporters, the cinema industry and so on. Many self-employed individuals, such as barbers, electricians and plumbers, also lost work. Very few, such as software developers, consultants, chartered accountants and some lawyers, could work from home. The media also suffered due to the loss of advertising and people not buying papers and magazines due to fear of the spread of the virus. Many in the media lost their jobs and most had to take salary cuts.

Educational institutions also shut down, creating a crisis of learning. Working parents faced a crisis in handling children confined to homes and classes taking place online. But the Internet divide in the country prevents everyone from participating in the process. Exams had to be cancelled and admissions were difficult to manage. All this put the future of children in jeopardy. With the economy in a limbo, job creation suffered, except in some areas, such as e-commerce. Overall, jobs evaporated and the future now looks rather bleak for the young entering the job market at this point of time. Those who have lost jobs are struggling to get new ones.

*Shape of Recovery—V, L or U*

With the decline in production, there is spare capacity with businesses. So they don't need to go for new investment and are likely to slow down any ongoing investment as well. In fact, as businesses fail, aggregate investment in the economy could turn negative. So investor confidence has sharply declined. But stock markets, after declining massively in March, have recovered. As company reports appear showing massive decline in profits or losses, the markets are likely to decline in due course. The financial markets have become highly unstable. The central banks have released a lot of liquidity but the rate of growth is still low. All this needs analysis.

Most of the well-off have suffered a loss of wealth and their business sentiment is on the wane. This will be further impacted as businesses fail and real estate property comes on the market. Rents will further decline and because there will be few buyers, property prices will fall further. This will further impact the sentiment of the wealthy. There will be a wealth effect—namely the rich will feel less wealthy and cut down on their consumption and investment. This will make recovery from the crisis slower and more difficult. This problem will be true globally and not just in India.

Businesses have been fed the idea that recovery will be quick—that it will be as sharp as the decline was, so the graph of growth rate will be 'V-shaped'. Various international agencies have reluctantly accepted that the rate of growth in the world will be sharply lower and unlikely to recover soon. Experts have been behind the curve as in 2007–09, during the global financial crisis. In May, when the rate of growth precipitously fell in India, the International Monetary Fund (IMF) predicted a 1.9 per cent rate of growth for 2020–21. The Ministry of Finance was still talking of the economy growing. But how can proper planning be done if the assumption about the data is incorrect?

The reason the ministry and the financial institutions are shy of admitting the reality is so that investor sentiment does not decline further which could make the markets crash even more. But how long can one carry on this charade? Not using the right statistics to make policy will result in its failure. For instance, all budget figures depend on the rate of growth of the economy, and if that is incorrect, the budget figures will not turn out to be correct. The deficit will be much higher and if expenditures are not immediately cut, later the shortage of resources will be even greater.

With the massive loss of employment in the unorganized sector, a decline in incomes of the farmers, salary cuts for workers in organized sectors and the wealth effect suffered by the rich, consumption has sharply declined and will not recover anytime soon. Further, with business failures and spare capacity in large swaths of the economy, investment in the economy is likely to be negative or very low. It may be buoyant in a few sectors such as the pharmaceuticals industry, a few FMCG producers, telecom, e-commerce and other technology sectors. But mostly everywhere else it will collapse, such as in retail, wholesale, automobiles, hotels, airlines, entertainment, etc.

Exports will also decline sharply, since most countries suffering a recession or depression will import much less than earlier. Policymakers have expressed the hope that foreign capital may relocate from China to India, since many countries are upset with China and do not want to depend too much on it for their supplies. This is unlikely, since most countries would like their industry to relocate in their own country. The president of the US has already said this (PTI, 2020d). He has anyway been pressing American industries to return to the US (Reed, 2019). Given the massive unemployment in all countries, they would all want investment in their own country and not elsewhere. So not much can be expected from there.

There is huge uncertainty about the future and the changing nature of work. Factories and offices cannot function like they did earlier. Physical distancing and sanitization will impose additional costs, and capacity will be redefined. Like in restaurants, where one cannot have as many customers as earlier and many more will prefer to cook at home rather than eat outside. Travel and tourism will decline due to the need for physical distancing. This will have a knock-on effect on airlines, taxis, railways, entertainment, outside dining, etc. So the economy will not return to where it was in January 2020—there will be a new normal.

With a decline in demand, prices will soften and inflation will decline. As production declines, commodity prices will also soften. This has already been visible in the case of petro goods, which collapsed and at one stage even turned negative for delivery a month down the line. This was unprecedented. With large-scale unemployment, wages are also likely to decline. In India, the unorganized sectors have always acted as a reserve army of labour, and this will be further accentuated. While some sectors may experience labour shortage in India due to the migration of labour to rural areas, most businesses, working at way below capacity, will not need that much labour. So with input costs and wages down, chances of a decline in prices are high. So the primary worry for the economy will be deflation rather than inflation. The concern is that deflation will lead to a further slowdown in investments.

In brief, with market-determined private consumption, private investment and exports all likely to sharply go down, recovery will be slow. It will be a shallow 'U-shaped' one. Actually, all major economies (except China) are in depression and not recession. In a recession, the economy declines by a small percentage for a short time, but in a depression the economic decline is much greater, and to get out of it takes quite a while, since expectations take time to normalize. Consumer confidence and investor sentiment do not rebound soon.

Economy is not like a rubber ball, which, if dropped on a hard floor, will bounce back to the height it was dropped from. Society consists of people, farms and businesses. Economic shocks have a deep impact on them and they have to bear heavy costs, which changes their behaviour. So there is an asymmetry between the economy going down and then coming back up. Those that are hurt badly cannot smoothly recover. If that could happen, there would have been a quick rebound in the economy—in the shape of a V. But that is unlikely.

## Government Policies

When markets fail, the government is required to intervene. The pandemic has led to all markets failing. The government and the wider public sector is the one source of demand in the economy, which can run counter to what the market is signalling. This is the counter-cyclical policy suggested by Keynes and Kalecki in the early 1930s during the Great Depression (See Keynes, 1936, and Kalecki, 1971).

This policy was implemented in the mid-1930s and in the post-Second World War era up to the mid-1970s, and, more recently, during the global financial crisis of 2007–09. Massive fiscal deficits were allowed in the budget of all major economies to boost demand.

In the mid-1930s in the US, it took the shape of the 'New Deal'. In 2007–09 in India, massive purchasing power was pumped into the rural economy via loan waivers, midday meals, MGNREGS and other such schemes (Kumar, 2009). The Fiscal Responsibility and Budget Management (FRBM) Act, 2003, was given a go-by and the fiscal deficit was allowed to rise sharply. That is why India was one of the few economies that did not have a negative rate of growth.

No wonder, then, that most countries have now announced big stimulus packages. The US, Japan, along with the European Union as a whole, have all gone for large packages to stimulate their economy. Central banks are pitching in by cutting interest rates to historic lows and flooding the markets with liquidity. But will this work in a lockdown and even after it is slowly eased in stages, when the rate of recovery is slow? What are the steps that could work during and after a lockdown?

In India, the government and the Reserve Bank of India (RBI) have also announced packages. But the amount of money allocated from the budget is small. Most of the packages consist of loans and credit to different sectors of the economy, such as agriculture infrastructure and the micro, small and medium enterprises (MSME) sector. Major changes in laws have also been announced as part of the packages. But these are mostly long- and medium-term policy measures that will have little immediate impact on an economy in crisis. Immediate support from the budget is only about 10 per cent of the packages. Further, many announcements made as a part of the packages were already in the budgets of the past few years. If they were not implemented then, will they be implemented now (See Kumar, 2020g)?

The package consists largely of supply side measures while what is needed is immediate boosting of demand in the economy. The government is not doing what it ought to be doing, namely supporting the vast number of people who have lost employment by giving them some money that would increase demand and help revive the economy.

Because of the misplaced priorities of the government, the social situation is deteriorating and India is having the worst of all worlds. Neither is the disease being contained nor is the economy reviving. The poor are getting the short end of the stick. But this disease is such that it neither respects borders nor class divides. As long as it exists, it will affect all countries and even the high and mighty can get afflicted, as was the case with British Prime Minister Boris Johnson and Brazilian President Jair Bolsonaro.

## Looking Ahead

The course of the disease is unclear, so one cannot predict when it will come under control. That would need a lot of social effort and discovery of either a vaccine or some medicine to counter its effects. Chances are that it will be a long haul, with high social and economic costs. The current best guess is that the world economy will be in severe recession/depression, like in the period from 1928 to 1933. This is indeed a scary prospect, and governments and analysts will have to think out of the box to tackle the situation.

The world will not recover to the pre-January 2020 situation any time soon, and, as mentioned earlier, there will be a new normal, with lots of economic, political and social changes. The pandemic has highlighted the importance of the collective, since the disease can only be tackled as a collectivity, with everyone contributing. The credibility of the government has become crucial for the population to follow its pronouncements faithfully. So society will have to tackle the widespread alienation of citizens and consider strengthening the sense of social justice. However, this will not be a one-way street, since there will be pressure for automation, use of artificial intelligence, etc., which could lead to growing unemployment among the marginalized and further alienation in society.

The pandemic has exposed the abysmal social conditions of labour, especially in India, with its vast unorganized sector and poverty. The dreadful social conditions prevalent in India and the government's apathy towards them have come in the way of making the lockdown a success. There is a need to rethink the causes of the vast disparities in our society and the poor living conditions of a gigantic number of Indians.

The upper classes have been exposed to the distress and hardship of the poor. What was under wraps has come out in the open and pricked the conscience of many of them. If this makes them question our model of development and the way society is organized, there is some chance of a basic rethink. People may need to reflect on the causes of underdevelopment, inequalities, the degrading environment and so on. The nature of the ongoing globalization and interdependence among countries will also come under scrutiny. The social and political aspects of consumerism and its impact on nature needs to be reassessed.

People now realize the importance of good governance and a robust public-healthcare system and that this is not possible without clean and representative politics. The link between political parties and vested interests may also come under deeper scrutiny so that true representation in legislatures becomes possible. The dichotomy between market and state will perhaps be reassessed and the role of the public sector may be revisited, given the recent experience of the evident failures of the private sector during the pandemic.

In this book, first health emergency will be discussed and then why the modern-day economy has been hit particularly hard by a lockdown. After that the macroeconomic aspects of the lockdown will be discussed, so as to emphasize the need for out-of-the-box thinking. Next will come the assessment of the impact of lockdown on the Indian economy. The discussion on government policies will follow, with a focus on what has been done and what needs to be done. Finally, the concluding chapter will summarize the arguments in the book and attempt to anticipate what lies ahead.

# II

# Nuts and Bolts of the Pandemic: Disease, Health and Lockdown

The SARS-CoV-2 virus, though highly contagious, has a lower mortality rate when compared to that of other contagious diseases. For example, in the case of Ebola, 50 per cent of those who contracted the disease died (WHO, 2020a). However, in the present case, the percentage of people dying in mid-October was around 2.5 per cent globally. While in Spain and Italy almost 10 per cent who had tested positive for the disease had died, in South Korea it was less than 1 per cent. In India it was around 1.5 per cent. Among those who have died, a disproportionate number is that of the elderly and those with pre-existing conditions or co-morbidities such as diabetes and high blood pressure. About 80 per cent of those who have tested positive have either a mild form of the disease or are asymptomatic. The rest who are hospitalized or put in isolation have mostly recovered. It has been found that the infection rate in children is very low and men are affected more than women. Finally, those who are obese are being impacted more severely.

## The Virus: What Are We Dealing With?

What is a virus and how is it different from bacteria that infects us and for which we take antibiotics? Why is there no medicine or a vaccine for this virus? These are some of the questions that the public has been asking.

Talking about viruses, the tobacco mosaic virus (TMV) was the first virus to be discovered in 1892. But except that it was much smaller than bacteria, not much else was known about it until much later. Typically, it is visible under an electron microscope and not the normal optical microscope. A virus is an inert particle, something between the living and the non-living. It needs a host to survive and multiply. It enters a cell and captures its replication mechanism to make copies of itself and multiply. It then escapes the cell to infect other cells in the body. This leads to disease in the body. COVID-19 is caused by the SARS-CoV-2 virus.

It is estimated that there are millions of types of viruses in nature that infect plants and animals. Some of them attack human beings and lead to afflictions such as the common cold, influenza and polio. Only a few thousands of the existing viruses have been analysed. So we do not know enough about the various kinds of viruses that exist in nature.

A virus typically has an RNA, which has the information to replicate itself and produce the remaining structure of the virus, such as its coating and the spikes on its surface. The surface of the virus is made up of a greasy membrane, which keeps the virus intact. On the surface, there are spikes that can latch on to certain parts of a cell surface (receptors) to gain entry. Usually, the spikes do not match the entry points of cells, so the virus cannot enter it—that is, they cannot infect the cells. Out of the millions of types of viruses, only a few are able to enter the cell of a human being, so we are relatively protected. However, mutations occur and that can result in the spike of the virus tweaking itself so it can latch on to a cell at certain points, like a key to a lock, to gain entry into the cell, infect it and that results in the disease.

The greasy covering of the coronavirus is susceptible to soap and alcohol-based sanitizers. They tear open the virus and the contents inside spill over. These remnants are no longer capable of infecting cells. No wonder the best defence against a viral attack is personal hygiene—washing hands and not touching the face with infected hands. When infected hands touch the face, the virus can enter the body through the nose or the eyes. The SARS-CoV-2 especially attacks the cells in the respiratory tract. This causes difficulty in breathing and other complications in the lungs, which can result in death.

Fortunately, COVID-19 is found to be mild in 81 per cent of cases, of moderate intensity in 14 per cent and virulent in 5 per cent globally. The first group is of asymptomatic cases, which do not require any treatment. But this group can spread the disease to others. The next group, of 14 per cent, require isolation and oxygen to help breathing. Some of them deteriorate into severe cases, which are the 5 per cent that require hospitalization with possible use of the ICU and ventilators (CDC, 2020).

So how do viruses differ from bacteria? Why is the treatment different? A bacteria can sustain itself without the need of a host, unlike the virus. It is much larger than a virus. It attacks cells rather than capture them, like in the case of tuberculosis bacilli. Antibiotics work to kill bacteria but do not impact viruses. Often, antibiotics are prescribed even for viral infections. The reason is that the viral infection weakens the body and makes it prone to bacterial infection too. So antibiotics take care of the secondary infection, not the viral one.

## Cure for Viral Infections

The human body can identify foreign bodies and attack them through antibodies. That is how infections such as the common cold are dealt with by the body. The infection can become deadly if the body's defence via antibodies becomes weak or if it has not encountered such a foreign body earlier and does not have the antibody needed to fight it.

In the case of COVID-19, when the virus bursts out of its initial host cell and starts infecting other cells, the body's defence mechanism is triggered. Antibodies are produced, but they start attacking the cells themselves thinking they are the foreign bodies. This further weakens the infected person's body. Since the SARS-CoV-2 virus attacks the respiratory system, the functioning of the lungs gets compromised both due to the virus and the triggering of the body's immune system.

Medicines and vaccines can help cure the infection, but in different ways. A vaccine triggers the production of antibodies, so the disease can be prevented. A medicine helps fight the disease once it has already infected the body. The medicine does not produce antibodies but breaks down the foreign particle itself, so the infection reduces. Thus, medicines and vaccines have to be specific to a particular foreign particle entering the body and leading to a disease. What works for polio may not work for influenza. A medicine that works for HIV may not work for Ebola. There is a global race to discover a vaccine and/or a medicine for the SARS-CoV-2 virus, with the Oxford, Moderna, Wuhan and Pfizer groups, along with Russia's Sputnik V vaccine, leading about 200 efforts. Seven Indian companies are collaborating with some of the well-known global companies on developing a vaccine.

Developing a medicine or a vaccine is a laborious process. It takes years, and sometimes, in spite of everyone's best efforts, nothing works. This is because the human body itself is a very complex system and may develop unwanted side-effects due to the medicine or the vaccine. Therefore, there is always the danger of the vaccine or the medicine, if not properly tested, leading to further problems, instead of just curing the disease.

A medicine is a molecule that disrupts something in the foreign particle, so it is unable to attack the cells in the human body. Alternatively, it may help the body's cells stop the attack altogether. So a molecule that can disrupt the foreign body or its actions has to be identified. We know that poison can kill; a medicine is nothing but poison for the foreign body, but it should not be poison for the human body. It is, therefore, important that it be tested in the laboratory to see what impact it has on the foreign body. After such a molecule is found, in different phases of trials, it is first tested on animals and then on human beings to check how safe it is.

This process, right from identifying the molecule to a medicine being created, is time-consuming and expensive. Drug companies say they spend billions of dollars in discovering a safe molecule. The safety of a molecule for use in human beings has to be certified by the drug regulatory body of a country. For example, the Food and Drug Administration (FDA) in the US and the Central Drugs Standard Control Organisation (CDSCO) in India are the regulatory bodies that certify drugs before they can be used for treatment. The drug companies charge an arm and a leg when they bring a new drug in the market claiming enormous developmental costs. Often, in the US, drugs are priced at many times (sometimes even 100 times) the cost of manufacture. Often, Indian drug manufacturers sell the same drug at a fraction of the price it sells for in the US, and this is objected to by the big multinational companies. India has also been supplying these cheaper drugs to other countries such as Africa.

Various vaccines have been in different stages of trials and it is hoped that a safe vaccine will emerge soon. Due to urgency, an accelerated process of development has been allowed by countries. Medicines that were developed against Ebola (remdesivir), HIV (antiretrovirals such as lopinavir and indinavir) or malaria (hydroxychloroquine) have been tried for COVID-19 as well. Now, with computers, simulations can be done to identify drugs that may be effective against a virus if its structure has been identified. The Chinese laboratories had worked out the structure of the virus by the end of January and published it. That has helped other scientists, who have been working on 5000 potential molecules.

Another line of treatment being tried is the use of antibodies extracted from the plasma of cured patients (Cunningham, 2020).

This is known as convalescent plasma treatment. Infected patients may take a week or two to develop antibodies in their blood. It may offer immunity for a short or a long time, depending on various factors. Specific antibodies have to be identified that can block a particular virus, which is why it is also called the monoclonal antibody treatment. These antibodies, which prevent the virus from entering the host cells, are called neutralizing antibodies. If that happens, the infection stops. How well such a treatment will work and whether immunity will be short- or long-term is being investigated. But in serious cases, even if it only brings down the intensity of the disease, it would be a big gain.

There has been much confusion around COVID-19 medicines and vaccines. This is best illustrated by the pronouncements on hydroxychloroquine, the antimalaria drug. US President Donald Trump called it a wonder drug in one of his early press conferences. But his advisers quickly distanced themselves from this statement and said that the drug was still in a trial stage and its impact on COVID-19 was not clear. The WHO also said the same thing. A French study soon showed that not only was it unhelpful but that those who were administered the drug had a higher death rate (AFP, 2020). After that, it was said, including in India, that this drug could act as a prophylactic and that front-line warriors could benefit from taking it. But even this has not been proven yet.

There was considerable drama when India, one of the chief producers of this drug, banned its export. Trump threatened to take action and the Indian government backtracked on the export ban and allowed it to be sold abroad. There was public concern whether exports would lead to short supply in India. In a display of desperation, the well-off sections began hoarding it and, soon, it was unavailable at most chemists.

Alternative medicines are also being suggested. In India, Ayurveda has claimed to boost immune systems and strengthen the lungs. This, along with yoga, is being prescribed by practitioners of traditional medicine. Homoeopathy has also claimed to help control the disease. Since the SARS-CoV-2 virus is new, it is not clear whether these alternative treatments and medicines will work on something that has not been encountered earlier. Only through proper testing can the efficacy of the alternatives be established. It is possible that to the extent that alternative medicines can boost the immune system, they could help the body deal better with the virus.

## Varieties of Viruses

There is a problem. Viruses mutate, and there may be many variants of a virus. Scientists have already identified at least three variants of the new virus we are dealing with. It is also suspected that what afflicted the Chinese population is different from what infected the Europeans and the Indians. Some of the variants may be more virulent than the others.

Mutations also explain how the SARS-CoV-2 virus suddenly emerged. Out of the millions of viruses in plants and animals all around us, some mutated version of an existing virus can suddenly attack humans even when its earlier version did not. Due to environmental degradation, many animals are now in close proximity to humans. Further, animals are kept in close proximity with other animals sold as food. When that happens, such as chickens stuffed in small cages at a butcher's shop or pigs bred in farms, new forms of a virus can develop rapidly via mutation.

The most accepted theory of emergence of the SARS-CoV-2 virus is that it emerged from the wet market in Wuhan, where all kinds of living animals are kept in small cages in congested conditions to be sold as food. It was initially thought that the virus jumped to human beings from bats. This has been the most widespread conjecture, since the first cases were reported from the Wuhan wet market. Bats are known to be hosts to a large number of viruses due to their peculiar immune system. But rodents are also known to host many viruses, and some researchers have suggested civets (cats) and pangolins (ant eaters) as the source of the virus.

## Origins of the Coronavirus and Bio-Engineering

In nature, mutations occur due to cosmic rays constantly bombarding the surface of the Earth. They are high-energy particles and can damage the molecules in cells and cause mutations. This also happens in the human body, where the DNA, the blueprint of our reproductive systems, gets altered and, at times, results in cancer. Over the past many decades, scientists have been experimenting with altering cells and tinkering with DNA via biotechnology, so as to carry out cloning, etc. It is well known that military forces all over the world have been interested in developing bioweapons to attack the enemy and incapacitate its population. For instance, military researchers are known to study the pattern of bird migration and butterflies to see if they can be used to spread deadly diseases in enemy territory.

White races practised biowarfare with natives of newly discovered lands in the Americas. They spread deadly diseases among natives by gifting them infected blankets. They created an epidemic among the locals that weakened them and enabled the whites to conquer huge swaths of land with very few soldiers (Diamond, 1998). For instance, the Incas and the Mayans, both very advanced civilizations, were looted and pillaged all too easily by the Spanish.

One theory originating from the US and often repeated by its president is that the SARS-CoV-2 virus escaped from a Chinese laboratory in Wuhan, where bio-engineering research was going on. However, some scientists have argued that it does not have the signature of a bio-engineered virus and seems to have naturally evolved from previously known strains of the coronavirus. Subsequently, these theories took on a political colour.

The US administration delayed taking action against the spread of the disease and, as a result, it became the worst-hit country in the world. Rather than accepting that there had been delay in decisive action against the infection, the US president tried to deflect the blame to the Chinese, saying that they were the ones who had delayed announcing the disease to the world and that it had deliberately been created in a laboratory.

It is true that China initially did not accept that a new virulent virus had emerged. This indeed delayed preparations that could have been made by other countries to protect themselves. The Chinese authorities, in fact, punished Dr Li Wenliang, the doctor who, on 30 December 2019, had first raised concerns about a new virulent virus afflicting patients. He noted that they were all from the wet market in Wuhan.

The authorities came down heavily on Li, accusing him of 'making false comments' and that his words had 'severely disturbed the social order'. He was made to apologize. Soon, he, too, was infected by the virus and, after struggling for three weeks, succumbed to the disease on 7 February 2020. China admitted on 20 January that there was human-to-human transmission and that the outbreak was an emergency. The local authorities realized their mistake and apologized to Li, but by then it was too late. This is the nature of authoritarian regimes—they first deny a problem and then admit to it when it is too late.

## The SARS-CoV-2 Virus: A Chinese Conspiracy?

Some people see a design in China's delayed announcement. China was the country where the disease originated and was tackled effectively through a brutal lockdown. Wuhan, and China, recovered by the end of March, when other large economies of the world were in the throes of chaos. It was said that the Chinese economy was on the rebound and that its companies were buying out valuable companies of other countries whose share prices had fallen steeply due to the fast-spreading disease.

In India, when China's central bank, the People's Bank of China, bought 1.01 per cent of the shares of HDFC bank at the end of March, the most valuable Indian bank at that point, it was seen as evidence of China wanting to make inroads into the

Indian companies. It is another matter that the bank already held 1.75 per cent shares of HDFC. Also, in the last few years, many of the new Indian e-commerce companies, such as BigBasket, Udaan, Zomato, Byju's, Paytm, Paytm Mall, MakeMyTrip, Ola, Flipkart, Oyo Rooms, Snapdeal and Swiggy, welcomed major investments from Chinese companies. The Indian government reacted by amending its foreign direct investment (FDI) policy, on 18 April 2020, to impose restrictions on companies from bordering countries investing in Indian companies. Since such a law already existed vis-a-vis Pakistan, this was aimed primarily at the Chinese.

But why would China attack the rest of the world by targeting itself first? It could easily have triggered the outbreak in the US, since it has a lot of trade with the US and exports huge amounts to that country. That way it would never have been suspected of deliberately spreading a disease. If China is clever enough to engineer a deadly virus, it would surely have the guile to engineer the start of the pandemic elsewhere.

It is now widely believed that the disease spread to the US through Europe and not directly from China. Apparently, travellers from Wuhan frequently visited northern Italy and Iran for business, and that is how the disease spread from China. From Europe it went to the US. The US delayed a lockdown. New York City, one of the most important travel hub in the world, did not put any restrictions on travel and ended up becoming the biggest centre of the spread of the disease. Seattle, the largest city in Washington State, was possibly the first to be directly infected by travellers from China, but the state acted quickly and controlled the disease.

Finally, China is a big exporter to the entire world and if it attacks the other big economies, which then tank, Chinese exports will suffer the most. This will slow down the Chinese economy considerably. Further, many countries are now wanting to shorten their supply chains and produce more at home, so that they do not have to depend on other countries, especially on any one country. This will impact foreign investment in China which in turn may reduce their export markets permanently. China cannot easily substitute the exports with its own internal market. So the many conspiracy theories that China has engineered the pandemic to be able to dominate the world economy without going for a war seem far-fetched.

The WHO organizes the global approach to diseases, especially a pandemic. It gets information from countries about any new virus or disease that may have been detected, analyses and disseminates it and then prepares a response. China informed WHO, which then passed on the information about COVID-19 to the rest of the world.

The US has accused WHO of playing ball with the Chinese government in delaying the dissemination of information about the new virus. Further, it has said that WHO ought to have declared the disease a pandemic much before 11 March 2020. It had declared the disease a 'Public Health Emergency of International Concern' on 30 January 2020. Trump at a press conference on 29 May announced the withdrawal of support to WHO, accusing it of collaborating with the Chinese. It was argued that the director general of WHO, Dr Tedros Adhanom Ghebreyesus, was close to the Chinese President Xi Jinping, who had backed the former's appointment. At a time when the entire world needed to pitch in, the largest donor to WHO withdrew its support. Fortunately, others stepped in to bridge a part of the gap.

But for a virus that does not differentiate between countries and classes, the solution has to be an international one. Thus, a global effort is needed to devise a vaccine and find a medicine to deal with the disease. The US by itself cannot control the disease and WHO is needed to coordinate the global effort against the disease. So this is hardly the time for blame games, which can only distract from the goal—finding a cure.

## We Forgot That Pandemics Appear Routinely

In the past few decades, there have been many virus attacks, such as HIV, SARS, MERS, Nipah, H1N1 and Ebola. The world has learnt to deal with them, but SARS-CoV-2 is still largely a mystery. It is highly virulent and has spread rapidly. What do we know about the earlier outbreaks?

The Spanish flu almost a hundred years back has been one of deadliest pandemics known to humankind, and the present attack is comparable in scale to it. The Spanish flu started in 1918 just at the end of the First World War and killed an estimated 50 million people worldwide by 1920 (All About History, 2020). It is said that 15–20 million people died in India itself (Biswas, 2020). The attack came in two waves and the second wave killed more people than the first.

Even in this pandemic there is a fear that there will be a second wave as winter sets in, which could kill many more people, unless a medicine and/or a vaccine is discovered. The Spanish flu came at a time when nations were considerably weakened by the First World War. There was censorship, so news of the pandemic was not allowed to be made public. Only Spain, which was not part of the war, could carry news of the flu. That is why, even though Spain was not the place of origin of the virus, the flu came to be known as the Spanish flu.

At that time, the understanding of what a virus is and what its attack meant was much less than today. Since then, medicine has made considerable progress and medical systems are far more developed, so better care is possible. Further, the production systems are far more advanced than in 1918, so manufacture of medicines and equipment can be ramped up quickly to meet contingencies. Finally, the understanding of how medicines and vaccines are to be developed is far more evolved now. So it is possible to tackle the disease better.

However, the negative aspect of modern-day life, as far as a pandemic is concerned, is the far greater mobility of people. Gandhi (1909) pointed out that the railways had enabled disease to spread more quickly, since people could travel faster and carry diseases with them. Now with widespread air travel, the speed of movement is even greater and disease can spread much faster—within hours it can cross continents. That is what has happened with the SARS-CoV-2 virus, which rapidly jumped from China to South Korea, Iran and Italy, and from there to other countries across the world. By the time it was discovered that a new virus had emerged and that it could lead to a pandemic, people had moved and the disease had spread.

In the case of Ebola or Nipah, travel was restricted and people were quarantined where they were and that helped control the disease. Fortunately, these viruses were not as virulent as is the present strain of coronavirus. So the clear lesson is that once it is known that a new virus attack has started, the movement of people has to be immediately stopped. It has to be quickly ascertained who the infected people are and who have they been in touch with (called contact tracing), and all of these people have to be quarantined. That is the only way to check the spread of the disease. The sooner this is done, the better the disease can be controlled.

## Experience of Key Countries

The experience with SARS-CoV-2 has also been similar to that with Ebola and Nipah. China imposed a drastic lockdown on the movement of people in Wuhan, where the virus originated, and the Hubei province in general. By the end of March, the disease had been contained in China. South Korea, the next country to report the spread of the disease, also went for massive testing and tracing, and controlled the spread of the disease. Germany did the same. The US and the UK delayed control by not stopping the movement of people, and they have some of the highest number of infected people. Brazil has not implemented a lockdown at all and that resulted in a large number of people being infected and dying. One saw pictures of mass graves being dug up for burials. Countries such as Italy and Spain, which were severely affected, in spite of a well-developed healthcare infrastructure, were overwhelmed, and the elderly were allowed to die so that the younger people could be saved. Only a very strict lockdown allowed these countries to deal with the pandemic. With the onset of winter, the number of cases have risen again all over Europe.

Many of the developing countries are poor, with weak medical infrastructure, and have been impacted the last, such as countries in Africa and Asia. While they benefited from the experience of the countries that faced the disease earlier on, they did not have the resources to deal with the crisis, so are having to face considerable hardship. The economic difficulties are also more severe than for advanced countries because of higher poverty levels.

Many diseases kill far more than SARS-CoV-2 had killed by March. So some argued that too much was being made of this disease and a harsh lockdown was not needed. TNN (2020) gives data on some of the big killers (annually) in India—15.4 lakh due to heart-related problems, 9.6 lakh due to lung-related problems, 7.8 lakh due to cancer, 7.3 lakh due to stroke, 7.2 lakh due to diarrhoea, 4.5 lakh due to tuberculosis and 2.5 lakh due to diabetes. Accidents of various kinds lead to 500 deaths every day on average. In fact, during the lockdown, deaths due to accidents declined because movement of people dropped sharply.

What is being forgotten is that the disease is virulent and that if it spreads unchecked, it will kill a lot more. If it is assumed that the disease quickly spreads to even 60 per cent Indians, it will infect 800 million people. Even if only 3 per cent Indians die due to it, it will mean 24 million dead in a short span of time—far more than the numbers from any of the above-mentioned major killers. Since the hospital system cannot cope with such a large number of people falling seriously ill, there will be social breakdown and chaos. So the comparison of numbers during the lockdown with other diseases is not valid.

## Do Other Deaths Decrease?

The coronavirus is virulent and can be fatal. So, along with deaths from other causes, did the total number of deaths increase during the pandemic? Actually, detailed data is not available for most countries. Giattino, et al (2020) give data on excess mortality due to COVID-19 for some of the advanced countries. It is measured as the number of deaths in a given month or week, compared to the average of deaths over the same week or month in the previous five years. It may also be given in percentage terms to compare across different countries, which will take out the effect of the population size differences. Data indicates a sharp rise in excess mortality across various advanced countries in March and April. They also give data on age-wise differences, which shows that all age groups showed excess mortality but that it was more for those aged above eighty-five years. Eurostat Statistics Explained (2020) gives more detailed data for Europe, including gender differences.

There is much confusion about what should be counted as a COVID-19 death. A person infected by COVID-19 may die due to it, due to secondary reasons independent of the disease or due to the aggravation of an already existing condition by the disease. In the US, between 1 March and 16 August 2020, there were 260,000 more deaths but only 169,000 were confirmed COVID-19 deaths (Giattino, et al, 2020). The picture gets more confusing because there are reports of fewer deaths due to other causes because a) accidents have come down, especially traffic-related ones, since driving has decreased substantially and b) people are following hygiene and physical distancing, so infections are less. For instance, deaths from diarrhoea and influenza may be fewer than earlier.

In the developed world, due to restrictions, people are living a more healthy life; they have more time for their families and to exercise. These could reduce stress and, therefore, could lead to fewer cardiac and neurological problems. So strokes and heart-related issues could also have been fewer.

However, it is also argued that many people are not going to hospitals for fear of catching COVID-19 and, soon, many more cases of other diseases could also surface. This is possible, but the number of deaths should have increased due to untreated pre-existing diseases that are not being treated. But evidence for this is not available. Many private hospitals in India are running at a loss, since their OPDs are closed, the number of patients has declined and elective treatments (such as surgeries) have been postponed. It is argued that to cover these losses, private hospitals are charging huge amounts for treatment of COVID-19 and, due to public outcry, the government in India has had to put a cap on hospital charges.

In India, some districts have reported an increase in the number of deaths in April 2020 compared to April 2019. But, in India, data collection is unsatisfactory, so one cannot tell what is happening at the state or the national level. For instance, in Delhi and Mumbai, it has been reported that the number of cremations and burials actually taking place is greater than what the municipal and state governments are reporting.

So overall, deaths have increased in the advanced countries but the picture for India is not clear due to lack of data. COVID-19 added to the number of deaths but there may be fewer deaths due to other existing causes—for three reasons. First, the number of COVID-19 deaths are fewer than they would have been without the lockdown. Second, due to better sanitation and hygiene, deaths due to other causes have come down. Finally, deaths due to accidents have come down.

## Test, Test, Test!

The WHO has, from the start, recommended that the strategy for control of the spread of the disease has to be based on extensive testing. As was said by its director general Tedros Adhanom Ghebreyesus, the only option without a vaccine or a medicine is to 'test, test, test!!!' (WHO, 2020b).

Countries successful in checking the spread of the disease initiated a programme of extensive testing, then tracing their contacts in the recent past, and quarantining everyone testing positive and those who were in contact with them. This is the only way to stop the spread of the disease.

India had one of the lowest testing rates in August (Graph 06). Italy was doing thirty times more tests per million of the population and the US twenty times more in late May. It is precisely for this reason that it is not known how many people are infected in India and, therefore, one does not know how many more coming in contact with these people are also getting infected.

India, in the early stages, did not show a large number of infections, unlike in Europe. It can be argued that this was because of inadequate testing (Graph 06). It is important to note that having fewer cases when testing is inadequate can be deceptive—we do not truly know how many have the disease. Further, India's low death rate (Graph I.2) is also deceptive, since many deaths have not been reported. In mid-June, it emerged that Mumbai, Delhi and Chennai were not correctly reporting the number of deaths. In the UK, many deaths of the elderly in care homes were not initially counted—only deaths in hospitals were. Thus, the correct picture was not available initially.

Initially, when a few are infected, testing and tracing can be used to effectively stem the spread of the disease, as was done in South Korea. However, a delayed response could lead to extensive spread of the disease, after which it becomes difficult to tell who infected whom. This is called 'community spread'. India has been in this phase for some time now but the government is not admitting to it. Further, as millions of migrants moved from cities where infection was high to their respective villages, they took the disease with them and it spread to the rural areas too. Districts that were not reporting cases initially soon started to.

Even though the state governments have been insisting on quarantining returning migrants, it has not been effective. Right from the start, migrants should have been allowed to travel only after being tested. In India, most of the migrants allowed to board trains and buses to return to their native places were not tested. Largely, only their temperature was checked, which is wholly inadequate.

Testing in India was low, since testing kits were not available. India had to import them and the ones that came from China were said to be unreliable. So it was like not testing at all. Similar complaints of unreliable kits from China were also received from Spain. It is possible that when these kits were mass-produced by China for export, they were not standardized and hence gave inconsistent results. India had to import kits from other countries for testing. This highlights the weakness of our medical industry that it could not manufacture the kits quickly enough, in spite of the emergency the nation faced. It was only in May that reports trickled in that made-in-India kits would soon be available.

The lack of testing kits has prevented India from testing on a large scale. It also led to enormous confusion as to who should be tested. Protocols kept changing even on a daily basis. Sometimes it was said that everyone should be tested if there was suspicion of infection; at other times, it was said that only those with serious symptoms should be tested and not those who could be asymptomatic. But if people are not tested when they have just contracted the disease, they continue to infect others until they are quarantined. In that case, community transmission occurs and the situation gets out of control.

India should have gone into massive testing right from the start, and resources should have been made available on priority. Everyone returning from abroad should have been tested at the airport and quarantined, so that the disease did not spread in the country. If not from January, when the first case was reported in Kerala and WHO declared the disease an emergency, it should have become the norm by mid-February, when the disease had rapidly spread to large parts of the world. While restricting travel from abroad was a good step, it was inadequate without extensive testing.

## Available Tests

There are several tests but the three main ones used are:

a.  RTPCR
b.  ELISA
c.  Rapid Antibody test

*RTPCR* (Real-Time Polymerase Chain Reaction) is used for individual diagnosis. It tells whether a person is infected. It is based on swabs taken from the nose and the throat. The test extracts the RNA from the virus and checks whether it is from SARS-CoV-2. It gives conclusive proof in 90 per cent of the cases. So it is possible that the virus may be missed and the test may have to be repeated. It is, therefore, suggested that the virus be extracted from sputum, or the fluid in the lungs. But that is a more tricky and time-consuming procedure. This test, moreover, is quite expensive and if the fluid is to be extracted from deeper inside, it can be even more expensive. Initially, labs were charging a high price for the test, so the government stepped in and fixed the price at Rs 4500, which is still quite steep for most. At this price, most of the poor and even the middle class may not go for the test. Not only would individuals have to be tested but entire families too, if there was suspicion of infection. And the tests might have to be repeated. That is why it was suggested (Kumar, 2020c) that the test be made free and that the government should pay the private labs. But this suggestion was not seriously pursued. With massive testing, the rate of infection could have been brought down substantially.

*ELISA* is an enzyme-linked test to detect the presence of antibodies in a blood sample. When a person is infected, the body produces antibodies. So, if antibodies are present in a blood sample, it is a sign that the person has had the infection. But it does not immediately tell if the person is infected at that point. It is typically useful in making population-based estimates. This test is relatively cheap and can be performed quickly.

The *Rapid Antibody Test* is similar to ELISA but uses different reagents. It is also less reliable. It can confuse the presence of antibodies from other diseases with ones from SARS-CoV-2. So it can give false positive results and has to be confirmed via an RTPCR test. Even a negative test result does not mean that the person is not infected with COVID19. Thus, it is only useful for population surveys.

The above suggests that there can be two strategies for testing—individual and mass. In the latter, the blood of many is pooled together and tested for the presence of antibodies. If antibodies are not found, it can be inferred that the people tested have not been infected and they can safely go to work without the fear that they could infect others. But if antibodies are found in the pooled sample, everyone has to be tested separately. When the disease has not spread much, it may work, but when it has spread extensively, most samples will show a positive result and everyone will have to be tested individually. In that case, it only delays the process of identifying the infected.

When businesses are to reopen, the problem is to identify who among the workers are infected and who are not. The non-infected alone should be allowed to work, lest the infected spread it to others, in which case the business will have to shut down again. This is when pooled testing is suggested. In fact, it is also suggested that workers may be given a card certifying that they are non-infected. But, at this stage of spread of the disease, this strategy may not work.

## Lockdown and Its Imperatives

While the rich countries have a well-developed health infrastructure, the poorer ones do not (Table I.1). Since the disease is highly contagious, it has to be contained early, so it does not spread rapidly and overwhelm the health infrastructure. It is argued that the healthcare system will not be overwhelmed if the number of those infected remain below the capacity of the medical system of the country.

A lockdown slows down the rate of transmission within the population. There is a term, called 'R-Number', which is the number of people that an infected person infects. So, if it is 2, each infected person can be said to infect two people. An R-number greater than 1 means that the disease will keep spreading and not slow down. A lockdown is a means of bringing it to below 1. Until a lockdown is implemented, the numbers can rise exponentially, but if a lockdown is effectively implemented, after fourteen days, the incubation period of the disease, the numbers start to taper off. This is called the 'flattening of the curve'. The spread of the disease finally reaches a peak, called the 'apex'. A lockdown helps keep the apex below the capacity of the health infrastructure. Otherwise there will be chaos.

Even if the number of individuals hospitalized is high after reaching the apex and the numbers remain high for a time, called 'plateauing', the healthcare system gets overwhelmed, with doctors and medical personnel constantly occupied over long periods of time. This is unsustainable. Therefore, to deal with the pandemic, there have to be more doctors and staff. This is not the case in developing countries, which have a shortage of personnel even in normal times—especially in rural areas.

For taking care of the infected patients, extreme caution is required, so that the caregivers do not themselves get infected. Personal protective equipment (PPE), masks, face shields, and keeping the temperature moderate and not cold are essential, but that makes working difficult. One has to stay in a PPE suit for an entire shift and there is a lot of sweating due to the temperature and the inability of the sweat to evaporate through the impermeable PPE suit. One cannot have water or food or go to the toilet during the shift, or another PPE suit is needed, which adds to both cost and time wasted.

Along with a lockdown, one also needs to consider the capacity of the public health infrastructure in a country. In the past forty years, this infrastructure has been weakened and privatized in several countries. In fact, in the recent past itself, many have talked of the possibility of a pandemic hitting humankind and the need to be prepared to deal with it. However, this has not been taken seriously, and, in the US in 2018, the administration disbanded its own global health security team, which was supposed to make the US more resilient to the threat of epidemics (Bilmes, 2020).

In brief, a lockdown is not a cure for a disease but it does prevent the medical system from getting overwhelmed. It does two things.

First, it prevents the number of infected cases from increasing rapidly and hopefully keeps the apex below the capacity of the medical system, as happened in New York City, where the numbers grew rapidly. Second, it gives the system the time to ramp up its capacity to deal with the crisis. For example, to increase the availability of hospital beds, medical equipment, increased testing and discovery of a medicine and/or a vaccine.

In India, unfortunately, the lockdown was not effectively utilized. To make it successful, special care needed to be taken of the less fortunate (Kumar, 2020d), who usually live in crowded and unhygienic conditions, and for them practising physical distancing is difficult. They do not have the savings to stock up on essentials. They buy their requirements on a daily or a weekly basis, but a lockdown puts strict restrictions on people's movements. Thus, the imperative for a successful lockdown ought to have included providing the poor with essential supplies at their doorstep—food, energy, soap and so on—to give them clean water to cook, bathe and wash hands, whereas, often, they are short of even water to drink. In the absence of all this, in India, they were forced to move around in search of essentials and the lockdown did not deliver what it should have.

Further, in urban centres, the poor live in congested slums, such as Dharavi in Mumbai. Often, there are ten people to a room, with people coming in shifts to sleep. During lockdown, they were all expected to remain confined to their rooms 24x7, which became impossible to sustain. In fact, they should have been allowed to migrate to their villages after proper testing. This was not done and the people travelled on foot, on cycles and crowded trucks in terrible conditions. Those who stayed behind ought to have been decongested. For this, empty school buildings, halls and tented colonies on open grounds could have been used. Undoubtedly, this is a herculean task but when the situation is worse than a war, this difficult task should have been carried out.

Since all this was not done in India, the lockdown failed to be as effective as it should have been. The number of infections continued to rise but the lockdown had to be relaxed (See Chapter IV). Even the medical system was not adequately ramped up and the situation has tended to get out of hand from time to time. Given the social and medical conditions in India, the lockdown was more difficult but also more necessary than in many other countries.

## Argument for 'Herd Immunity'

Another line of argument regarding how the spread of the disease could evolve is that there will be more than one round of the disease, as was seen in earlier pandemics. Till a medicine and/or a vaccine is developed, more and more will continue to get infected. China witnessed another round of infection after a lull. New Zealand was free of the virus for 100 days and suddenly two new cases turned up. As argued earlier, the solution is to free the world of the virus.

It is argued that when a large number of people are infected by the disease and get cured, they develop immunity to it, like in the case of flu and the common cold. This breaks the chain of spread. The infected would have developed antibodies and will not spread it to others, so the yet-uninfected will be protected from the virus. This is referred to as 'herd immunity'. It is said that for this to work, 60 per cent of the population needs to first get infected. If a vaccine is developed or a medicine found to cure the disease, things can be brought under control more quickly. Trials are going on but according to experts, for a vaccine to be ready, it takes at least eighteen months to develop it (Grenfell, R. and T. Drew, 2020).

The issue is that spread will occur, herd immunity will happen, but over what time frame? The lockdown slowed the spread of the disease and delayed its peaking but is not stopping the movement towards herd immunity.

The UK initially experimented with achieving herd immunity, but within days, as the numbers rose alarmingly, it had to reverse its policy and implement a lockdown. But the delay almost overwhelmed its National Health Service. In the US too, the delay in lockdown in New York resulted in the number of cases rising rapidly, making it the country with the largest number of cases and deaths in the world. Further, the US was lax in implementing the lockdown in several of its states and that led to a surge in cases, as shown in Graph 01.

The number of people getting infected matters and has to be kept low, because a percentage of them will die. Suppose only 2 per cent of the infected die and only 5 per cent need ventilators. Even if the number of infected individuals is 1 lakh, 5000 will need ventilators and 2000 will die. If 10 million get infected, 500,000 will need ventilators and 200,000 will die. If this happens in a short period of time, the medical system will get overwhelmed.

In India, to reach herd immunity in one year, 60 per cent will have to contract the disease, which would be 800 million citizens. If 5 per cent need hospitalization, ventilators and oxygen supply, the number would add up to 40 million. India does not have that kind of hospital capacity or medical personnel to tackle such a situation effectively. Deaths would be much more than 2 per cent, which would itself mean 16 million—a huge number. This could lead to societal breakdown.

In India, the pressure to go for herd immunity is both from the government and businesses (See Chapter IV for more detail). Businesses realized that they would fail on a large scale because of a lack of sales and revenue during lockdown. As a result, they wanted the lockdown lifted sooner rather than later. They felt that once sales started, losses and failures would be limited. They argued that there was a trade-off between 'life and livelihood'. They said that workers without jobs and incomes would die of hunger if not from the disease. So it was argued that starting work was crucial. The government seems to have been in agreement, since it realized that the situation had slipped out of its control, because it did not do what was required during the lockdown. If it lifted the lockdown, it would not be blamed. It could argue that it was trying to save lives by allowing workers to earn, so they could sustain themselves.

But this argument is flawed. As the governor of New York said in his press conferences, if there is life, livelihood can be taken care of. He argued for first saving lives by controlling the disease and only then opening up the economy. In India, too, we have enough food stock and essential supplies to feed people for a year. However, we did not mobilize as a nation to do so and the lockdown did not achieve what it should have.

In brief, without adequate testing, it is difficult to end or ease a lockdown and economic costs will keep rising. This is a catch-22 situation. If a lockdown is imposed in parts of the country to prevent the spread, economic costs rise. Starting economic activity prematurely, which leads to the disease flaring up and requiring another lockdown, is costly. Thus, an optimum strategy is required, which takes care of both the health aspect of the pandemic and the economic costs—the former ought to take precedence.

## Weaknesses of Healthcare and Related Infrastructure

India's lack of testing and the near-breakdown of the medical infrastructure in major cities are testimony to the country's weak medical infrastructure. This is a result of sheer neglect since independence. It is not that the infrastructure has not improved since Independence, but it has lagged behind the requirements of a vast and poor population. It is concentrated in a few urban pockets but very weak in the rural and semirural areas. The pandemic is showing that even where it was better developed, such as in Mumbai, the NCR and Chennai, it was often not able to cope with the requirements of the vast population. The implication is that even in these pockets, it is not up to the mark.

In most developing countries, the healthcare infrastructure is very weak (except for in Cuba, which has been investing a lot in healthcare). Further, as pointed out earlier, physical distancing is difficult, since the vast underprivileged population lives in cramped and unsanitary conditions. That is why, in spite of a lockdown, there was community spread of the disease in India, even though the government does not admit to it.

In the US, a disproportionate number of African Americans have contracted the disease and died. India is also likely to face similar problems, with the marginalized sections of the population getting hit more than those better off. There is a huge unorganized sector that employs 94 per cent of the workforce (Kumar, 2018) at low wages, who live in poverty and are the marginalized. They are being acutely afflicted by the disease.

Healthcare infrastructure also includes the availability of medicines, hospital beds, ventilators, testing kits and protective equipment for medical personnel. It is not fully known how this disease spreads and new theories are being propounded every so often. At first it was believed that the disease did not spread through air and a physical distance of 3 feet was considered adequate, but this was later increased to 6 feet. Later still, it was said that microdroplets in the air can persist for hours and even across 8–10 feet. It was also said that droplets on floors can stick to shoes and that could lead to the transmission of the disease. It was earlier said that masks were needed only by medical personnel but later it was made mandatory for everyone to use one, once outside their homes.

Protocols for dealing with the pandemic need to be in place, but these have taken time to evolve. That is the reason why many doctors, nurses, paramedics and policemen have died from COVID-19. This has happened both in the developed and the developing countries, including India. In the US, even with its well-developed medical systems, medical personnel were initially not getting enough protective gear to treat patients. In India, the shortage was even more acute. Here, the production of masks and PPE was ramped up in May, with garment manufacturers and tailors being roped in.

Production of medicines and ventilators, along with oxygen-monitoring and oxygenation equipment, was ramped up May onward. The government converted halls and hotels into hospitals from June. Private hospitals were reluctant to treat COVID-19 patients, but the government had to force them to do so. In the meanwhile, people had to run from one hospital to another to find beds to get patients treated. There have been heart-rending stories of people dying in ambulances or just waiting for a bed outside hospitals. Doctors in public hospitals were overworked.

There were also reports of profiteering by the private sector. Taking advantage of the desperation of families, some private hospitals charged them an arm and a leg. It was reported that some hospitals demanded lakhs of rupees as down payment before admitting a patient. The government had to step in and regulate the prices being charged. Private hospitals and facilities also complained that their normal business had suffered, since patients were postponing coming to them out of fear of being infected. Since foreign travel was banned, many hospitals that used to thrive on patients coming from abroad for treatment in India suffered losses. Hospital managements claimed that they had incurred losses on the massive investment they had made on their facilities.

Many infected individuals preferred to self-quarantine at home, given the conditions of public-sector hospitals and the profiteering by the private-sector hospitals. Pharmacists charged high prices for normal equipment and medicines needed for treatment. In India, a disaster is called the third crop after the rabi and kharif crops. So, whenever there is a flood or a drought, traders, officials and politicians make money. That seems to be happening during the pandemic too.

Globally, there has been a weakening of the public sector since the mid-1970s. It has been argued that it is inherently inefficient. This has led to a wave of privatization and promotion of markets everywhere. Where markets did not exist, they were created. The role of the state was redefined as 'market-friendly state intervention'. Following this philosophy, resources were withdrawn from the public sector and concessions were given to the private sector to help it advance (Kalecki, 1971). This move towards market-based functioning and retreat of the state was applied with disastrous consequences to two noble sectors—education and healthcare.

This has proved to be detrimental to the wider interest of society and is now visible during the pandemic.

It is hard to value these two services. How much should a teacher or a doctor be paid? What should be the fee for a procedure at a hospital or the tuition fee charged from a student in an educational institution? If society pays more to the schoolteacher, the tuition fee would be higher. Poorly qualified teachers could accept a low salary but the quality would suffer. If one wished to have highly qualified teachers, they would have to be paid a high salary and the cost of education would go up. But that would rule out most of the poor and the middle class from such education and a subsidy would be required.

Similarly, in the case of healthcare, if one paid the doctors and other staff high consultation fees, the hospital charges would be high. If hospitals required doctors to recommend expensive tests that are not needed, the hospital bill would be high. If the doctors called in consultants to look at a patient even if they were not needed, the bill would go up.

As a result, in the private sector, to make a profit, there are high bills for medical treatment and high tuition fees in educational institutions. This has resulted in a growing social divide in healthcare and education.

In most countries, the move for privatization starting in the late 1970s was accompanied by reduced funding for public-sector institutions; so their quality deteriorated. The elite sections of society moved to the private sector and later to institutions in advanced countries. In a vicious cycle, this led to further segmentation and deterioration of the public sector institutions.

In India, the private sector in healthcare infrastructure grew rapidly after the launch of the New Economic Policies (NEP) in 1991 (Kumar, 2013) and the underfunded public sector deteriorated swiftly. There was overcrowding in the public sector and a breakdown of facilities.

The private sector, set up with the profit motive, does not feel obliged to cater to social needs. All manner of malpractices have proliferated here, such as the sale of organs and blood, C-sections rather than normal deliveries, recommending tests that are not needed and calling in of consultants that are not required (Kumar, 1999). Many doctors get a cut on tests recommended and for prescribing medicines of a particular brand. The social commitment of the medical profession has declined rapidly in the face of the profit motive. This is not just true of the private sector but also for the public sector, with malpractices proliferating and callousness growing over the years. Social commitment has declined all around. This is not to argue that everyone is dishonest—many have remain committed to society and their professions, but the number of such personnel is dwindling fast.

Now, in a pandemic, where the life of the medical personnel is on the line, why would those working for profit risk being on the front line of the fight? This is primarily the reason that, in India, many private-sector hospitals and clinics tried to excuse themselves from becoming COVID-19 hospitals. They agreed only under duress, rather than come forward on their own to take on the social challenge.

In brief, with privatization of the healthcare sector in India, the social commitment of the healthcare system has weakened. This is visible in the reluctance of the medical system to voluntarily take up the challenge during this time of social crisis.

### Pandemic, Isolation and Their Psychological Impact

The pandemic has created fear in the population. The disease seems to be everywhere and infects silently, so one does not know how one gets it. It can impact friends and family, and that is one of the major worries. It has brought about much uncertainty in life. It has restricted movement and disturbed the daily routine of large number of people.

Fear, uncertainty, loneliness and isolation have left a deep psychological impact on people. Many have lost their jobs and are not certain they will get it back. They may be getting some income from social security (in the developed world) but that is less preferable to having a job. People are getting depressed, and confined to their homes; thrown together 24x7, tensions are building up within families. Differences, which were attenuated earlier when people went out and met others, have got accentuated. At times, this has even resulted in violence. Children are also on edge, since they cannot go out and need to be entertained. Their social interactions with other children have also been restricted. While this does offer an opportunity for families to be together and bond with each other, in such depressing times even that is not easy. People need psychological help to deal with this new situation.

Tensions and uncertainty have led to many people spending a lot of time listening to news or searching social media for the latest news. This has resulted in what has been called an 'infodemic'. A large amount of fake news and half-truths are also floating around on the media and that has added to confusion and worries. Often, it has reinforced one's prejudices or traditional unscientific views about the disease. This has led to a deterioration of the psychological makeup of individuals. People fearing the worst have resorted to panic-buying, emptying out shelves of essentials in stores.

For the poor, the situation is worse. As mentioned earlier, confinement is an ordeal to them. Uncertainty is worse for them, since they have no one to fall back on. Among migrants, there was panic at the thought of dying away from their families. Many said that if they had to die, whether because of the disease or of hunger, they would rather do so in the presence of their families. So they tried to go back to their villages in spite of unavailability of transport. Pictures of hungry families carrying their few belongings ready to trudge a thousand kilometres home were heart-rending.

Thus, the pandemic has resulted in a high level of stress all around. Suicides seem to have increased. Fault lines of all kinds have simultaneously been accentuated. For instance, commitment to society, which had anyway weakened due to privatization and the celebration of greed and self-centredness (Kumar, 2013), has only declined further. This is a social and not an individual issue and requires a strong leadership to give guidance if it has to be tackled. However, unfortunately, that has been missing in many parts of the world. Leadership is not playing the role it should to galvanize and motivate people.

## Success Requires Transparency and People's Participation

Governments have to be transparent and take citizens into confidence for a successful fight against the pandemic. People will follow the government's strict instructions and the lockdown will be successful only if the people trust the government. But in India, with its weak and corrupt governance, people do not usually trust the government. Governments have promised relief to the poor in normal times but many have never received any. Similarly, during the lockdown, the government promised that it would take care of the poor, but that did not happen. That is why people wanted to return to the safety of their villages, back to their kin.

In India, there was much confusion about policy and that eroded the government's credibility. Politics continued to play itself out, which meant that there was no united effort by the various political parties, and the central as well as the state governments. False accusations were made to corner opponents, and this further confused the people. For some time, a certain community was sought to be blamed for the spread of the disease. They were accused of holding meetings and not practising physical distancing. It turned out that many other communities were doing the same thing and even important politicians were holding rallies, and birthday and marriage celebrations in disregard of the rules. On social media, all kinds of fake news was being circulated to target the opponents. This added to the confusion and resulted in the weakening of any commitment to make the lockdown successful.

Initially, the middle classes came out in support of the government by lighting lamps or clapping from balconies in appreciation of the front-line warriors and medical staff straining to tackle the disease. The military also saluted the front-line workers through fly-pasts, marching bands, etc. Some of these steps were the replication of steps taken in developed nations. The prime minister addressed the nation several times before and during the lockdown. He opened his address every time with an exhortation to the public to rise to the occasion, to boost the public's morale. But given the scale of the problem and difficulty of delivering on promises, the public mood swung to despondency and scepticism.

However, musicians played music from their rooms and balconies to cheer people up. Groups got together to perform symphonies or dance routines, and beamed it live on social media. Art and poetry to capture the mood of the people were also created. Classes for children and official meetings moved online to keep people engaged. So new forms of creativity did become visible. These are positive signs in the midst of trying times.

But, above all, what is needed is informed opinion and proper education for all, so that the basics of sciences and social sciences are better understood. This is sorely lacking in India today and that is why people are more prone to misinformation, which makes it difficult to cope with the crisis facing them. The lesson for the future is that along with better healthcare facilities, quality education for all is essential and that society has to invest massively in these sectors.

*Environment and Consumerism*

The spread of the disease is being linked to global environmental degradation. As already argued, animals have been forced to come in close proximity to populated areas, which enables viruses to mutate and jump to humans. It is also said that live animals sold in wet markets are the source of the virus. This is also linked to their being kept in cramped cages, where mutation and jumping of viruses to humans get accelerated.

All this, in turn, is the result of rapidly growing consumerism in society. Consumerism is the consumption for the sake of consumption (Kumar, 2013). It involves massive use and waste of natural resources. The lockdown showed us that life does not require the extent of consumption human beings, especially the elite in society, have got used to. Consumption of fruits, vegetables, milk, sugar, etc., have dropped and their prices have crashed in rural areas. Sales of many items of discretionary consumption have dropped, such as clothing and consumer durables. Due to the drastic fall in consumption and production during lockdown, pollution levels had also fallen sharply.

The question is how much can consumption be reduced without impacting the welfare of people? As far as the vast number of the poor are concerned, they only consume the basics, so they contribute little to consumerism. It is the middle and the upper classes that mainly indulge in consumerism. They have the incomes to do so. There is also a tremendous waste of resources in the corporate sector and the government. Kumar (2013) points to this 'social waste' in the economy, which can be eliminated without affecting people's living standards. Bowles, et al (1984) showed that in the US in 1980, 50 per cent of the GDP was a waste. In India, in the mid-2000s, 25 per cent of the output could be reduced without lowering the welfare of the people (Kumar, 2006).

In brief, since the disease has not been fully understood yet, it is better to be cautious in implementing the lockdown, and then in easing the restrictions, lest one is hit by another wave of the disease. The virus does not know borders and class distinctions. It cannot be controlled by any one country. The social elite cannot protect themselves while the disease continues to spread among the marginalized. A global effort is, therefore, called for. Some basic rethink of social attitudes is also essential once the disease has come under control.

# III

# Modern-Day Economy: Why the Lockdown Hits Hard

In the previous chapter it was argued that to slow down the rapid spread of the virulent COVID-19, countries had to implement lockdowns. This was needed to keep the numbers of the infected at levels manageable by the existing healthcare infrastructure. But lockdowns meant that people could not go to work, in factories or in offices. As a result, production came to a halt. This had serious consequences for the economy. But why more so in present times?

The answer to this lies in the working of a modern-day economy. The structure of an economy today is very different from what it was during the previous big pandemic, the Spanish flu (1918–20). That is why the impact is also different from what it was a hundred years back. This chapter presents some of the key features of modern-day economies, which are leading to some of the worst consequences the world economy has ever faced. In fact, the situation is unprecedented.

## Specialization and Self-Sufficiency

Explicitly or implicitly, individuals talk about what kind of work they are good at—their specialization. There are musicians, doctors, businessmen, carpenters, politicians, actors and teachers. Each of them may know something about a few other things but they are mostly as asides and not as the main source of their livelihood. To work and to earn a living, people specialize in a particular line of work. Those who do not specialize find it difficult to earn a decent living.

There is a huge division of labour in society, with different people doing different kinds of work, and together we provide all the goods and services the world consumes. We produce little of what we consume. Most things used at home come from outside the home, produced by others. For example, most of us would not even be able to produce a spoon on our own, starting from scratch. A miner would mine the iron ore, someone would convert it into pig iron and yet another would convert it into steel, which would then be moulded into a spoon by someone else. In between, there is transportation, storage, accountants, traders and so on. This shows that we are deeply interconnected and no one is self-sufficient.

At home, we do perform a variety of tasks for ourselves, such as cooking, cleaning, taking care of our children, etc. But that does not mean we are self-sufficient. Our homes are filled with goods, and we use so many services—all obtained from outside. They enable us to do the tasks we do at home but that does not get us any income. Income comes from what we do outside the home.

In an earlier era, there was greater self-sufficiency, since many things were produced at home and not bought from outside. In fact, villages in earlier times were quite self-sufficient, since they produced most of the things they needed for daily life. Only a few things came from outside. The farmer produced the food with seeds produced on the farm; manure was produced from animal waste; the bullock was used to till the field, etc. The village blacksmith produced the implements, and the carpenter and the weaver produced the cloth, etc. Thus, a village in an earlier era could continue life even if it was cut off from the rest of the world because the essentials were largely produced within.

In a modern-day village, most things come from 'outside'. Farmers may produce the wheat they eat but get the manure, implements, pesticides, etc., from outside—the earlier self-sufficiency of village life is gone. City life is even less self-sufficient. Food is brought from outside and the drinking water may come through pipelines from a lake or a river hundreds of miles away. Electricity is transmitted over long distances from big power plants located near a source of energy. In fact, in modern times, a village or a city cut off from the outside will find it difficult to survive.

## Division of Labour and Welfare

The story of Robinson Crusoe we read in our childhood can help explain matters. Crusoe was shipwrecked but was fortunate enough to land on an island. But there was no one else on that island. He was lucky there was fresh water and food available, so he could survive. But what kind of life was that? He had to do everything himself—get food, fetch water, make a shelter, get energy and so on. He had to constantly work for a very rudimentary life. He could not produce metal to even make a spoon. If he, by chance, had a knife, he could maybe carve a piece of wood. For cooking, if he needed a vessel, he would need the skill of a potter and the energy to bake earth. Even lighting a fire was tedious. Life was tough.

We are not Robinson Crusoe marooned on an island. We live in a society that has a lot of people with different kinds of skills. They operate capital of all kinds, with which all that society needs can be produced. If production were robotized, human labour would not be needed but that is not the case yet. Labour is required to run machines and offices to produce what is needed. Human presence is still required for production, even if less of it is needed than in the earlier less-mechanized era.

During the lockdown, people could not go to their workplaces, factories and offices, which led to a stoppage of production. Only the workers producing essentials were allowed to go to work.

For instance, workers producing milk, bread, drinking water and electricity continued to work. Others were required to isolate themselves at home to prevent the spread of the virus.

Modern-day production is also about scale economies. It is often concentrated in pockets that are themselves geographically widely dispersed. This necessitates that produce be moved to where the consumers are—that is, all over the globe. It, therefore, takes time to produce and then to move the produce to the consuming centres. From the time production starts to the time the consumer buys the product, there is a big gap. This means that the producers have to invest money till the final sale takes place and revenue is earned. This requires finance. Further, trade, transportation, storage and various services are required to deliver the product to the consumer. This creates the need for more specialization to effectively carry on production and distribution in modern-day societies.

The result of such specialization is that today, no country or region is self-sufficient. Global supply chains have emerged, and most nations, since they are not self-sufficient, rely on global supply chains. Of course, smaller nations have little chance of being self-sufficient, since they produce very few things and import mostly everything else. For example, Sri Lanka cannot produce a large number of the things it needs and has to import them. Even big nations such as India are only relatively self-sufficient and have to import a lot of things. The biggest economies, the US and the EU, import most items of common consumption, such as textiles and electronic items, from the developing world. They import the inputs (energy) for many of the things they produce. Even their machines may be imported. That is why the share of import in the GDP has gone up everywhere since the 1980s.

MNCs have created global supply chains to maximize their profits. China, for a variety of reasons, has increasingly become the hub of global supply for a large number of manufactured items. That is why when it locked down due to COVID-19 in the beginning of 2020, production got globally impacted. Further, as the disease spread, more and more countries declared lockdowns, and that further disturbed global supply chains and impeded production in various countries. Countries are now talking of reassessing these models of long supply chains, which, if disrupted for any reason, can damage their economies.

## Market, Money and Income

Due to specialization, the 'outside', from where one obtains what one needs, is called the 'market'. It is a place for exchanging what we produce with what others produce. This is true for both a society of an earlier era or a modern one. Earlier, people would barter what they produced with what others produced. Farmers would give grains or lentils they produced to the weaver in exchange for cloth they required and so on. This requires a double coincidence—the weaver has to find the farmer who needs the cloth he/she has woven and is willing to exchange his produce with him/her.

As specialization increases, this double coincidence of needs becomes more and more difficult to work out. A lawyer needing a piece of cloth would have to find just the right client who has spare cloth and needs to file a case. Next, having got the piece of cloth from the client, the lawyer would have to give her clerk a certain amount of it for the work done in the office. But the clerk may not need the cloth and, instead, may need shoes. The clerk would then have to look for someone who would be willing to exchange the cloth for shoes. This chain of double coincidence becomes longer and longer as specialization grows in society. That is where money enters the picture as the common medium of exchange in the market. A lawyer does not need to find the right person who wants to file a case in a court in exchange for the cloth he/she has.

Similarly, the farmer who has wheat to sell goes to the market and sells it for money. The weaver, who has cloth to sell, also sells it in the market for money. Now both go to the market and buy whatever they need. The farmer may not need to buy cloth now but may want to buy a mobile phone, and the weaver may need to buy a water filter now and not wheat. Also, the wheat bought in a Kerala village may be coming from Punjab and not the village itself. The Malayalee does not have to travel to Punjab to exchange what she has for the wheat. The cloth sold by a weaver in Rajasthan may sell in Chennai, but the weaver and the farmer do not have to meet to exchange what they produce—double coincidence is no longer required. In brief, goods and services are paid for in money and that can be used to buy whatever else one needs.

Technological development has led to production becoming more and more sophisticated and complicated. It is also broken down into its components for greater efficiency. Production of each component is assigned to a different person within a factory or an office and may even be at different locations. This means meeting each other for the exchange of what each has produced becomes more and more difficult. Exchanging components is also futile, since by themselves they do not fulfil any need of the other person. For instance, workers producing the glass casing of a car headlight exchanging their produce with someone producing the pig iron does not make sense. By themselves these things are not useful to either of the two. Money simplifies this task of exchanging products. That is why money starts to play a more and more important role in life as specialization grows in society. It also starts to play more and more complex roles and takes on a life of its own as the world of finance.

Finance dominates the world today. During the global financial crash of 2007–09, it was said that Wall Street dominated Main Street—meaning that real production in agriculture, industry and so on was secondary to what happened in the financial markets. The financial markets determine what happens in an economy and government policies are very sensitive to their dictates. Often, the finance ministers (in the US called the secretary of treasury) are people who have served in big private financial institutions. For example, in the US, many of them have been from Goldman Sachs. The current secretary, Steven Mnuchin, is also a former partner and chief information officer of Goldman Sachs.

The central banks issue currency and regulate the financial markets, and this has played a more and more important role in the economy. Their policies have become crucial in guiding an economy. Not that they determine the rate of inflation and the growth rate of an economy, but they have an impact on these and other important variables. For instance, in determining the availability of credit to businesses and the interest rates at which they can get loans, central bank policies play an important role.

The central banks globally have tried to play a role in boosting the economy during the lockdown. All of them have cut interest rates in the hope that more investment will occur and have released liquidity in the market to enable businesses to get credit. But the way the money market works in a developed economy differs from the way it works in a developing economy because of structural differences. India's central bank, the RBI, is less able to influence growth or inflation, since agriculture is still very important to the economy and its production depends on the monsoons, which, in turn, determines food inflation, an important part of the overall inflation in the economy. It also impacts growth prospects.

## National Income and Welfare

Activities performed by individuals at home do not fetch them an income. For example, a spouse taking care of the home and children does not get paid. If they are asked what work they are doing, they usually say they are not working. Actually, they are working very hard but because society says work means working outside the home to earn an income, they think of themselves as not working. The maid who comes from outside the home is paid a salary for the work she does, and she is said to be working. In the process of her working, her labour (outside her home) is exchanged with our labour performed outside our home.

The activity carried out by a person outside the home results in an income earned, and that is used to buy what one needs from the market. What the weavers produce for consumption at home cannot be exchanged outside and does not earn them an income. They have to sell their surplus production to others and that becomes their income. Note, money is used as a medium of exchange. But it is not to be confused with the income that is earned from the work that one does to produce something that is exchanged in the market.

Aggregation of what everyone produces for the market is called the annual production of a nation, the Gross Domestic Product, or the GDP. The traditional thinking is that higher the GDP, greater is the well-being of citizens. So prosperity is measured by the GDP per capita. That is the average income of citizens or the average amount of goods and services available to each person each year. Why average? Some may have a command over a lot of it while others may get little of it—that is, disparity among people may be high.

The link between the GDP and people's welfare can be tenuous because of several reasons (Kumar, 2013). First, production leads to pollution, which adversely impacts people's health, and, therefore, their welfare. Second, a high degree of inequality means that the average does not represent the welfare of those at the bottom. Third, greater inequality may lead to social and political consequences, which lowers welfare. Fourth, much of the work done at home (called free labour) is not counted in the GDP while that may be the biggest source of welfare for the family. And so on.

So during a lockdown, when people cannot go out to work, they can continue to work at home. But most of the work (except for production of essentials) that gets counted in the market and in the GDP stops. As a result, people's incomes fall, which, in turn, leads to a fall in their capacity to buy what others produce. So demand falls.

## Changing Production Structure

Specialization has brought about big changes in the production structures of all economies in the world and made them more vulnerable to lockdowns. Freezing of supplies anywhere affects production downstream. An economy can be divided into three broad components—the primary, the secondary and the tertiary sectors. The primary sector consists of agriculture, forestry, etc., which are gifts of nature. The secondary sector processes the produce of the primary sector. For instance, sugarcane is used to produce sugar, and iron ore to produce iron. The tertiary sector produces services such as trade, transport, education and health.

At present, the tertiary sector, dominates the economies of the world, including in most developing economies. In 1950, the Indian economy was largely dependent on agriculture, which produced 55 per cent of the output and employed 88 per cent of the workforce. It was not until 1980 that the weight of agriculture became less than that of the services that were rapidly growing in India (Kumar, 2013). Currently, agriculture makes up only about 12 per cent of the GDP while services contribute to 55 per cent (See Tables II.1 and IV.1). This has now become the global trend. In the US, in 2019, agriculture contributed 0.9 per cent to the GDP while services contributed 77.4 per cent. In 1948, the shares of the GDP for the US were 20 per cent from agriculture and 60 per cent from services (Ott, 1987).

Agriculture is the major component of the primary sector. In the developed world agricultural production takes place in large, open farms or in greenhouses, which means people do not work in close quarters with each other. Even in India, where most farms are small, work takes place in the open and people do not need to work close to each other. Due to mechanization, very few farm hands are required in the developed world. This trend is catching on even in the developing countries, such as India. The implication is that whether in the US or in India, work in agriculture can go on with physical distancing.

So, during a lockdown, work or production need not stop in agriculture. Since agriculture produces one of the essentials of life, this gives us the assurance that in spite of a lockdown, when most work comes to a halt and people are unemployed, life can continue.

India, with its huge surplus foodstock, a bumper crop in April (rabi crop) and continuing production in the next crop cycle (kharif crop), can feed its population without difficulty, even when work stops in other lines of production.

The services sector is the biggest contributor to the GDP. It often requires people to be in close proximity to each other and, therefore, poses a serious problem of continuing production during a lockdown. For instance, health and education require people to be in reasonably close proximity. Doctors have to see patients and classrooms are mostly full of students. Similarly, barbers, retailers, restaurants, movie halls, taxi drivers, bankers, lawyers, etc., have to have people in close proximity to work. Even e-commerce, where people need not go to an establishment, requires big warehouses where people work near each other and delivery workers who have to drop packages at the buyers' addresses come in contact with others. In the case of many services, therefore, contact among people is required and these activities need to stop during a lockdown.

Only in the case of some services, work can be done without coming in contact with others—from home. Like in the case of software developers, share brokers, chartered accountants and insurance agents. A lot of banking can be done via the Internet but some bankers are needed in offices for routine work. Patients can consult doctors via teleconference but that also has severe limitations and is often unsatisfactory. Working from home can also be distracting, since one has to balance work and family life, and efficiency may decline.

Some work may be done remotely, such as running the courts of justice, but even that requires work at the registry and some contact with people. It is important to note here that the amount of work that can be done from a distance in the case of courts is small, compared to their normal working. During the lockdown in India, the courts took up far fewer cases than before and the pendency of cases which was already high in Indian courts has increased further. Litigants were not able to meet lawyers and, therefore, filing of cases declined, compared to normal times. This also implies that seeking justice has become more difficult. In fact, the current situation has resulted in many young lawyers being forced to look for alternative career options as legal work has dried up.

In the case of education, online classes have been tried but are proving to be difficult for a large number of children who do not have access to smartphones or laptops, and sometimes even the Internet and electricity. Also, teachers are not used to delivering lectures or notes online. Much experimentation is going on but it is still work in progress. Getting the attention of children in a classroom even in the presence of a teacher is difficult; it can only be imagined how much more difficult it could get when the child only has a screen to look at. While mature students or those pursuing higher degrees may be able to use the Internet effectively, it is difficult for the average student to do so. Hence, the gap between students from better-off families and poor ones, and the motivated students and the less-committed ones, is likely to increase. Very often, parents have to supervise the child at home and that prevents them from going to work.

A lockdown, thus, means that many of the services cannot be produced or delivered. In India, in April 2020, during the lockdown, the Purchasing Managers' Index (PMI) for services dropped to a historic low of 5.4. A value of 50 means no change; anything greater than that means expansion while any number less than that means contraction. Thus, 5.4 stands for extreme contraction of the services sector—it implies the collapse of production of services.

The third part of the economy is the secondary sector. It includes manufacturing, construction, electricity, and gas and water supply. It basically uses the raw materials provided by the primary sector, which comes from nature, and converts them into products—such as sugarcane converted into sugar, cotton into cloth and iron ore into steel. For the US economy, the contribution of this sector has been fairly stable, around 20 per cent of the GDP for a long time (Ott, 1987). For the Indian economy, it is currently around 28 per cent (NAS, 2019).

This sector requires people to work in factories and workshops in a closed environment. Even though a lot of automation has taken place so that fewer and fewer workers are needed to produce goods, workers are still needed. For instance, in automobile factories, a lot of robots are used but people are still needed for various tasks, such as taking care of machines and the assembling of cars. If production could be completely robotized, workers would not have been needed, but that is not yet the case anywhere. Even in the case of restaurants, where robots are being used to serve customers, workers are needed behind the robots. Similarly, robotized surgery requires a skilled doctor to supervise and take over in case anything goes wrong. Drones may be able to do deliveries but they have to be centrally controlled.

Thus, during a lockdown, most workers are not allowed to go to work and production comes to a halt both in the services sector and in the secondary sector. Only essential work takes place, such as production of food and medicines, and carrying out of medical services and civil administration to implement the lockdown. Most of the other government work also stops.

### The Marginalized Unorganized

The Indian economy is complex. Its intricacy cannot be completely captured by the three broad sectors mentioned in the previous section. Each of these broad sectors is further subdivided between the organized and the unorganized sectors. Even though 55 per cent of production is generated by the former, it hardly employs 6 per cent of the workforce (Kumar, 2018), while the latter produces 45 per cent of the output but employs a whopping 94 per cent of the workforce. Most of the economy, therefore, consists of workers from the unorganized sector, even though they produce a small share of the output of the economy.

The organized sector works with advanced technology, uses skilled labour and pays them well by Indian standards. The unorganized sector typically works with low technology and pays little. For example, compare a waiter at a five-star hotel and one who works in a dhaba. Despite similar work, the salary differential between the two sectors can be a factor of 5 to 10. So, of course most workers want to work in the organized sector but, because of higher automation, few new jobs are generated there. Perforce, workers have to work in the unorganized sector. Often, it is the residual sector, where people are forced to generate work for themselves (Kumar, 2013).

Due to paucity of work, workers may push a cart, drive a rickshaw, sell vegetables on the streets and so on. In the cottage sector (the unorganized sector in which family-based work is done), family members may pitch in with work, such as making envelopes, quilts or potato chips at home. In small auto-repair shops, lathe machine shops or electrical-repair shops, there may be one or two helpers. This is the micro sector of the economy, where each unit works with a small amount of capital and a few workers. The average employment is 1.7 persons per such micro unit.

During the lockdown, work in the unorganized sector stopped, since most of the workers were not able to go to work. Also because of lack of capital, the units were not able to buy raw material. These small units were not able to sell their products, since markets shut down and consumers could not buy. Most of the micro units work from very congested areas in the cities, such as Dharavi in Mumbai, and because of the danger of the disease spreading, these areas were shut down.

Google can track mobility data showing where people are going—to markets and to work. It compared the mobility data of January and February 2020 with that of the lockdown period of March, April and May. The comparison showed a marked decline in activity. But this does not give the full picture, since a lot of the unorganized-sector workers stayed in slums close to the place of work or at the workplace itself—in shops, establishments and dhabas. Also, due to their poverty, they may not have a smart phone or several family members may share a common phone. So the decline in activity would be more than that indicated by Google.

The workers in the unorganized sectors are characterized by not only very low wages but also an insecure tenure of work. They can be removed from work any time. If there is work, the employer hires them, otherwise they are left high and dry. Many of them are daily-wage earners who stand at street crossings (chowk) every morning in the hope that someone will offer them an odd job. Many are self-employed, such as a barber or a rickshaw puller. In a lockdown, the work of all these workers stops and so does their income.

Most of these workers live close to the extreme poverty line, if not below it. They are barely able to meet their day-to-day essential expenditures of food, clothing, housing and so on. Most of them hardly have any savings. It's day-to-day survival for them and, as such, any shock in their life can lead to their slipping below the poverty line. During the lockdown, they could not meet even the basics of survival—they had no savings to stock up on essentials, unlike the well-off sections of society.

As mentioned earlier, a large number of workers in the unorganized sector are migrants from villages. Due to technical changes and growing mechanization, agriculture does not generate new employment. So to get better incomes, a large number of them migrate to cities to improve prospects for their families. Whatever savings they make are mostly sent to their families in their villages.

Without savings, as soon as the lockdown started, many migrants started to starve, with little access to food and water. Often, to save money, five or ten migrants rent a room together so they can share the rent. In some places, people even have to sleep in shifts. One worker told me that they were five to a room and could not even afford to stretch out and sleep, so they stayed awake till they couldn't anymore and then curled up and slept. Most workers did not even have the money to pay the rent for the little room in which they lived. Further, in many cases, the landlords worried about the spread of the disease asked the workers to vacate the rooms.

The lockdown was a disaster for them. They had to face either hunger or the disease. Often, they were heard saying it was better to be with their own families if they had to die. They were also heard saying that they would not return to the cities because of the way they had been treated during the lockdown. While some have returned, many are still in the villages. After all, there is little work in the villages, and that is why they had come to the city in the first place. The situation in the villages became worse with so many workers returning. Once again, this highlights the desperate situation of most workers in India.

## Supply Chains

No production is possible without input. For example, to produce utensils, steel is required—which requires pig iron as input and which is made from iron ore. This is an example of a supply chain to produce a relatively simple product. When more complex things are produced, such as, say, a mobile phone, the supply chain gets more complex, since various components are required that may be supplied by vendors from across the globe. A variety of raw materials, such as gold, rare earth elements and ceramics, are needed from across the world. An aircraft is even more complex, and has an even longer supply chain. Modern-day economies consume a lot of different inputs, and to produce them, long supply chains stretching across the globe are needed. That is the reason trade has proliferated, which is what is referred to as 'globalization'.

If supplies get disturbed at some point, it impacts the entire chain. Trade and transport have to function efficiently for raw materials to reach producers and for the finished products to reach the consumers. During a lockdown, all this gets disturbed and production gets curtailed. Production stops not only because of the inability of workers to reach their factories or offices, but also because of the disruption in supplies. This impacts even essential goods, which are allowed to be produced during a lockdown.

Without trade and transportation, even essential goods cannot be produced, even if workers are available. This means that raw materials required for the production of essentials also have to be treated as essentials for them to be produced and supplied to the population. For instance, to supply packaged food items or frozen food items, packaging and refrigeration have to also be treated as essential. The implication is that packaging material such as cardboard, aluminium and plastic also need to be considered as essential. Repair of refrigerators becomes essential and so does repair of electrical equipment needed in retail stores. The point is that in an integrated production system, it is difficult to say what is 'non-essential'.

If the lockdown is short, all production can be halted for that period and the inventory of essentials in the pipeline can be used to supply to the public. But in a long lockdown, the availability of essentials may become problematic and shortages may develop. If production of these items is to restart, many associated lines of production may have to be allowed to operate but under strict conditions of physical distancing and other precautions.

So managing supplies in a lockdown is tricky and administration has to monitor the situation carefully. Both the lockdown and the supply of essentials are necessary. Globally, China has been at the centre of much of manufacturing. In January 2020, when the pandemic spread across China and it went into a lockdown, global 'supply chains' were disrupted. That impacted production across the globe, including in India. For instance, more than 70 per cent of the inputs into medicines, a large percentage of mobile phones and inputs into electronics come from China. Several countries, therefore, are rethinking their dependence on only one source of supplies—the thinking is to keep the supply chain within one's national boundary, as far as possible. This will impact the nature of globalization the world has been witnessing the past few decades.

## Inventory and Working Capital Requirement

Businesses hold some amount of inputs in stock so that they don't have to face a shortage of input that can force production to stop. Even what is produced is held in stock until it is sold. For instance, one sees pictures of a large number of cars parked outside an automobile factory or a car dealer. Stocks of input and output are called the inventory.

There is a cost attached to inventory. Loans are taken from banks to hold the inventory. As sales take place, revenue is earned and the money borrowed from banks can be returned, along with the interest accrued on it. But because the inventory is constantly held, the loan taken is called the working capital and it is a rolling loan that is not returned—only the interest is regularly paid to the bank. In effect, interest is the cost of holding the inventory.

Businesses try to minimize their inventories to lower costs and maximize their profits. The new concept in this context is 'just in time'—namely, getting raw materials daily, producing daily and selling daily, so that the working capital requirement becomes less and the interest outgo gets minimized. But, in this case, one has to be sure of getting supplies every day, or else production will come to a halt and costs will rise.

If sales stop, revenue is not earned but interest payment has to continue. Further, as sales decline, inventory builds up, since the factories hold the raw materials and the unsold finished products. Additionally, workers and managers still have to be paid and other overhead costs have to be borne. This leads to increased borrowing from banks and increased interest-payment obligations.

Some well-run businesses have reserves. These are their savings from past earnings. These reserves can be used to take care of current requirements of cash, but it also means that losses rise and savings are depleted. Not-so-well-run businesses that do not have reserves find themselves in greater losses and may either default on interest payments or become sick companies. In turn, this results in difficulties for the banks, since the loans on which interest is not paid are called non-performing assets, or NPAs. So the banks' financial position also deteriorates.

Some businesses run on a lot of borrowing compared to their equity. They are called 'highly leveraged'. They have a high interest burden relative to their sales and are the first businesses that collapse when the economy slows down or if it shuts down during a lockdown.

Small businesses work with small amounts of working capital. Often, the banks impose onerous conditions on them or these businesses borrow from informal money markets at high interest rates. If the owners of these businesses have some savings, they use it as working capital. When the economy shuts down, these businesses exhaust their working capital quickly. Further, they need to continue consumption and use their savings for that purpose, the result is that they don't have capital left to restart business. Finally, small businesses are often suppliers to big and medium businesses that do not pay them on time. Thus, their need for working capital increases. When production stops, payments are further delayed and more working capital is required, which is not available—and that leads to the collapse of these businesses.

It is, therefore, easy to conclude that in a lockdown, the likelihood of failure for small and weak businesses and companies in the financial sector increases. Even after the lockdown was lifted, these businesses have found it difficult to restart on their own. Failure of these units leads to a permanent loss of employment and a crisis in the lives of their workers. Since most of the employment in India is in the small and cottage sectors, if they fail, the crisis of unemployment aggravates.

## Modern Economy: Role of Supply and Demand

As argued earlier, the economy of the earlier era was simple, with barter taking place within a small community such as a village. Modern-day economies, with much greater complexity and difficulty of finding double coincidence, use money as the medium of exchange. This shift also produced a big change in the way the economy works.

The role of supply in an economy can be understood with the following examples. In earlier times, the production of wheat was used both for consumption and for planting in the next season. The latter is both savings and investment. In such an economy, consumption, investment and savings were all in the form of physical goods. With more wheat sown, there was more investment and more production in the next crop cycle. Similarly, the cloth produced by the weaver, in such an economy, was entirely consumed. So the more the cloth produced, the more was its consumption in the community.

The discussion above implies that in earlier times, where money played a minor role in the exchange of goods and services, the important thing was how much society produced—that is, supply. This is captured in Say's law as, 'Supply creates its own demand.'

In a modern-day economy, where exchange is through the medium of money, a major change occurs. Keynes (1936) pointed out that things were turned on their head. Demand now matters more and that is what turns the wheels of the economy. Only if people go to the market to buy things will sales occur and producers be able to sell their products. If people do not demand a product, sales will not take place and producers will have to stop producing that product. If they don't stop, they will have unsold inventory, which will lead to increased costs and possible losses.

More importantly, investment is not automatic. Producers have to make a decision on how much demand there will be and how much they will need to invest to meet any extra demand. So expectations about the future become crucial. Very often, these expectations turn out to be incorrect since these are guesses and, consequently, one finds that one has overinvested or underinvested, resulting in losses. When investment is short, not enough employment is generated and incomes fall. So does demand and, resultantly, production declines further. Thus, investment is the crucial variable for growth of the modern-day economy, and its extent depends on the expected future demand.

It is not the number of people that matters but the demand they generate. India has a huge population but since most earn very little by world standards, demand is low. Demand is not to be confused with need. People may need many things but may not have the income to buy them, and so demand may be short in spite of large numbers.

To generate demand, advertising is used. Where need does not exist, it is created. For instance, fashion was created to sell more clothes, so people opt to give up their old clothes (which can easily last much longer) to buy newer ones. Car models are changed so that people buy new cars even if their earlier cars can last many more years. This is consumerism—consumption for the sake of consumption. Consumption of basics is necessary but one can do without inessentials. The result is social waste and environmental degradation.

There are essential and non-essential goods and services. Life can continue without the non-essential goods and services but not without the essential ones. One needs water but can do without aerated drinks, demand for which is created via high-pressure advertising. Good public transportation is necessary but private ownership of vehicles is not. Basic clothing is necessary but closets full of dresses is not.

In the modern-day economy, production of the non-essentials is what keeps demand high, so that production takes place and employment is generated. Is there no alternative? People have got so used to this waste that they treat any advice against consumerism as paternalistic. No matter how apparent it is that the environment is deteriorating and leading to climate change, these are not seen as immediate threats but something to be concerned about in future.

However, the difficulties that a large number of people now face due to the pandemic may make society rethink this. Due to lockdowns around the world, a large number of people had to survive only on essentials, either because that was the only thing available or because that was what was provided as support to the unemployed. Further, if, due to environmental damage, animals are transmitting disease to humans, and pandemics keep occurring, people will see this as an immediate threat. So they may be willing to cut down on non-essential consumption. This would be a permanent gain for society.

### Globalization, Capital and Labour—Rising Inequality

Kumar (2013) points out that globalization is a long-standing process. It is not a recent phenomenon starting in, say, 1979, when Margaret Thatcher became the prime minister of the UK, or 1991, when India introduced the New Economic Policy (NEP). But the phase since the 1980s is characterized as one of marketization. It is accompanied by great flexibility enjoyed by capital, which can move around quickly from one jurisdiction to another. A new financial architecture has emerged that affords capital such mobility and often in secrecy, which the national governments cannot check.

It is based on the large number of tax havens that enable capital to hide its identity and move quickly (Tax Haven Team, 2014). Mobility of capital has strengthened it, compared to labour. National governments are now required to formulate policies as per the desires of capital so as to retain it. These policies are called the Washington Consensus (Williamson, 1989). Capital's high degree of mobility makes national governments compete against one another. If one jurisdiction offers a concession, others have to follow suit. India has had to lower its corporate tax rates because other countries have a lower tax rate. Capital gains tax had to be lowered, even though it leads to speculative activity, because other countries have a lower tax rate.

This is why even the European governments have had to lower tax rates since the 1990s. As the Soviet Bloc collapsed, the east European countries offered lower tax rates to attract capital. This forced the west Europeans to also lower tax rates. This has come to be called the 'race to the bottom'. Ireland cut its rates the most and got many major companies from the US to set up businesses there. For instance, Google, Starbucks and many other companies have located their businesses in Ireland. This is called base erosion and profit shifting (BEPS). The consequence of this competition has been that governments have lost tax revenue and there has been a shortage of revenue for public services. For instance, India has one of the lowest expenditure (as per cent of the GDP) on education and health and one of the smallest size of police, judiciary and the bureaucracy compared to many other countries. The impact of this is visible in the current pandemic as the weakened public healthcare system finds it difficult to cope with the virus.

The global financial architecture is governed by global financial firms and institutions. There are credit-rating agencies such as Fitch and global financial institutions such as the IMF, the World Bank and the Asian Development Bank (ADB). They put pressure on governments to toe the line dictated by finance. If a country strays from the path dictated by them, it is punished with capital flying away from that country. The stock market declines rapidly as capital is withdrawn and a balance-of-payment (BOP) crisis follows. The currency depreciates and interest rates rise. Inflation soars and growth slows down. Therefore, economies, especially those of developing countries, are forced to toe the line dictated by global financial institutions.

The result of these trends has been the weakening of labour in society and a dramatic rise in inequalities across the globe (Kumar, 2013). The pandemic has highlighted this, since a large number of workers don't have a living wage and have no savings and, therefore, find themselves unable to cope with a lockdown. In brief, the problems of globalization as marketization are now starkly visible.

# IV

# Lockdown and After: Understanding the Macroeconomic Aspects

The previous chapter highlighted the role of the division of labour, money, income generation, supply and demand, financial architecture and globalization. All these refer to the big picture of an economy, as opposed to the nitty-gritty of what happens to an individual or a firm. The former is referred to as macroeconomics and the latter, microeconomics.

## Why Macro First

Macroeconomics takes precedence over microeconomics, since the former sets the stage for the latter. That is what the Keynesian revolution was all about. If the macro is right, the micro can be geared to be what is needed by the economy. If the macro is not set right, contradictions emerge among the micro aspects. Hence, there is a need to understand the macroeconomic aspects of the lockdown first, before one can analyse the micro aspects—namely what will happen to individuals and firms.

Some economists feel that the individuals and the firms make up the economy, so understanding their behaviour will help one understand the big picture. This is called building the macro from the micro, or the micro foundations of macroeconomics. In economics, this does not work, as Keynes (1936) has illustrated. There is the 'fallacy of composition', which implies that the sum of parts does not add up to the whole. This not only applies to economics but to other fields as well, such as physics. For instance, the behaviour of an individual molecule outside a crystal is quite different from when it is part of the crystal.

In economics, take an individual, say, Robinson Crusoe again, and add up 'n' of such individuals. Would that be the macro of a society consisting of 'n' individuals? Indeed not. For Crusoe, there was no division of labour and no exchange, since there was no one to share the work with or produce anything that was needed—he had to do all the work himself. There would be no need for money. Similarly, there would be no language, since there would be no one to communicate with and so on. So multiplying his behaviour by 'n' would not give us the behaviour of society.

Keynes illustrated this by talking of the 'widow's cruse'. If everyone decides to save more, ceteris paribus (with other things being equal or unchanged), demand will come down and production will decline. As a result, the amount of savings will not change. The amount of savings in a monetized economy is determined by the amount of investment (Kalecki, 1971). So to increase the total savings in such an economy, the total investment will have to be raised. For instance, if animal spirits (investor exuberance) are high during a boom and businesses invest more than earlier, savings in the economy will go up.

In brief, macroeconomics can be counter-intuitive and needs to be understood before the other aspects of the economy can be discussed. This is also true in the context of a lockdown. Therefore, in this chapter, the macro aspects of a lockdown will be discussed and then, in subsequent chapters, the micro aspects will be taken up. The analysis of macroeconomics is based on the understanding of what happens to macroeconomic variables—incomes, investments, savings, exports, imports and the growth rate of the economy.

*Classification of Countries Affected by the Pandemic*

Due to the COVID-19 pandemic, countries can be classified into three categories. Those that got the disease early and quickly recovered from it, such as China and South Korea; and those that are going through different phases of easing of lockdown, called 'unlock', while the disease is still spreading fast, such as India. Finally, those that had controlled the disease and opened up but are now facing a second round of spread of infection, such as Italy, Spain, France and the UK. India and the US were more or less in lockdown till May. The US presented a mixed picture across its various states. New York was in strict lockdown and recovered, but many of the southern states did not practise strict lockdowns and saw cases rise dramatically. Brazil did not practise a lockdown at all and its case count rose, quickly making it the second-most affected country after the US [See Graph 01].

In India, too, the lockdown was gradually relaxed from around the middle of April, but substantially only from June. However, in India, unlike the other two categories of countries, the lockdown was lifted even when the disease had not been substantially brought under control; in other countries, the number of new cases and deaths had peaked and then declined substantially before the lockdown was lifted. In these countries, testing and tracing had been ramped up. Unfortunately, in India, relaxation took place when the number of tests were still way below what was needed in such a large country (Graph 06).

As argued in Chapter I, the pressure to lift the lockdown came from businesses. This is true for all countries. Businesses realized that they were likely to fail if the lockdown continued for long. In the US, Trump threatened to lift the lockdown way before some of the badly hit states wanted to. In Brazil, as mentioned earlier, Bolsanaro refused to order a lockdown at all. In both these countries the number of cases rose rapidly. India has followed that path in spite of the lockdown.

The countries in the first category, the ones that recovered, give hope that others can also recover and get back to near-normalcy. But as argued earlier, normalcy is unlikely until the disease is controlled globally. China and Singapore have experienced a second wave of the disease due to returning citizens. How have the economies of these countries performed after they lifted the lockdown?

China was initially reported to have ramped up production after the lockdown ended. In the first quarter of 2020, the rate of growth of the Chinese economy slipped from about +6 per cent in the previous quarter to -6.8 per cent. This is in spite of the fact that they quickly and brutally imposed a lockdown in the Hubei province and prevented the spread of the disease to the rest of the country. This also ensured the lockdown could be relaxed quickly in the country. As a result, in the second quarter, the economy recovered to +3.2 per cent growth (BBC, 2020b).

Full recovery to pre-pandemic levels will be difficult for China because it is a large exporter. As mentioned in the previous chapter, it is a big supply hub and has huge exports. Since production in other big countries has declined drastically due to lockdowns, they will import less from China, which will put a dent in China's overall exports. While exports of masks, PPE kits, ventilators and similar items may increase due to the pandemic, this is a tiny part of their overall exports. It cannot compensate for the decline in the rest of the export items. Production, therefore, cannot be ramped up to full capacity and investment will also not pick up any time soon.

In brief, because the rest of the world is in deep recession and there is little prospect of revival in the short run, China, as a large exporter, will also face lower growth due to a decline in export demand. The big difference is that when China underwent a lockdown, it was alone, while afterwards, when China recovered, a large number of big economies (such as the US, the EU and India) were in lockdown at the same time. So when the world economy is in deep recession, China is trying to emerge from its own downturn and may have certain advantages. It can try to increase internal demand, but that is not going to be easy for a population that has passed through traumatic times. It can try to increase public investment, but it remains to be seen whether that can overcome the decline in exports and consumption.

## Worse than a War or a Global Financial Crisis

The economies of the world have faced crises from time to time and weathered the storms. There are wars in which production gets disturbed and there are recessions when the economies go into reverse gear. The question is: Will the experience of how to deal with these crises help in the present situation?

The countries in lockdown were producing a fraction of what they used to in pre-pandemic times. As a result, income generation fell drastically. However, consumption has to continue. Savings are the difference between income and consumption. So, as incomes fall and consumption falls less, savings decline. Those who lose work and have no income have to dissave—that is, they have to use up their past savings. Investment by businesses almost stops due to decline in demand and the uncertainty prevailing about the future. These are conditions that have not been experienced since the Great Depression. So, will the experience of the recessions and depressions help now?

Actually, the situation is worse than what had happened during the depression of the 1930s or during the world wars.

During wars, production does not fall—it only gets reoriented to the requirements of war. For example, in Germany during the Second World War, a chocolate factory started to produce airplane propellers. In the US, car factories started to produce aircraft. Further, there was no unemployment because people were drafted into the war effort. This is the opposite of what is being faced during the lockdown now. There is massive unemployment since production has stopped, and people have been laid off.

During recessions and depressions, demand is down and unemployment is high, but it is not that supply stops. There is no curb on producing things. Production is down not because people cannot go to work but because their demand for what is being produced declines. In a lockdown, production cannot take place, so both supply and demand collapse.

Simultaneously, workers get laid off and their incomes fall, and most businesses close down and their profits fall and even turn into losses. The result is that a large number of people lose their incomes and, therefore, demand falls drastically. This is a unique situation and past experiences of dealing with crises are no guide to predicting what will happen in future and how one should deal with the present situation.

In brief, during a lockdown, there is voluntary stoppage of production by society and that leads to a shrinkage of the resource base of the economy. Such a situation is unprecedented.

Therefore, there is need for a new macroeconomic understanding of the situation (See Kumar, 2020i). The macro-variables—output, employment, prices, savings, investments and foreign trade—need to be reformulated and studied in the light of the changed situation.

## Lockdown and Macro-Variables

Unemployment, Compression of Profits, Wages and Consumption

During lockdown, as production of most goods and services stops, incomes fall drastically. A large number of workers lose employment since businesses are not able to pay salaries, given that a) their revenue falls to near zero b) they have to bear the cost of holding inventories c) they have to maintain basic upkeep of factories and offices and d) they have to pay interest on their borrowed capital. So businesses start incurring losses even if they were profitable earlier.

In brief, both profits and wages fall in the economy during a lockdown.

In India, it is the large unorganized sector that immediately shut down and a majority of its workforce lost work and incomes.

They have no social security and little savings. Even many employed in the organized sector are contract workers from the unorganized sector. They can be fired any time without any notice as businesses face difficulties. These workers were the first to lose employment as businesses in the organized sector shut down.

In brief, most of the unorganized-sector workers lost employment in India. This would also be the case in most of the developing countries. In the developed world, this category would comprise of the small businesses, which also shut down and retrenched workers.

A vast majority of Indians who are working in the unorganized sector and/or are poor, have low incomes and hardly any savings. So when incomes stop, their consumption drastically falls. The small- and cottage-sector producers are also like the unorganized workers, with little savings that quickly get exhausted when production stops. That makes it difficult for them to restart their businesses when the situation normalizes.

Those in the organized sector have some protection and social security. But all across the world, workers in this sector also lost work as businesses closed down. In the US, by mid-June, 44 million people had filed for initial jobless claims in twelve weeks—in spite of the relaxation in the lockdown and many being rehired (Davidson, 2020). This is an unprecedented number and many times larger than during the global financial crisis of 2007–09. This again illustrates that this crisis is different from the earlier crises faced by the world.

In India, too, workers in the organized sectors lost employment. They were asked to go on leave, told to resign if they did not want to be fired, told to take a salary cut and, in many cases, simply given the pink slip. The government, on 29 March, mandated by notification that employers should pay full salaries to workers but the matter went to the Supreme Court, which said that the government could not force employers to pay full wages (Mathur, 2020). In the US too, employers were told to pay a certain percentage of the income to workers, and this amount was given to businesses from the budget as a support. But in spite of that, a lot of people were simply laid off. The US government also gave money to people so that they could continue to buy food, pay rent and so on. However, this was inadequate and many people queued up in their cars at food-distribution centres.

Businesses that were shut down or worked only partially during the lockdown incurred losses, as explained in the previous chapter. Thus, owners of capital, who are usually well off, also suffered a loss of income. As a result of expectations of business losses, stock markets and financial markets declined. Initially, all over the world, in March and April, the stock markets fell by record amounts. They picked up subsequently in the hope that government interventions will revive the economy. But the stock market recovery has been narrow and looks unsustainable, and may peter out (See Chapter IV for a more detailed discussion).

A decline in the stock markets makes the rich feel less wealthy. This has a negative impact on their consumption and investment. This situation in economics is called the 'wealth effect'. Due to the wealth effect, the rich cut back on their luxury consumption. In India, the sales of luxury cars fell sharply both during and after the lockdown. Further, during a lockdown, as businesses close down or incur losses, properties are either vacated and/or landlords reduce rents. Thus, not only rentals but the capital value of properties, too, see a decline, since they come into the market but there are very few buyers there. Those who depend on their interest income from bank deposits for a living also find their returns declining as the interest rates are cut. So, again, the rich feel less wealthy and cut back on consumption and investment, even though they have the savings to continue their usual consumption.

Those who do not lose employment in the organized sector—such as government servants, medical professionals, and those working in FMCG and other essential sectors—continue to earn incomes like before. They also have savings. In anticipation of the lockdown, these people and the rich went to stores and emptied out the shelves of essentials. So the demand for essentials shot up—to the detriment of the poor, who do not have the capacity to stock up. But this increase in demand can only be a temporary blip, since, as the situation normalizes, people who had hoarded these supplies will reduce their demand for these items.

The implication of the organized-sector employees continuing to get their salaries in spite of production stopping is that companies dissave—but this cannot last for long. The self-employed and the retired elderly have eaten into their savings. Small savers who had invested in the stock market directly or via mutual funds have suffered losses and a lot of their assets have evaporated.

Overall, consumption collapsed, since even the well-off mostly bought the essentials and not the non-essentials. Whenever there is so much uncertainty, as created by the pandemic, people turn cautious and postpone buying discretionary items of consumption. They can always buy a car or a shirt later, when things are more under control. Under the circumstances, given the uncertainty, most consumers prefer to spend only on essentials and save for the future.

There is also fear of a second wave of the disease (like in the case of the Spanish flu, when more people died in the second wave) and the possibility of another lockdown. There is also the fear of losing one's job in the second wave, when things could be worse than in the first wave. All this causes a lot of uncertainty in the mind of the public and turns it conservative as far as unnecessary expenditures go. This is reflected in the decline of 'consumer confidence' (RBI, Monetary Policy Report October 2020).

As discussed earlier, most services are difficult to deliver while maintaining physical distancing—such as in the case of parlours, salons, restaurants, hotels, and the entertainment, tourism and travel industries. Thus, a large chunk of consumption is ruled out or greatly restricted, and these businesses find it difficult to revive themselves. The fear is that as these businesses restart after a lockdown, they will not be able to function as earlier. They are faced with low demand, which means revenues will fall but costs will rise due to the need for physical distancing and maintaining sanitary conditions. Therefore, many of these businesses will go into losses and ultimately fail.

Agriculture, which can function with physical distancing, has also suffered in the current situation. With large numbers of people unemployed, restaurants and hotels closing, and entertainment and festivities brought to a halt, demand for food has fallen. Many farmers were not able to sell their produce and ploughed it into the field rather than harvesting it. Due to transportation stopping, fruits and vegetables could not be moved from farms to cities. Prices collapsed at the farm gate while they rose in the urban consuming centres due to shortages and hoarding. So a large number of farmers lost their incomes, even though they could continue farming. Their consumption of non-agricultural goods and services also declined. Many in rural areas who depended on remittances from their relatives in the cities would also have lower incomes because their relatives returned to the villages and then they also had to be taken care of.

In brief, due to the lockdown, almost every segment of society lost incomes—the organized sector, the unorganized sector, farmers, many in the middle classes and the rich. This loss of income meant that even consumption of essentials came down during the lockdown. Demand for a majority of services and for discretionary items collapsed even more. Therefore, there was loss of incomes and work and as a result, overall consumption will not revive any time soon. This is at the heart of the demand problem.

Dissaving during a Lockdown

Savings are the balance of income left after consumption. If incomes collapse, savings also fall. Even if incomes drop, consumption has to continue at a rudimentary level. This forces people to tap into their savings—that is, they start to dissave. Small businesses use up their savings for current consumption. Deposits in banks are withdrawn to keep cash in hand. Still, deposits increase as people withdraw from other investments (such as the stock market and mutual funds) and put the money in the banks so as to remain liquid. Thus, deposits increase while credit demand falls, since production and investment decline and banks end up with excess funds.

That is why the interest rate reduction by the central bank does not give a boost to investment and the economy—businesses that are shut do not need credit. Banks park their excess funds with the RBI to earn a return.

In Chapter II, it was argued that producers hold some raw material in stock so that even if supplies get affected for some reason, they can continue producing. But inventories have a financial cost, since working capital is borrowed from banks and interest has to be paid to them. As a result, companies minimize their inventories. But then, even a small supply disruption due to a lockdown quickly shuts down production in the entire supply chain and income generation stops.

For instance, if cotton is unavailable, thread cannot be produced, and because of that, cloth production stops. Further, the processing units do not get work. In turn, garment manufacturers and cloth merchants get impacted. Less transport is used, accountants become idle, and so do shopkeepers once stocks have been exhausted. Workers all through the chain lose work.

Healthy companies have reserves (savings), which they can use for a while, but that is not the case with weak companies or smaller units that have little savings. Both the strong and the weak companies have to dip into their savings. For instance, a profitable airline company that operates fewer flights, has aircraft, pilots and crew idle, and the company and its employees lose incomes and, therefore, savings are correspondingly less. The airline has to use its reserves to continue operations and is hence dissaving.

A lockdown does two things. First, workers cannot go to operate the machines or produce services; and second, supplies of inputs are disrupted and, consequently, production gets impacted. So, even though workers and capital both exist, production declines, and incomes and savings fall.

As businesses fail, their loans from banks turn into NPAs. This impacts the income and the savings of the banks. Banks borrow from their depositors who may not get interest or in an extreme situation many not be able to get the money deposited by them. So both the banks and their depositors lose their savings.

The smaller units and cottage industry usually do not get loans from established institutions (banks and non-banking financial companies, or NBFCs). There are several reasons for this—such as lack of collateral or the institutions finding it too expensive to give out small loans or just plain and simple corruption. So these smaller units often depend on private lenders (who charge high interest rates) and/or invest their own savings in their ventures. When they close down or curtail production, they are unable to repay their creditors or have to consume their savings. Either way, savings decline or dry up completely.

In all these cases, whether it is the rich or the poor, big or small businesses, savings decline as production declines or stops, resulting in dissaving.

## Investment Falls

Working capital is part of the investment in the economy and, as argued earlier, production cannot take place without it. So investments are more important than consumption to keep the economy going. When consumption takes place, demand is generated. But that requires people to have an income and that, in turn, requires production, which crucially depends on investment. As discussed in the previous chapter, in a monetized economy, demand is the key to growth and what is being argued here is that investment is the more crucial part of demand.

So, if investments decline, demand falls, production is cut back and incomes decline—so do consumption and savings. In this vicious cycle, demand falls further. The result is idle production capacity and, due to that, investing more does not make sense.

Why do businesses invest more? They anticipate an increase in sales due to a rise in demand and feel they need more capacity to produce. If one is producing 100 cars but selling only 70 (capacity utilization is 70 per cent), one can meet demand without further investment. If it is selling 90 cars (capacity utilization is 90 per cent), it may think of investing in expanding capacity to 110 cars in the anticipation that demand will go up further and a capacity to produce just 100 cars will fall short. So capacity utilization is an important determinant of investment by businesses. If capacity utilization is 70 per cent, 30 per cent of the installed capital is not being used, which leads to losses or low profits. In such a situation, adding to the capital can only lead to more under-utilization of capital and more losses, because the capital already invested is only partly utilized, since sales are short and profits get stressed. Therefore, new investment will not be made.

During a lockdown, when only essentials are produced and all other production comes to a halt, there is huge spare capacity in everything, other than essentials. Now, this may be ignored and investment may take place if it is clear that the economy will revive and demand will continue as before. But, as discussed in the previous chapter, instead of a V-shaped recovery, there is likely to be a shallow U-shaped recovery. In other words, for most lines of production, there will be spare capacity for quite some time. That is why there will be little investment in most lines of production.

Public investment can continue even when capacity utilization declines, since it can bear losses. But as will be discussed in Chapter V, due to a shortage of resources in the budget, even public investment will have to be cut back, except in COVID-19-related areas.

Business Failures and Investment

Even in the case of essentials such as food and FMCG, there may be spare capacity for quite some time and little investment may occur. This may not be the case for telecom, hospitals, medicines, e-commerce, software and a few such things. However, some of these lines may grow at the expense of existing businesses that are likely to fail due to a shift in demand. For instance, if e-commerce displaces brick-and-mortar stores, there will be business failure among the latter and little net investment. Due to shortage of working capital, shift or reduction in demand and increased cost of business, many other businesses may also fail. For instance, many airlines and restaurants may close down. All these business failures leading to their shutdown would imply negative investment.

Businesses that were already stressed prior to March 2020 because of the decline in the Indian economy now face failure due to prolonged shutdown. Businesses that depend on a lot of borrowing (highly leveraged) will be the first to fail. Many firms in the financial sector are in this category. Further, financial-sector entities are all interlinked via credit. Therefore, when one delays returning a loan, the next one cannot return its loan to its creditor and there is default. This chain is long, and as many financial-sector entities start to fail, there is a domino effect—as was the case in 2008 when Lehman Brothers failed.

The policy of allowing a six-month moratorium for payment of interest to banks will help check business failures during this period. But this may not be enough because production and income generation stopped during the lockdown and the revival of business is uncertain. As argued earlier, the moratorium only postpones the day of reckoning, because the interest burden continues to mount. If after the lockdown, businesses start gradually, losses will still mount and the capacity to repay loans will be limited. If businesses fail and NPAs build up, the financial sector will face failures. Businesses that had large reserves (savings) to begin with are the ones that will feel less pain but they, too, will be in trouble if lockdowns are imposed repeatedly.

To sum up, in the case of essentials, investment will continue, but, in most other lines of business, new investment will not occur due to uncertainty, the existence of spare capacity, the slow start of businesses after lockdown, the rising costs of business, shortage of working capital, business failures, etc. Investment by the public sector will decline due to a shortage of resources. Finally, business failures will imply negative investment. So, in the aggregate, investments will decline sharply and will be close to zero both during and after lockdown.

### Three Phases

When an economy that was running normally, like in December 2019, suddenly goes into a lockdown, it experiences a shock. It can be said to have entered a new phase and its dynamics change. When the lockdown is lifted, another phase begins. So the three phases of the economy are:

1. Pre-lockdown
2. Lockdown
3. Post-lockdown

The lockdown and the post-lockdown phases are considered separate, since their start is marked by a shock to the economy that delinks them from Phase 1. Also, the economy is unlikely to go back to Phase 1 post-lockdown, since there is likely to be a new normal.

Phase 1 can be used as a benchmark for comparison with what transpires in the subsequent phases and, since that is well understood, it is not being discussed here. The characteristics of the latter two phases are first presented to help the analysis of the change in the economy. Analysis of phases 2 and 3 also helps understand what policies may or may not work to enable the economy to recover. For instance, what would the role of a stimulus (See Chapter V) be and how much of it would be needed?

One needs to begin by capturing the cessation of much of production and the decline in profits and wages. Further, since there is a large unorganized sector in India, where wages are low, no income tax is collected from them. Even the organized-sector workers who pay income tax are now facing a cut in incomes and will pay less tax. Due to the loss of business for months, most businesses have incurred losses or have had little profit, so they are paying less of taxes. Businesses that failed will not pay any tax at all. The decline in rents and interest incomes on deposits also mean lower tax payments. This implies that incomes all round will be less and much less tax will be collected during the year 2020-21.

## Characteristics of a Lockdown

1.  The most important aspect of a lockdown is that the production of goods and services is severely curtailed.
    a.  Except for essentials, all other production comes to a halt. Production continues in agriculture and of the very basic essentials, such as medical items and some FMCG. There is minimum of trade, transportation and administration.
    b.  Capacity utilization in non-essential sectors falls to zero, such as for automobiles.
    c.  Unsold production stuck in the pipeline becomes inventory and its cost mounts.
    d.  Even for essentials, production declines below full capacity due to supply bottlenecks and fall in demand.
    e.  In agriculture too, production of perishables falls due to its perishing consequent to decline in demand. Demand for eggs, meat, flowers, etc., also declined due to closure of hotels, restaurants and sweet shops.
2.  Employment falls drastically. This is indicated by the sharp rise in social security payments in developed countries such as the US and the increased demand for work under the MGNREGS in India.
3.  Due to low capacity utilization across most businesses, fresh investment becomes zero.
    a.  In the public sector, too, investment falls due to budget constraints.
    b.  In the private sector, working capital limit is exhausted, reserves are used up (dissaving) and depreciation increases due to business closures, so investment becomes negative.

4. Households dissave, since their incomes decline (organized sector) or become zero (due to unemployment in both the organized and unorganized sectors), while consumption of essentials has to continue.

5. Prices soften due to excess supply, except in the case of essentials. All commodity prices fall due to reduced demand. But they rise in urban areas due to shortages and hoarding.

6. Agriculture prices fall at the farm level due to shortage of demand but rise in urban areas due to hoarding.

7. Overall, there is a tendency towards deflation in the economy.

These features can be used to study the impact of a lockdown on the macroeconomy. From the above it is clear that all macro-variables decline sharply, except for fiscal deficit (See Chapter V). The latter is the excess of expenditure of the government over its own resources. It is financed by borrowings.

8. Incomes Fall:
   a. Organized-sector wages drop substantially due to wage cuts and unemployment.
   b. Unorganized-sector wages drop to zero due to closure of businesses and cessation of work.
   c. Private-sector profits decline sharply because production is substantially reduced and businesses run at a loss due to cessation of activity, while interest payment and loans have to be repaid and fixed costs continue.
   d. There is profiteering in essentials by trade, which generates black incomes but this is much less than what was generated prior to the lockdown.

9. Deflation Likely:
   a. Due to a sharp fall in demand, all commodity prices fall. Petro-goods are an example.
   b. Except for sectoral prices, where there may be shortages, prices fall so there is a tendency for deflation rather than inflation.

c. Further, during a lockdown, the consumption basket is limited to essentials. Their prices rise in urban areas but fall in rural areas (Kumar, 2020f). Since the consumption basket contracts to mostly the essentials, only their prices need to be considered for measuring inflation. In the aggregate prices fall.

d. Due to massive unemployment, wages are likely to fall resulting in a softening of prices.

10. Consumption Drops Sharply:

a. Due to a decline in share prices, real estate values and decline in the financial sector, there is a wealth effect, which causes consumption by the rich to drop.

b. Workers in both the organized and the unorganized sectors consume much less than earlier and, that too, mostly the essentials. Consumption of discretionary items is postponed and falls drastically.

c. Consumption by unorganized-sector workers, who mostly lose employment, is entirely based on transfers of various kinds from the government.

d. In India, the unorganized sector shut down, and since it employs 94 per cent of the workforce, its consumption of essentials was large but less than before the lockdown.

e. In the aggregate, consumption declines drastically during a lockdown and, given the uncertainty of employment and incomes, it only picks up gradually post-lockdown.

11. New Investment and Dissaving:

a. Due to a shortage of resources with the government, public investment declines and is negligible during the lockdown. It can only pick up gradually after the lockdown.

b. Due to huge unutilized capacity, new investment by the private sector becomes negligible during and post the lockdown.

c. As working capital is consumed by the cottage sector and it gets eroded for the organized sector, private investment turns negative.

d.   As incomes of all sections drop, savings fall, even though consumption is less than earlier. There is dissaving by most sections of society except by fixed-income employees who do not lose their jobs and continue to receive a salary.

e.   Only those sectors (essentials) that continue to function and generate incomes manage to continue to save.

f.   Businesses that are closed use up their reserves and dissave.

g.   Banks, the creditors for businesses, dissave, since they pay interest to their depositors but do not receive interest due to a moratorium on payment.

h.   Workers losing work have no incomes but continue to consume, so they too dissave.

## Characteristics of the Post-Lockdown Period

Some sectors that had to stop production during the lockdown start operations gradually. But demand does not revive any time soon due to reasons discussed earlier. Some analysts have argued for a 'V-shaped' recovery because of pent-up demand (PTI, 2020, and *Business Standard*, 2020). Graph III.1 shows the trajectory of the economy under different assumptions. Only the most optimistic one, with immediate recovery, has a V shape; others all show shallow recoveries—U-shaped.

The production capacity of the economy is redefined due to the need for physical distancing in production. This means the full workforce cannot be deployed in factories and offices. In some sectors, work can be done from home (called Work from Home) but such work is not yet a significant part of the total economy. Primary sectors such as agriculture and forestry continue in full since they are in open areas, but their contribution to the GDP is small and cannot compensate for the big decline in other sectors.

Post-lockdown, there are two opposing tendencies as far as prices are concerned. Input costs decline due to the fall in commodity prices and, because demand is low, prices tend to fall further. Due to unemployment, wages are likely to decline, putting pressure on prices.

Factors that can put an upward pressure on prices are a) a shortage of specific skilled labour due to migration, leading to an increase in wages in some industries b) the need for physical distancing and other precautions, which may lead to a rise in costs and c) the raising of prices by lines of production such as travel and tourism, and sports, to make a profit, since their production cannot go back to full capacity.

The factors causing prices to decline are stronger than the ones leading to an increase in prices. So prices tend to fall, which can lead to business failures (Kumar, 2020d). This tendency is accentuated by the shortage of working capital, exhausted during the lockdown. BusinessLine Bureau (2020) quotes Confederation of All India Traders (CAIT) as saying that up to 30 per cent retailers are likely to close down. Saluja (2020) quoting All India Manufactures' Organisation (AIMO) says that 35 per cent of small businesses may shut shop. So, for quite some time, the pre-pandemic level of output may not be achieved.

Except for sectors producing essentials, new investment remains nearly zero due to continuing large unutilized capacity.

Consumption demand remains muted because:

1. Due to wealth effect, the well-off sections consume less than earlier.
2. Those who have suffered unemployment and those whose salaries have been cut do not increase consumption for some time.
3. The employed (even with wage cuts) are fearful and uncertain about the future. This leads to weak consumer sentiment and reduced purchase of discretionary items.
4. Demand for many services, such as tourism, travel and entertainment, is weak, due to the fear of infection and need for physical distancing. This has an impact on other related businesses such as, taxis, hotels, restaurants, food, milk and poultry industries.

In a nutshell, post-lockdown, with both consumption and investment down, demand remains low and production is likely to rise only gradually, so any recovery will take time (Graph III.1).

## Post-Lockdown Lessons from China and the US

The US economy is the largest in the world and possibly has the most extensive healthcare infrastructure in the world. So what happens to it is important when it comes to understanding what is likely to happen to the world economy. Since it has a massive healthcare infrastructure, it can relax the lockdown with greater ease than, say, a country such as India. Therefore, it is important to refer to the US to understand what India faces as the lockdown is progressively relaxed.

Kirsch (2020), Valinsky (2020), Voytko (2020) tell the story of massive business closures, lay-offs and cuts in wages and salaries across the board in March, April and May 2020. Annexures III.1 and III.2 give a list of companies that were globally impacted by May 2020; a large number of them are US companies. It is also suggested that the impact is likely to be long-lasting and a quick recovery may not take place. In June and July, there were further lay-offs and closures. The US opened up prematurely and the disease asserted itself in the south and the west, and lockdowns had to be imposed again in these states. What has now come to be seen as the most important symbol of the mistake the US made in dealing with the pandemic was when its president, who had asserted all along that masks were not necessary, put on a mask for the first time in public on 12 July 2020.

China was the first economy to emerge from the lockdown after containing the disease. For most of April and May, China had no new cases of COVID-19. When the lockdown was lifted and travel allowed, cases again started being registered. So post-lockdown lessons may be learnt by studying what happened in China. A Bloomberg (2020) headline suggested that the Chinese economy could recover quickly post-lockdown. But inside, the story is quite different. Based on surveys, it is said that there is a decline in investment and consumption. These are not likely to recover for some time, so any recovery will be gradual at best.

The contrast cannot be clearer. The US made the mistake of not taking the lockdown seriously. Therefore, even though it has the best medical system in the world, it was overwhelmed. It could have recovered quickly and restarted businesses but that is not likely to happen, and recovery will be shallow. China took the lockdown seriously and substantially controlled the disease and was able to open up the economy smoothly. However, it also faced a shallow recovery due to the severe impact on its economy during lockdown, post lockdown and on its exports. But China is in a much more advantageous position than the US, in spite of being a smaller economy. This is due to the difference in their approaches to the pandemic, the clarity of approach and the display of determination by the leadership. India needs to learn from these contrasting examples and follow an appropriate strategy, as suggested in Chapter I.

## Conclusion

In this chapter, it is argued that to understand the nitty-gritty of the impact of the lockdown, its broad macroeconomic impact needs to be analysed. It is pointed out that the situation is worse than during a war or during the global financial crisis of 2007–09.

The situation is unprecedented, since in a lockdown, society voluntarily shuts down production in most of the economy. It results in an adverse impact on consumption, savings, investment, exports, government revenue and growth of the economy. This has pushed much of the world into depression, and not just recession. That is why even as the lockdown is eased, recovery is slow. Due to dissaving and closure of businesses, the resource base of the economy contracts.

This chapter shows that the economy goes through three phases. From the normal phase, it declines dramatically during a lockdown, but even when it is eased, it is unlikely that the economy will immediately bounce back, since demand will remain low due to continued unemployment and cuts in wages. As a result, many business will fail, the cost of doing business will rise and many lines of production will not revive immediately. Medhi (2020) points to the big impact on tech companies in India. E-commerce and similar companies should have been the least impacted, but given that even these were badly hit, the brick-and-mortar companies are likely to be even more deeply disrupted, as CAIT and AIMO have pointed out.

It is also argued that India can learn from what happened in the Chinese and the US economies. They are likely to recover slowly to the pre-pandemic level. This is also likely to be the case with the Indian economy, with its large unorganized sector, which will cause recovery to be much slower than in the US. A V-shaped recovery is highly unlikely for any economy in the world.

# V

# The Indian Economy's Performance

Cases in India started rising rapidly in June 2020—and so did the deaths (Table IV.1 and graphs under IV.1). The economy continued to show signs of stress. So, in spite of rising infections, Unlock 1 was implemented on 1 June 2020. Soon, the lockdown had to be reimposed in Chennai, Bengaluru, Pune and a few other cities. In most countries where the number of new cases fell, the lockdown was relaxed, such as in China, South Korea, Italy and Spain. In the US, in New York State, the worst affected place in the world, relaxation came after the curve had declined. But many states, such as Florida and Texas, did not go for strict lockdowns and soon became COVID-19 hotspots. Brazil, which also did not go for a lockdown, saw a surge in the number of cases and its hospital system reached a state of collapse. How did India fare?

## The Lockdown

India cancelled the visas it had issued and stopped people coming from abroad after the WHO declared COVID-19 a pandemic on 11 March 2020. By then, more than a lakh had been infected globally, 4,000 had died and, in India, 60 cases had been diagnosed as positive.

Not much, but the graph was rising (See graphs IV.1.1 to IV.1.4).
By then Italy and Iran had become the hotspots of the disease. But
the spread was already global. On 18 March, travel to India from the
EU, the UK, Turkey, etc., was stopped. A *janata* curfew was imposed
on Sunday, 22 March, as a prelude to the lockdown. The prime
minister, in a speech to the nation on 24 March, announced the
lockdown from midnight.

By the time the pandemic was announced by the WHO,
it was clear that the disease was going to spread in India too, but a
lockdown had not been announced yet—the government waited till
25 March. Thus, fourteen days were lost. Kerala was the only state
that recognized the gravity of the problem because it had earlier dealt
with the Nipah virus (May 2018) and had brought it under control.
It started testing people arriving from abroad and quarantining
them, so the spread of the disease could be controlled. This was not
done in the rest of the country, so infected people kept arriving and
spreading the disease.

Many parliamentarians wanted the Parliament adjourned,
since physical distancing could not be practised there—members of
Parliament (MPs) sit just inches apart and no physical distancing is
possible. The government quickly passed Budget-related legislation
on 25 March and adjourned the Parliament sine die (with no
appointed date for resumption). Some state legislatures continued to
function for political reasons. Thus, there was an inordinate delay in
implementing the lockdown.

The lockdown hit citizens out of the blue—they were not
prepared for it. There was massive rush at stores for buying essentials,
so, again, physical distancing was not possible. The poor did not
realize what the lockdown meant and what trouble they would face
in the coming days.

The government was also not prepared for implementing the
lockdown. It thought it would be enough to prevent people from
moving around, except for those performing essential services or those
out to buy essentials. The police, asked to implement this curfew-like

situation, went about beating up the poor if they were seen on the streets. While police brutalization is common in India, reflecting a lack of sensitivity towards the poor, it also indicates poor governance. As mentioned in Chapter I, no arrangements were made for the poor. They were not provided with proper transportation and testing facilities. Since the poor in India live in congested conditions, efforts should have been made to decongest them by housing them in empty school buildings and tent colonies constructed in open areas. Needless to say, the government should have quickly ramped up the medical infrastructure, including testing, before locking the country down.

## Late Lockdown and Early Relaxation: Situation Not in Control

So little is known about the virus that ascertaining what would work for India is not clear. Many in India thought that luck would favour the country because a) the virus would die due to the intense heat of summer b) Indians take the BCG injection in childhood and they would have some immunity c) Indians have a naturally higher immunity because they mostly live in unhygienic conditions and d) Indians are, on average, younger, so will be less impacted by the virus or will by asymptomatic. As the rising number of cases shows, except for possibly c) and d), none of the other factors seem to have helped.

As mentioned in Chapter I, expansion of the medical infrastructure could have been planned, such as setting up hospitals in vacant hotels and halls or even in open grounds. One good initiative was that of the Indian Railways which converted some of its idle rail coaches into hospital wards. But the heat in the coaches was not taken into account. Ways to overcome a shortage of equipment, such as ventilators and oxygen concentrators, could have been worked out by getting factories to alter their production mix. A shortage of PPE kits and masks could have also been taken care of by getting garment-making factories to make them as per specifications. This did happen later but in an unplanned way and without proper standards being maintained. Test-kit production needed to be ramped up quickly but the country remained dependent on imported kits until the end of June.

The above-mentioned steps were obvious but not implemented until June, when the country went into Unlock1, even though these suggestions were made by me in a TV programme in mid-March, even before the lockdown. It is true that these are difficult to implement at short notice but the situation was worse than even during a war and these steps ought to have been implemented urgently. Everything else should have been dropped and dealing with the pandemic should have been the only focus.

Further, there was little coordination across the states and the Centre, so much confusion was created. Different states issued contradictory instructions and often changed them on a day-to-day basis, leading to more confusion. This points to poor leadership and governance capability of the country. If ever there was a time for cooperative federalism, this was it. The Centre and the states needed to follow a common approach, allowing for flexibility for state specificities.

A council of chief ministers under the PM is needed to coordinate actions. At a minimum, a well-run administration is required for policies to succeed. There could have been a committee of chief secretaries and DGPs of all states, under the Cabinet Secretary. It must be stressed that policing has to be humane—brute force should not be used, which alienates those who are already in distress. Further, there is need for complete transparency, so that the public develops faith in the administration and voluntarily follows the rules sought to be implemented.

Be that as it may, the lockdown was needed and worked to slow down the spread of the disease, but it failed to control the spread altogether. As graphs IV.1.1 to IV.1.4 and Graph IV.2 show, the number of daily new infections, recoveries, active cases and deaths in India rose rapidly. Yet, the nation relaxed the lockdown in stages since 14 April. With people moving around, a lack of testing and tracing, and a weak medical system, the disease spread. The numbers declined after mid-September (TNN, 2020d). They fell from an average of 92,830 cases a day from 9–15 September to 70,114 a day from 7–13 October.

As discussed earlier, there was pressure from businesses to ease the lockdown and allow them to function, so they do not fail. The government succumbed to this pressure. The government, also did not have an option because it was not able to implement the lockdown in the way it should have. Finally, even after the lockdown was eased, many businesses were not able to operate as before, and quite a few of them failed or are on the verge of failure.

In brief, India did not implement the lockdown in time, did not do what was needed to implement the lockdown successfully and lifted the lockdown prematurely without the disease having been controlled (under business pressure). But, as discussed in Chapter III, in spite of the relaxation, the economy remains subdued due to a lack of demand. Hence, India is experiencing the worst of all worlds.

## Trade-Off between Tackling the Disease and the Economy Stalling

Nations are confronted with a dilemma: If there's a lockdown, the economy will stall, as depicted in the previous chapters, but if it is not implemented early, a large number of people will contract the disease and may even die. The only solution is to implement an early lockdown before a large number of people get infected and continue it till the numbers decline.

China initially delayed the lockdown and the disease spread. But then it imposed a brutal lockdown and controlled it before it could spread too widely. The US initially did not implement a lockdown and became the country with the most number of cases and deaths. Even much later, fear was expressed that if the lockdown is lifted prematurely, the disease will reassert itself and another lockdown will become necessary, with all its adverse social and economic implications. That would be more painful than an early and strict lockdown.

Lifting of the lockdown is feasible if there is capacity for widespread testing. One needs to know who has been infected and who needs to be isolated so that they do not spread the disease further. That is what South Korea did as soon as cases started being reported there.

There is also the fear of a second wave of the disease as people move around as is now being witnessed in much of Europe. Further, the spread aggravates with the onset of winter, as had happened with other virus attacks. There is another peculiarity that has been noted with this virus—some of those who have been cured and tested negative for the disease ended up testing positive a little later. So people may not be developing long-term immunity to the disease and can get reinfected and, in turn, infect others. The implication is that people who have been infected once also need to be careful and may require to be isolated. Finally, this implies that 'herd immunity' may not work and caution needs to be exercised in the relaxation of a lockdown. This state of affairs will prevail until a medicine and/or a vaccine is discovered.

Successful countries present the model of a sharp and brutal lockdown, followed by relaxation with testing and tracing. India has not done this and, as argued above, has had the worst of both worlds. Is another complete lockdown inevitable? But that is going to be even more difficult to implement. A premature relaxation has also led many to believe that the initial lockdown was not needed because cases were very few and that more deaths occur due to other diseases. Such people have not taken the disease seriously and are casual in their approach. This is true especially among the young, who want to go out and have fun. In many places, such as Delhi, this has brought about a second wave of attack.

One line of argument is that the young should be allowed to start work and the disease, if contracted by them, will be largely mild and there will be fewer deaths among them. It is argued that during this phase of relaxation, special care will have to be taken of those with comorbidities, especially those above the age of 60. But society is integrated with elderly parents and grandparents often either living with younger people or staying in touch with them. So if the latter get infected, the elderly will invariably get infected too. Their isolation is not feasible, so they will be at greater risk of dying.

In brief, an optimum strategy is required, in which both factors—health-related consequences and economic costs—are taken into account. Businesses would like the latter to be more important, but for society as a whole, the former should be more important. The strategy should have been a sharp and brutal lockdown, with imperatives for its success implemented, as spelt out in Chapter I, and then relaxation with testing and tracing. Unfortunately, this was not followed in India, with the result that partial lockdowns have had to be imposed, which again disrupted business, which nullified the advantages of opening up in the first place.

## Progression across States, Cities and Districts

In India, the number of infected people was low in March and April. It appeared that India had managed to control the disease well. The first case was of a student who had returned from China to Thrissur in Kerala on 30 January 2020. The first death from COVID-19 was of a 76-year-old man on 12 March in Kalburgi, Karnataka. He had returned from Saudi Arabia. At that time, there were seventy-three cases in all in India.

In March, the disease was limited to a few states and among those returning from abroad, such as in Kerala, Karnataka, Maharashtra, Delhi and Haryana. But by the end of the month, it had spread to the entire country (Wikipedia, 2020). Maharashtra has been the worst affected state so far, with the largest number of infections and deaths. But by the end of June, the situation in Maharashtra seemed to be coming under control, with the number of deaths declining, even though the number of cases kept rising. But, again, in July, the disease reasserted itself. At one point, Gujarat was doing badly, but by the end of June, it was not in such a bad shape. The same month, the situation in Tamil Nadu, Delhi and Haryana deteriorated. Tamil Nadu had to reimpose the lockdown in mid-June. Assam and West Bengal also reimposed lockdowns at the end of June. Graph IV.2 shows the situation in six badly affected states in June-July.

Metros such as Mumbai, Chennai and Delhi saw a surge in cases, since observing the lockdown in congested slum areas was difficult, as discussed earlier. The medical systems in Mumbai and Delhi were overwhelmed, with horror stories of people not even getting ambulances to go to hospitals, not finding beds and then dying in their cars and ambulances. There were reports of people abandoned on hospital beds and dying in toilets because there was no help; of bodies lying next to patients, since there was no one to take them to the mortuaries. Mortuaries were also full, so bodies piled up on corridors. There were cases of families receiving the wrong bodies or when bodies were cremated without the families being informed, so they could not trace their loved ones. In some cases, people were scared and did not come forward to claim the bodies of their relatives. These abandoned bodies were often cremated or buried without any thought of dignity to the departed. These were the signs of a breakdown of society as the medical systems in metros got overwhelmed.

To begin with, many districts did not report any cases, probably due to low testing. As migrating workers returned to their villages, the number of such districts declined. Migrating workers were often quarantined by the villages and the states. Those who arrived by train—the Shramik Specials, which started ferrying migrants after 1 May—were screened at both the originating and the destination stations. They were required to produce medical certificates showing they were COVID-19-free to buy tickets. But, obviously, none of this worked, since checking was cursory and the medical certificates could have been obtained for money. Also, many of the infected workers were most likely asymptomatic. So, during the journey, the disease spread to others as well.

There was much confusion about the extent of the spread of the disease, since testing was inadequate even in major metros such as Mumbai and Delhi. As testing was ramped up, more and more cases were reported. Many suggested that massive testing was not the answer because most of the infected were asymptomatic and would be automatically cured. They would not require hospitalization and could quarantine themselves at home. But without testing, one cannot even know who should be quarantining themselves. The danger is that people carrying the disease may spread it to someone who is vulnerable and who would then have to be hospitalized.

In brief, the disease has now spread across the country and unpredictable as it is, even when it appears to be under control, it can suddenly reassert itself. This has happened in the case of Bengaluru and Agra. Thus, as is often said, the virus has to be eliminated everywhere and not just in parts. It can spread from one part of the country to another. This is also a lesson from other countries, specifically the US.

## The Broader Aspects of the Lockdown in India

### Anaemic Growth Prior to the Pandemic

The Indian economy had been floundering even before the pandemic hit. The official quarterly rate of growth fell consistently from near 8 per cent at the start of 2018 to 3.1 per cent in the last quarter of 2019–20 (Graph 02), just before the pandemic hit India. But this data does not give the correct position of decline. Kumar (2018) has pointed out that since the demonetization of the economy in November 2016, the method of estimation of the quarterly GDP needs to be changed. Demonetization was a huge shock to the economy and especially impacted the unorganized sector. But this is not captured in the official data, which is based largely on the organized sector data.

The data for the unorganized sector is collected once in five years (called the reference year), when a survey is conducted. So, in the intervening years, it is mainly the organized sector that is used as a proxy for the unorganized sector. Various ratios are derived in the reference year and projections carried out on the basis of these ratios to get the annual estimates of the GDP. But when the economy is subjected to a major shock such as demonetization or the current lockdown, the ratios change and the old ratios are no longer valid. The unorganized sector sharply declined after demonetization, so that the growing organized sector can not represent it.

For the quarterly estimates, even less data is available—and all of it is from the organized sector, except for agriculture. Thus, the quarterly estimate mainly represents the organized sector. Hence, after a shock to the unorganized sector, such as the one due to demonetization, the quarterly data on the GDP is not at all representative. Alternative data have to be used to estimate the GDP.

After demonetization, the economy was hit by a second shock in July 2017, when the faulty GST was implemented (Kumar, 2019a). This further damaged the unorganized sector. After this, there was another shock in 2018 due to the crisis in the NBFCs that cater to the loan requirements of small and medium businesses, and the consumers.

Thus, I have been arguing that the economy was already in recession before the pandemic hit India in March 2020 (Kumar, 2019c). Supply chains started to get disturbed by February 2020, when the Chinese economy shut down. As argued in Chapter III, the pandemic has hit the unorganized sector very hard, since it has little savings. So this was yet another shock to this sector and the economy has gone into a tailspin since.

Experts behind the Curve

When there is adverse economic news, the officialdom usually does not admit to it until much later, so it is behind the curve. This is also true of international agencies, since they don't have independent data and depend on the national governments to give them the data.

In 2008, until the Lehman Brothers moment, the IMF had predicted a positive rate of growth for the world economy, while the world economy was already in a recession.

Only when the Index of Industrial Production (IIP) data for April 2020 pointed to a decline in output of more than 40 per cent did the chief economic adviser admit that the economy would contract in 2020–21 (Noronha and Sikarwar, 2020). The GST Council meeting in June discussed inadequate tax collections and growing fiscal problems. But, the officialdom remained in denial even though there was evidence all around. This denial is costly, since non-admission of the extent of economic decline results in flawed decision-making and a delay in applying correctives—and the problem just becomes more acute.

In India, two months after the lockdown was enforced, the official agencies were only giving vague statements about their estimates of the damage to the economy. The RBI governor said that the rate of growth would be negative but did not give a number. The Ministry of Finance also did not give a number. Non-official agencies that estimate the real rate of growth of the economy kept lowering their growth projections in quick succession (Table IV.2). Indeed, this has been a global trend. Without knowing the extent of the crisis, how is a nation to deal with it?

The IMF had, in January 2020, estimated that India's growth rate would be 5.8 per cent. In April, it scaled it down to 1.9 per cent and, on 24 June, it further scaled it down to -4.5 per cent. For the world as a whole, it predicted that the economy would shrink by 4.9 per cent, while it had predicted a shrinkage of 3 per cent in April. China reported a shrinkage of its GDP by 6.8 per cent in the first quarter of 2020 but the IMF projected that it will grow by 1 per cent in the full year.

The American credit rating agency Fitch Ratings projected a growth rate of 2 per cent on 3 April, 1.8 per cent on 20 April and 0.8 per cent on 23 April. Its calculations were based on the growth of 4.4 per cent in the January–March quarter, -0.2 per cent in April–June, -0.1 per cent in July–September and 1.4 per cent in

October–December. These are highly unrealistic figures. In June, the projection was scaled down to -5 per cent for this fiscal. But for 2021–22, it has given a figure of 9.5 per cent without stating the basis of this prediction.

S&P Global Ratings, another American credit rating agency, slashed the growth rate for the year 2020–21 from 1.8 per cent in April to -5 per cent in May. It is predicting a rebound to 8.5 per cent for next year. CRISIL, at the end of May, lowered the growth rate to -5 per cent from 1.8 per cent at the end of April. Earlier it had predicted a 3.6 per cent growth rate. At the end of April, Moody's Investors Service predicted a 0.2 per cent rate of growth for the economy, whereas in March it had projected a growth rate of 2.5 per cent.

The Confederation of Indian Industry (CII) has given a range of 1.5 per cent to -0.9 per cent growth for the Indian economy in FY 2020–21. To get to -0.9 per cent from where the economy was in April, and assuming an immediate rebound in June, an average growth rate of 12.8 per cent would be required in the next ten months—an impossibility.

In brief, the experts at the IMF, credit rating agencies and the CII have quickly been downgrading their growth estimates since March, when the lockdown was announced. How could they be so wrong? Even these projections do not seem right and are likely to be further lowered. The reason simply is that they are not factoring in the massive decline in output, consumption, investment and exports, as pointed out in Chapter III. For their projections to be correct, the economy would have had to rebound rapidly starting June 2020, which did not happen (See Table IV.3 and Graph III.1). So what would be a realistic scenario, given the collapse of the Indian economy during the lockdown and after?


Production: What Can and Cannot Work during a Lockdown

During a lockdown, production of essentials has to continue, or there will be societal breakdown. Some business, such as those producing medicines, medical equipment, toiletries and soaps, packaged food products, etc., have to be allowed to continue production. Agriculture, which produces grains, vegetables, fruits and milk, has to be permitted to function so that a shortage of these essentials does not occur. Trade and transport of these essentials also have to be allowed so as to make these items available to citizens.

The entire non-agriculture unorganized sector, constituting 31 per cent of the GDP, came to a halt during the lockdown—which included daily-wage earners, dhabas, rickshaw pullers, auto and taxi drivers, small transporters, construction workers and the cottage sector; people who have to be in contact with clients, such as barbers, tailors, beauticians and gym owners; and those who have to visit homes, such as for the repair and maintenance of household items, courier services, delivery of food, etc. None of these services were allowed during the lockdown.

In general, businesses where IT can be used and work done from home, such as software development and chartered accountancy, can continue to operate. But in most cases, efficiency is affected as people are not used to working from home and there are also distractions due to family responsibilities. Further, because the mind is distracted due to the prevailing situation, it becomes difficult to focus on work as in normal times.

A certain amount of administration is required to maintain law and order, impose curfews and provide essentials to the destitute and the unemployed. Energy, water and gas utilities have to continue to function. Other than these, most of the administration that is not considered essential also shut down.

Coming to the organized sector, a large segment of it requires workers to go to their place of work to produce, such as in manufacturing, trade, transport, finance, education and many professional services such as lawyers and chefs. Education to a certain extent is possible via the Internet but the poor cannot access it. Some banking is possible via the Internet but not everything can be done online. The auto sector and their dealerships, travel by air, road and rail, tourism, hotels, restaurants, shops and malls, cinema halls, etc., have to be shut down. If not, there cannot be a meaningful lockdown.

Sectors producing essentials such as medicines and FMCG did well, since the well-off hoarded these items. They bought months' worth of supplies in one go, lest it becomes difficult to go to the stores later or production of these items is disturbed. But it is quite possible that after the initial spurt, demand suddenly collapses as people stop buying these items because they have already stocked up. Traders taking advantage of the shortages raised prices of essentials such as foodgrains and vegetables.

With the easing of the lockdown by June, some activity revived in the organized sector (Table IV.3). But the unorganized sector could not start work due to a shortage of working capital.

One can get a crude estimate of activity taking place in different sectors of the economy by combining data from the following sources:

1. Decline in the index of industrial production
2. Decline in core sector activity
3. Purchasing Managers' Index (PMI) for manufacturing and services
4. Decline in rail passenger traffic
5. Decline in air traffic
6. Stoppage of public transport, such as bus, auto, taxi and rickshaw services
7. Decline in the arrival of fruits and vegetables in mandis
8. Decline in the demand for milk, meat, eggs, poultry, flowers and sugar
9. Shutdown of retail trade
10. Closure of hotels, restaurants, wedding venues and pubs
11. Stoppage of all entertainment, including sports and cinema
12. Stoppage of construction activity
13. Decline in the consumption of energy
14. Closure of government offices

15.  Closure of educational institutions
16.  Closure of many private healthcare centres

This is tabulated in Table IV.3, where it can be seen that in April 2020, the GDP was likely down 75 per cent as compared to April 2019, and in June it was possibly down 60 per cent as compared to June last year and in September down 30 per cent compared to that month last year.

## Unemployment

During the lockdown, with activity stopping in large parts of the economy, unemployment rose dramatically. As already argued, the non-agriculture unorganized sector shut down completely. Contract labour in the organized sector was fired. A section of permanent workers in the organized sector also lost their employment. Migration of labour from the villages of Punjab, Haryana, Kerala, Karnataka and Maharashtra back to the villages they came from (such as in Bihar) suggests that even rural employment declined during the lockdown.

In India, only those above fifteen years of age are counted as workers. There are about 450 million workers and, of them, 94 per cent, or roughly 422 million, are in the unorganized sector. The rest of the 28 million are in the organized sector of the economy. About 42 per cent—roughly 190 million—are in agriculture. So those in the non-agriculture unorganized sector are about 232 million.

Assuming that in agriculture everyone kept working (even though that is not true) and in the organized sector no one was fired (again, not correct, as data in Annexures IV.1 and IV.2 suggests), most of the 232 million lost employment. Very few in trade and transport continued to work, since these sectors were also down by 90 per cent. Many workers who were employed as house helps, drivers, gardeners and so on lost their jobs, even though their employers could afford to pay them. This was out of fear of the disease spreading. In brief, at least 200 million lost employment in India during the lockdown.

Centre for Monitoring Indian Economy (CMIE) estimated a loss of 122 million jobs in April 2020. Of this, 75 per cent were small traders and wage labourers. About 18 million each of salaried employees and entrepreneurs also lost work. The only category that gained employment was the farmers, whose number increased by 6 million (The Hindu Data Team, 2020 and ENS, 2020).

But there are problems in interpreting the CMIE data when there is a shock to the economy (Kumar, 2020h). Their survey is based on a sample drawn from the total population. Investigators visit households and ask their members the status of their employment. Workers on the rolls of their employers but not getting wages may say they are working. Further, the sample from which the data was taken may have been vitiated by the mass migration of workers in March and April. Not only they would not be counted but they are the ones that lost their employment. Another problem would have been counting those who were being paid but not working—such as government servants, teachers and corporate managers. They would have been counted as employed but were actually not working, hence included in estimating the national income but that is incorrect, since, for the size of the economy, it is the work that is important.

Counting employment in rural areas poses a different problem. The additional number of farmers counted suggests that disguised unemployment may have risen. Also, the additional workers under MGNREGS count as employment but represent a displacement from the work that these workers may have been doing earlier. It does not represent revival of employment in the economy. In fact, for the past three years, the allocation under MGNREGS had been growing due to the crisis in the unorganized sector and the return of the workers to the rural areas in search of work (Kumar, 2019a).

In brief, due to the shock, the survey would have neither captured work being done nor its nature. So the unemployment estimate of CMIE is likely to have been a gross underestimation of the loss of employment/work during the lockdown. If all this is taken into account, at least 200 million from the unorganized sector lost work and many in the organized sector either lost employment and/ or could not work even if they were not fired.

## The Plight of Labour and Migrants

As discussed in Chapter II, the pandemic has brought into the open the terrible plight of the unorganized sector and its workers. They are the marginalized in society and policy seldom caters to their issues. They could not cope with the lockdown and now continue to suffer even with the lockdown eased under business pressure.

As discussed earlier, without adequate testing, a large number of people will get infected as lockdown is eased. For herd immunity, if 60 per cent get the disease and develop immunity, 5 per cent of those infected will be serious, requiring hospitalization. That would be 4 crore people and most of them will be workers forced to go to their place of work. The poor are malnourished and don't have the resources to get tested or get proper medical treatment. Even if only 2 per cent die, and this number will be larger if India's weak medical system fails, 1.6 crore people will die—and most of them will be the poor.

## Uncivil Conditions That the Urban Poor Live In

Due to inadequate testing, the full extent of the number of people already infected and spreading the disease is not known. No wonder the number of cases has been rising rapidly since June 2020. Why was our medical system so weak and testing inadequate even months after it became clear in March that the disease would spread? It is a reflection of a political system and an executive that has hardly ever prioritized the welfare of the vast majority of the people it is supposed to serve. They are the residual, or the one's marginalized in policymaking. If some benefits trickle down to them, that is well and good. If the poor rise above a given poverty line, the system claims it an 'achievement'. The elite make it out that the poor ought to be grateful for the gains they have made since Independence.

The 'achievement' hides the uncivil conditions in which the poor live, especially in urban areas, and this now stands exposed thanks to the pandemic. They live in cramped and unhygienic slums, with little access to clean water and sanitary conditions. How are they to observe the lockdown and practise physical distancing? They live cheek by jowl and share toilets and water tankers. They have little savings, so they have to earn and spend on a day-to-day basis. With the pandemic, their earnings have stopped and they have turned destitute—this highlights the precariousness of their lives. One shock and they slip below the poverty line; one major illness in the family and they fall below the imaginary poverty line (Kumar, 2013). They had always been poor, but for policymakers, 'progress' was that they had jumped above the poverty line (APL).

As argued earlier, for policymakers, the poor don't count. So the prerequisites of the lockdown were not put in place for the poor. It is as if the poor exist to be exploited, to provide cheap labour to factories and homes of the well-off, and to act as the 'reserve army of labour' to keep wages low.

## Coercing Migrants to Return to Cities

During lockdown many businesses were on the verge of failure. They knew that if they did not restart, they would go under. So they put pressure on the government to ease the lockdown, even if people died. They knew that the poor would have little choice but to work, but if they got infected, it would be a cost the system would not care about.

The government's 'relief package' (Chapter V) is largely to enable businesses to survive, with little immediate relief for the migrants and the unemployed (only 10 per cent of the package). The additional allocation to MGNREGS is measly, compared to the numbers who have lost employment. The free allocation of food is not reaching many of the poor. Is all this deliberate? Is it a way of forcing workers who have migrated to their villages to return to the cities and to the work they left? This may accentuate the crisis for the poor, but it is unlikely that many who left the cities in dire circumstances will return soon.

But all this indicates confused thinking on the part of businesses and policymakers. As already argued, businesses facing a demand shortage consequent to a dramatic fall in consumption and investment (except for those producing essentials) cannot restart full steam until demand revives. Restarting at a low level of capacity utilization will only help them reduce their losses. The large number of micro units, 99 per cent of the MSME sector, will be in no position to restart, having exhausted their working capital. The package announced by the government is for the medium- and small-scale industries but not the micro ones that are part of MSME. Policy has hardly ever catered to this vast sector—it has always been a residual. So, even if migrants return, few will get jobs in the cities.

So the vast number of the alienated poor, like always, have little choice. They could not fully comply with the lockdown, given their uncivil living conditions, and now they have to face extreme poverty and be the guinea pigs for achieving 'herd immunity', thanks to pressure from businesses and because the government is unwilling to do what is required.

## Cause of the Mass Migration

In India, the migration of a large number of workers from the rural areas to the cities is a result of lop-sided investment since Independence. Most of the investment goes into urban areas and into the organized sectors. But due to growing automation, few jobs are generated in the organized sectors. So most of the migrants are forced to work in the unorganized sectors at low wages. They may also be self-employed as rickshaw pullers, drivers, cart-pushing vendors, etc. They have no savings or, even if they have, it is invested in their small businesses or sent home to support their families back in the villages. They often come alone to the cities and live in shanties and slums in unhygienic conditions—often five or ten people in a small 10x10-foot room.

This is the situation most Indian workers face even seventy years after Independence. True, conditions are not what they used to be in 1947. There is more education and better health facilities; child mortality has dropped; and longevity has increased. Many of the poor own mobile phones and don't have to walk barefoot any more. Electricity and tapped water have reached many villages. But this is expected in an economy where the GDP has grown by 32.2 times and the per capita income by 8.2 times since 1950, and some fruits of development have trickled down to some of the marginalized.

Industry and ruling elites capitalize on the poor working and living conditions of labour to lead their own comfortable lifestyle and make higher profits. Consequently, neither the state nor businesses grant workers their rights. For instance, a large number of workers do not get a minimum wage, social security or protective gear at worksites. They mostly have no employment security; often their wages are not paid in time; muster rolls are fudged; and there is little entitlement to leave. Given their low wages, they are forced to live in uncivilized conditions in slums. Water is scarce, and drinking water more so. Access to clean toilets is limited and disease can spread rapidly. There is a lack of civic amenities such as sewage. Their children are often deprived of schools and playgrounds.

Now, using COVID-19 as an excuse, state after state has reduced even what little security was available to workers, by eliminating or diluting various laws to favour businesses. In Uttar Pradesh, at least fourteen of the Acts have been changed, such as the Minimum Wages Act, 1948, the Industrial Disputes Act, 1947, and the Payment of Bonus Act, 1965. It's the same thing in Madhya Pradesh and Punjab. The plea is that this is needed to revive economic activity. The chief minister of Madhya Pradesh has said that this will lead to new investment in the state (Singh, 2020).

Whether or not new investment comes, when businesses are unable to restart or face a situation of low capacity utilization, what this will ensure is competition among states to dilute or eliminate labour laws. Thus, the poor working conditions of labour will deteriorate further.

In India, workers are characterized as either organized or unorganized. Those in the former category work in larger businesses and have some formal rights (which are being diluted) but, often, they find it difficult to have them enforced. Increasingly the big and medium businesses are employing contract labour provided by labour contractors from the unorganized sector, rather than permanent workers. Businesses pay contractors, who then pay the labourers part of the money they receive. So businesses claim that they are paying the minimum wage but the workers aren't getting it.

In a scenario where even the minimum wage is inadequate for a worker to lead a dignified life, what chance do those receiving even lesser stand to lead a civilized existence?

Businessmen who now talk of livelihood have never shown such concern for the workers in the past. They have paid low wages to earn big profits. How else, at such a low level of per capita income, could India have had the fourth largest number of billionaires in the world? Clearly, most of the gains of development over the past seventy-five years, more specifically since 1991, have been cornered by businessmen. They have made money not only in white but also huge sums in black (Kumar, 1999).

Businesses have manipulated policy in their favour—before 1991, by resorting to crony capitalism, and since then by bending policy in their favour, curtailing workers' rights and pressurizing the government to weaken its support to the marginalized sections on the plea that the markets be allowed to function. Now using COVID-19 as the shield, workers' rights are being further curtailed. No wonder, then, that the country collects only about 6 per cent of the GDP as direct taxes despite huge disparities. The burden of taxation falls on the indirect taxes, such as GST and customs duty, paid by everyone, including the marginalized.

The lesson to be learnt from the pandemic is that India has not been able to cope with it because of the adverse living conditions of the majority of its people, namely the poor. Now labour laws are being diluted (such as increased working hours and reduced wages), which means a worsening of their living conditions (Kumar, 2020g). This will ensure that the country will flounder again when the next pandemic strikes. The tragedy is that India is today headed towards societal breakdown for short-term gains of some sections of society. But it appears that a rethinking of the prevailing ruling ideology always comes at a heavy cost.

## Inflation or Deflation?

When production declines drastically, usually prices rise. But when demand falls, prices tend to fall too, whether directly or indirectly. Indirectly when discounts are offered by producers to increase sales. For instance, during much of 2019, big discounts were offered by car manufacturers to boost their sagging sales.

Due to the lockdown, both supply and demand plummeted. Post lockdown, both supply and demand for non-essentials stayed low. For essentials, the picture was mixed, because demand increased while supplies faced bottlenecks. To produce goods or services, labour, energy and inputs are required. Inputs can be basics and intermediates. For instance, to produce cars, one needs steel, plastic, wires, lights and so on. An office needs computers, paper, chairs and so on. What happens to the prices of these items also determines the prices of the final goods and services.

When demand falls, as during a recession, the demand for basics and intermediates falls too. So demand for energy and its prices fall. That is what happened to the price of petro goods as soon as the lockdown was announced in the major economies. Take the collapse in the prices of crude oil, for instance. At one point, the price for one-month future delivery became negative, since no place was available to store the crude oil that was being shipped. Prices of all commodities fall when demand plummets. Wages also fall, since labour becomes surplus as people lose employment. These two, raw material and labour, are the basics that determine the price of the final goods. Since these two fall, prices of all goods and services tend to fall too.

So a deflation of prices is likely. As argued in Chapter III, the consumption basket changes, so the inflation index needs to be recalculated. Unfortunately, this has not been done in India.

Consumption of essentials continues, and this is what should be included in the basket for measuring inflation during a lockdown. Essentials also need to be segregated into agricultural and non-agricultural items for inclusion in the basket. The former would consist of milk, vegetables, foodgrains and so on; the latter would consist of medical supplies and FMCG items such as packaged food and toiletries.

As already argued earlier, the demand for essentials from the well-off sections with savings shot up due to hoarding during the pandemic. But due to massive loss of employment and incomes, overall demand fell. Further, agricultural supplies could not come to the wholesale markets, so prices in rural markets fell and farmers received a low price for their produce. But since there was a shortage in the urban markets, the prices went up and traders made money.

Table IV.4 shows that the arrival of fruits and vegetables in the largest wholesale market in India, the Azadpur mandi in Delhi, fell dramatically in April. Table IV.5 shows a similar pattern for mandis in Punjab. So demand and supply both fell, and consumers did not benefit as retail prices remained high. For commodities procured by the government, such as wheat and oilseeds, the farmer selling in the market received a price less than the minimum support price (MSP) (Table IV.6). Demand for items such as sugar and milk also fell and agriculturists lost on these items too. In brief, the prices of agricultural commodities fell in rural areas but rose in urban areas. So farmers lost incomes while urban consumers faced a higher retail price.

The essential non-agricultural items carry a maximum retail price (MRP) on their packages. Usually, these items are sold at less than MRP but, during the lockdown, they were sold at MRP or even higher. In the case of medical supplies, such as masks, sanitizers, oxymeters and oxygen concentrators, prices were marked up hugely, their retail prices went up and traders made money.

The prices of petroleum goods such as diesel and petrol should have fallen. But the government, falling short of resources, increased taxes and raised the prices of these commodities. Many state governments also imposed extra excise duties on liquor and the prices of liquor rose sharply. There were attempts to raise the charges for education and hospitals but these were resisted and the government capped them. Landlords had to come to agreements with their tenants on lowering rents when business stopped. So there was a mixed pattern of price changes.

It has been argued that due to a fall in revenue and rise in expenditure, the fiscal deficit of the government has risen massively (See Chapter V)—and that will lead to inflation. The underlying idea is that this will increase demand and prices will rise. Actually, there is not much chance of this happening, since the decrease in private demand has been be far greater than the effect of the rise in fiscal deficit. So, overall, there will still be a fall in demand (Kumar, 2020i).

In brief, the measure of inflation has to be revised, since the consumption bundle of various segments has changed. At the consumer level, the prices of many essential items have risen in urban areas. In rural areas, the prices received by farmers have decreased due to a glut. The traders and manufacturers of essentials made extra profits because input costs went down but prices were not lowered. Finally, as businesses restart, because costs of labour, energy and inputs will be lower than earlier and demand will not revive soon, the chances are that prices will fall, that is, there is likelihood of deflation.

## The Importance of the Public Sector in a Crisis

It is now clear that a strong public sector is needed to tackle a crisis. The role of the public sector in healthcare has been discussed earlier. In India, the image of the public sector is one of inefficiency and corruption due to poor accountability and crony capitalism. But does a poor country such as India have an alternative, especially in a crisis?

The public sector represents the interest and the will of the collective. When accountability is weak, the public sector gets hijacked and becomes inefficient. The private sector operates solely with the profit motive and does not work unless assured of profits. This has also been quite clear during the pandemic. The private-sector medical infrastructure charged high prices for tests to be done, for medical supplies and for hospitalization until the government stepped in and capped prices. Many private-sector clinics, rather than pitching in voluntarily, asked to be exempted from COVID-19 duty.

The situation is referred to as market failure—namely that markets will not deliver 'efficiency'. Efficiency implies that society will achieve the best possible position (optimum) it can. So market failure is a situation when markets cannot take society to the optimum position and the government has to intervene to achieve the optimum. For instance, in the current situation, the private trade selling medical supplies at monopoly prices means that many people are being deprived of these goods. Traders selling food items at high prices when the wholesale prices have dipped means that many among the poor have to go hungry unless the government intervenes.

The public sector can operate at a loss but the private sector will shut down when losses occur. Many essential activities have to continue for society to survive, even if no profit can be made on these. For instance, to reduce pollution in cities, public transport may have to run at a loss and be subsidized by the government. Food has to reach the poor even if it has to be heavily subsidized. Education for young girls is essential for the country and its future, even if parents do not want to spend much on their education. So their education has to be subsidized. Most infrastructure in a poor country such as India cannot generate a profit, so infrastructure has to come up in the public sector.

The public sector's critical role was realized during the pandemic, since it was required to perform various tasks assigned to it. For instance, Air India brought back stranded Indians from Wuhan and other places. The mass movement of migrants back to their villages was aided partly by the railways and public buses. Public-sector banks were used to put money into the accounts of the poor. The public distribution system was used to distribute grains and lentils. Gas cylinders were also distributed via the public-sector undertaking (PSUs). Procurement from agriculture was done by public agencies. Loans to the MSME sector were arranged largely through the public-sector banks.

The public-sector financial institutions, such as the Life Insurance Corporation of India (LIC), intervened in the stock markets to prevent them from collapsing by buying shares when the private sector, and especially the foreign portfolio investors (such as pension funds), were withdrawing from the markets. This is a role that the LIC and other public-sector financial institutions have been playing for a long time. At the time of every Budget presentation, these institutions buy shares to boost sentiment. In brief, these public-sector financial institutions have intervened to stabilize the markets, even if they suffer losses in the process.

The government is thinking of investing in failing firms to prevent them from collapsing. There is a moratorium on interest payment and repayment of loans, which, as argued earlier, will lead to failures in the financial sector and the government will have to bail them out.

The RBI has been lowering interest rates and boosting liquidity in the markets (See Chapter V). This is to try and bolster investment. But this liquidity is going into the stock markets, one of the reasons the stock market rose in spite of a tanking economy. Again, this is a public-sector intervention to prevent the economy from collapsing.

In brief, given that India is a poor country and the market cannot deliver many of the essentials, the government has an important role to play via PSUs. During the pandemic, even businesses and the well-off have needed support from the government. So, in spite of inefficiencies, mismanagement and corruption in the public sector, it became the principal instrument for tackling the pandemic and the resultant crisis.

## An Unstable Financial Sector

As discussed earlier in Chapter II, one of the most important roles of the financial sector is to provide working capital and loans for establishing businesses—building factories and setting up offices. As production and investment decline (Chapter III), the demand for credit falls. The banks have cut interest rates but the demand for credit has continued to fall. People turn cautious during times of uncertainty, so they withdraw funds from other investments and deposit them in their banks to increase their liquidity. So, while the well-off keep more cash with them to face medical emergencies, to buy essentials or just to face the uncertainty, they also deposit more in their bank accounts. In brief, in the face of uncertainty, people go liquid.

Consequently, banks have excess liquidity, which they then deposit in the RBI to earn a return, called the reverse repo. It is a way of earning returns rather than keeping the money idle with themselves. The RBI does not want that; it wants the banks to lend to the investors so that the economy can get a boost. To encourage that, the RBI has repeatedly cut the reverse repo rate to make banks lend to businesses. But what do the banks do when the demand for credit has fallen?

This brings home the ineffectiveness of the RBI policy to boost the economy when demand is short, and production and investment have greatly declined. Only when production revives can demand for credit increase. Not the other way around. It is not that if credit is available, production will increase. So monetary policy fails to deliver in a situation of depression.

The stock market, an index of how private investors view the future, collapsed quickly in March as news of the pandemic spread. It has recovered much of the losses in the hope that the economy will revive soon. The US markets, which led the global market collapse, have recovered. But this is likely to be temporary, since the pandemic is not yet over and lockdowns are being reimposed in many parts of the world—and in India too. The economy will take another dive when the second wave hits and businesses shut down again. In these big market swings, the small investors suffer, whereas the big ones with their clout take advantage because they can manage the markets.

The upswing in India has been narrow, based on a few stocks doing well. As mentioned earlier, companies in technology, telecom, FMCG, medical supplies and a few essentials will continue to do well in spite of the pandemic. Their stocks will do well. Funds will shift from other stocks to these. This narrow rise in the stock market is a dangerous trend, since it cannot be sustained, given that the economy as a whole is doing poorly. Also, it raises the price to earnings ratio (p/e) that tells the investor what the price of a share of the company is, compared to the profit it earns per share. It gives an idea of the return that the investor can earn from the company. The higher the p/e, the lower the return from the company. If the p/e is 20, the return will be 5 per cent. So one has to depend on the capital appreciation of the share for a good return. But if the share price starts falling, the return may turn negative. Then the price of the share can collapse equally quickly. In the US, too, it is the technology stocks that have led the rally, which makes the rise narrow, especially given that a large number of firms are failing and/or downsizing (See Annexures III.1 and III.2).

Banks are likely to face a deep crisis, since, as businesses fail, they will not be able to pay interest or repay the loans taken from the banks. So, in spite of the moratorium on repayment and the change in the definition of an NPA, bad loans will rise above the already high level reached before the pandemic hit. Table IV.7 gives an idea of the stressed loans in various sectors of the economy. This will hit the profitability of banks further. In India, the NBFCs, which are like shadow banks, were already in a crisis due to some of the large entities (such as Infrastructure Leasing & Financial Services [IL&FS])

failing in 2018. Some more of these entities may fail as businesses fail and are unable to repay their loans post the moratorium.

The failure of the PMC bank in Maharashtra in October 2019 brought to the fore the weaknesses of cooperative banks. Now they have been brought under the supervision of the RBI. The failure of the high-flying Yes Bank just before the pandemic also brought to attention the fragility of small banks. Depositors in other smaller private banks have been flying to safety, weakening them further. Thus, before the pandemic, there was a growing instability in the Indian financial sector. But now, with the economy in depression, this instability is only going to grow. As argued above, the steps taken by the RBI are pushing funds into some shares that are rising inordinately and this is adding to the instability.

The instability is being aggravated by the fact that the financial sector is like a chain of links, one connected to the other. Lending takes place from one institution to another. If one fails, the previous one which had lent the funds, also begins to fail and then the one before that. So failure, at one point, results in the failure of other entities, like in a collapsing house of cards. This will be a big challenge for the revival of the economy. The RBI has tried to deal with the emerging crisis by allowing a moratorium on the repayment of loans but the situation is so dire that it may not be enough as businesses fold up.

The poor in the country have got access to banking via their Jan Dhan accounts. Apparently, there are more than 38 crore such accounts. Most of them are in rural areas. These are being used by the government to transfer money to the poor. For instance, the support of Rs 500 to poor women during the pandemic was announced by the PM in March and has been transferred to their accounts. There are many problems in the working of this scheme (Kumar, 2018) but it has given some support to those who get the money. Further, why is their money lying in these accounts when the poor lack money to feed themselves? Chances are that many of these accounts are proxy accounts or operated on behalf of others. During demonetization, a lot of cash was deposited in these accounts by those who had black money. This was a way of legitimizing black hoards. So such schemes are useful to some of the genuine poor but also impose a burden on the already stressed public-sector banks that have to bear the cost of keeping these accounts operational.

In brief, the already-fragile financial system of the country has become even more so, and will need a lot of support from the RBI and the government to stay alive and recuperate. The government will have to announce a package of relief to the financial sector to prevent it from collapsing. The government may also have to invest money in failing businesses by taking up equity. This could lead to an increase in crony capitalism, which is anyway rampant in India.

## Unlock 1 Onwards

As the country relaxed the lockdown and announced phases of Unlock (Annexure 01), some people started going to work and production of non-essentials restarted. The economy slowly started to recover (Table IV.3). But because of factors discussed in Chapter III, consumer and business confidence improved slowly—and so did exports. As a result, the country continued to remain in depression (Graph III.1).

Most of the industry and offices are in big metropolitan centres or in their proximity, and that is where the spread of the disease has been the highest—Delhi, Mumbai, Chennai, Bengaluru, Pune, Indore, Ahmedabad, etc. So from time to time, they have been in various stages of lockdown, making it difficult to open up completely. Further, a large number of activities have not been able to fully revive, leading to a shortfall in demand. Consequently, as discussed in Chapter III, neither consumption nor investment has revived fully and recovery has been shallow. Table IV.3 shows that only about 40 per cent of economic activity is likely to have taken place in June 2020 and 70 per cent in September.

The primary sector of the economy, consisting of agriculture, etc., will mostly be able to work and initially be the biggest contributor to the economy. The hitch during initial phases of Unlock was the availability of workers and the slow revival of trade and transportation of produce to the trading centres. Yet, one can assume that this sector could more or less be fully operational even though there were reports of fruits and vegetables rotting in the fields and a decline in demand for sugar, milk and eggs. The closure of schools has meant that children are not getting midday meals, where they used to get milk, eggs, etc., daily. So, in spite of bumper rabi and kharif harvests, production in this sector may remain short of earlier levels for some time.

Industry and services are the major components of the GDP. They typically operate from confined spaces, with many people working together, so that the chances of spread of infection are high. That is why it is difficult to restart them unless one is sure that the workers are not infected.

Due to the loss of incomes of a large number of people—workers and businessmen—demand for both non-essentials and essentials has been slow to revive, except for a few items for which there was pent-up demand. To produce most items, certain basic inputs are required, and these are clubbed together in the core sector. It consists of power, coal, cement, petroleum products, etc. When output declines, demand for most core-sector items falls, and this is what India has seen. Production of many FMCG items has not revived to earlier levels, as the unemployed consume less of these items.

Lots of discretionary purchases, such as clothing and appliances, have been postponed. Further, due to failure of businesses, incomes will further plummet and demand will go down even more. Even though demand for personal vehicles increased, since the well-off wanted to avoid using public transport—which is still risky—this is not enough to compensate for the overall decline due to the fall in incomes. So the manufacturing sector will remain subdued.

Many businesses that face a headwind have argued that they should not have to pay rent to landlords, or want to pay a lower rent in the future. So landlords have also lost incomes. Further, as businesses close down and vacate property, there is excess availability of rental property and there are few takers. Thus, rents have gone down and, along with that, the value of property. So the real estate sector, ownership of dwelling, etc., have continued to decline, let alone recover. The construction sector has also declined, since demand for new property has fallen.

Large uncertainty in the markets has impacted the financial sector. Further, if there is failure in this sector due to overleveraging, as suggested in the previous section, this sector's contribution to the GDP will fall. The first quarter reports of many companies have shown a massive decline in profits, and this has continued in Q2 of 2020–21. This is impacting the stock markets and making investors pessimistic. Thus, financial-sector activity has remained below last year's levels.

In India, there are about 5500 companies listed in the stock markets, and most of these stocks are held by the owners of the companies and the institutional investors (both domestic and foreign). When the stock markets decline, the well-off lose wealth. In March, trillions of dollars of global wealth evaporated, leaving the well-off feeling poorer. This, along with the decline in other asset prices, such as of real estate, has aggravated the negative sentiment of the well-off sections. So these people are suffering from a 'wealth effect', which results in their reducing their consumption and investment. This, in turn, has resulted in a decline in demand for luxury goods and consumer durables, even though the well-off have the savings to buy these items.

There are only some services that can be performed from home, and they will continue. E-commerce has grown, as people are buying more at a distance rather than from brick-and-mortar establishments. But that has displaced the latter and lowered employment there. Demand will also be restricted, since people will mostly buy essentials and that will further impact brick-and-mortar stores. E-commerce also involves delivery and people do worry about the danger of the spread of the disease through delivery agents. Restarting industry and services requires massive testing. Or activity may restart in districts that are infection-free, but that can only be determined through testing widely. In its absence, full activity cannot start anytime soon.

Physical distancing has to continue during unlock—and that is impacting many businesses. For instance, few are visiting restaurants or seeing movies or going for sporting events. Travel remains restricted and, though not initially but in due course, will become more expensive due to the need for physical distancing. Airlines and railways have not revived to pre-pandemic levels, since people are worried about being in close proximity and catching the disease. So the revenue of these businesses has remained low and they are incurring losses. This will put pressure on these sectors to raise their prices. But that could be counterproductive, as it would further impact demand. This will feed back into related businesses, such as the travel and food industry, which will also not be able to recover.

Public administration and the education sector will work below capacity due to the need for physical distancing. So they will also contribute much less to the economy than before.

In brief, as shown in Table IV.3, most sectors have operated much below pre-pandemic levels. One of my neighbours said to me three days after the lockdown started that he had only then realized 'with how little consumption life can go on. Why go to malls and buy unnecessarily?'

## Sectoral Aspects

While all sectors of the economy have been impacted by the lockdown, only a few sectors are discussed below. Whereas every industry and business has its own specificities, what is true for these economic activities also applies with greater or lesser force to others as well. The most important sector to look at is agriculture, since that is the largest employer and produces one of the most essential items of consumption for society to survive.

## Agriculture

Food production has to continue during a lockdown. It is also feasible to allow agriculture to operate, since it can function in a dispersed manner. It is carried out in open areas and not in closed ones (such as offices), which are more prone to infections. The issue is to maintain hygiene and that should be possible through strict dos and don'ts.

India has been lucky in that it had a huge surplus of foodgrains in March 2020. There were 75 million tonnes of stock when the requirement was 25 million tonnes. The bumper rabi crop further bolstered stocks by 25 million tonnes. Thus, there was no shortage of food during the lockdown—and the problem was neither production nor foodstock. The problem was marketing. This is especially important for fruits and vegetables, which are perishable and have to be harvested and marketed without delay. Storage is not easy, since cold storage and processing plants are few and far between. There were reports of farmers allowing vegetables and fruits to rot in the fields because they were not able to sell them. Table IV.4 shows that the arrival of these items in the biggest wholesale fruit and vegetable market was way below normal. Prices of these items at the farm fell sharply during the lockdown, as mentioned earlier. So both quantities and prices dropped, and farmers suffered losses.

Foodgrains and many other commercial crops can be stored. But, often, farmers need immediate cash for consumption and planting the next crops, and need to sell their produce. The traders take advantage of the plight of farmers and pay less than market prices for crops. In the case of many crops, the government announces an MSP. The MSP assures the farmers that they will get at least this price even if the market price falls below it. However, Table IV.6 shows that the market prices were below the MSP, so most farmers got a lower price. While the well-off farmers could hold on to the crop for some time, the real sufferers were the marginal farmers who could not wait and had to sell at the low prices. The lockdown came precisely when the crop had been harvested and was ready to go to the markets. But due to lack of transportation during the lockdown, the produce could not reach the big markets.

Demand for higher-value items such as milk, sugar, meat and chicken dropped as eating out declined, and restaurants and hotels closed down. Events were not held and entertainment stopped. Sweet shops closed down. So there was an all-round decline in demand and a softening of prices for these higher-value items. In fact, in the case of meat, chicken and eggs, there was even fear that the virus could spread through animals, so their demand fell further.

The result was a lot of wastage and destruction of these items. So even though production took place, part of the produce got wasted and did not contribute to the GDP, thus lowering the contribution of these items to the GDP. The crash in prices in rural areas also meant that farmers were in distress and in the next planting season, would put less of inputs thereby impacting agricultural output in the next season. It also meant that demand for labour on farms declined, leading to more unemployment and an increased demand under MGNREGS.

In brief, agriculture and agriculturists faced a crisis, even though they could hypothetically work normally with physical distancing. This was due to the collapse in demand in the economy and problems in trade and transportation.

## The Media

India has a vibrant media industry—print, electronic and social. This is crucial for a democracy. So even though there are problems due to its increasing corporatization and growing susceptibility to government pressure, it plays a positive role in preserving democracy. There are a large number of TV channels, magazines and newspapers—national and local—competing for news. So if one gets an important news item, others follow suit. Of course, each may give its own slant to the news but they cannot ignore it.

COVID-19 has posed the biggest threat to the media. The media covers most of its cost from advertising, which comes from businesses and the government. With businesses closed and suffering large losses, advertising budgets were severely curtailed. If car showrooms are shut and customers missing, what good would advertising one's car do?

Newspapers are handled by people and many feared that the virus could be on the surface of the paper. So a large number of people stopped buying newspapers, resulting in a decline in both sales and advertising in newspapers. This led to losses and some newspapers folded up. Some editions of national dailies also closed down. This has resulted in many papers and magazines offering their electronic version free of cost so that at least circulation remains high.

Many people in the media lost their jobs or faced salary cuts. One way of reducing salary is to let go of a senior person and make do with a junior one at a fraction of the former's salary. Something like this had also happened at the time of demonetization in 2016. This impacts the quality of the publication. Newspapers also reduced the number of pages. Since many small local papers closed down, the watchdog role played by the media waned—it strengthens accountability of those in power and this role got diluted.

As far as possible, mediapersons worked from home. But that is not always feasible, especially in TV journalism. Journalists can file reports from home but when they have to interview people in the field or get visual shots of events, they have to venture out. Journalists had to take a lot of precautions to avoid getting infected but some did catch the virus.

Given the fear of the spread of the disease, the public was hungry for information on it. Also, during the lockdown, with people confined to their homes, TV-watching and the use of social media went up. In fact, increasingly, news is being obtained via social media. There has been anxiety about whether and when there will be a cure, what to do to ward off the disease or things to follow if people do catch it.

So all kinds of people (doctors, social workers and gurus) have been active on social media, offering solace, remedies and so on. People have also been offering alternative medicine remedies that may boost immunity but may not be the cure. But their efficacy cannot be ascertained, given that this disease did not exist in earlier times, when these remedies were evolved. One virus is not the same as another and what may work with one may not work for another. That is the lesson of the allopathic medicine system. As is well known, what works for polio does not work for HIV.

Much fake news spread on social media and people panicked. For example, the news of buses being available to take migrants home. So, at the Delhi border, hordes of desperate migrants gathered and physical distancing was thrown to the winds. Similar things happened everywhere—in Surat, Mumbai, Bengaluru, etc. Such fake news made people more despondent, such as that the virus can spread through newspapers. The PM, in one of his speeches, batted for the print media but with little effect. The real danger of fake news is that it can misinform and reinforce prejudices and dogmas.

Publishing is also related to the media. It also faced a crisis because printing presses closed down. New books got delayed due to disruption of work in publishing houses. Publishing houses had to devise new strategies to survive. As educational institutions closed down and learning moved to the electronic mode of instruction, sales of printed material suffered. Exams were postponed or cancelled so material linked to exams, such as mug books, could not be sold.

In brief, the media and publishing have suffered grievously and will have to refashion themselves in the post-COVID-19 world. The impact is likely to last long. There will possibly be a shift to the electronic platform for both the media and publishing, but it is not clear how fake news can be tackled.

## The Education Sector

Education is crucial to the future of any nation. It had to be shut down, since it required a lot people to be in close proximity. Also, children could not be expected to be very careful about physical distancing and hygiene. So, even though it is said that proportionately fewer children and younger people are prone to the disease, they can pass it on to the older generation. So the reopening of schools and colleges closed since March was uncertain in spite of unlock (Annexure 01). Syllabi could not be completed and exams had to be postponed repeatedly—and, in many cases, cancelled. The start of the new educational session or new admissions also faced uncertainty and postponement. Most parents have not wanted to take a chance with sending their children to schools and colleges. So both new admissions and the beginning of the new term were disturbed.

All in all, the education sector is floundering. Institutions have tried to innovate by holding classes via the Internet, making course material available to students and so on. But this has not been satisfactory, since in a poor country such as India, many households do not even have electricity, let alone the Internet, computers and smartphones. Some children committed suicide because they could not attend classes and were afraid of falling behind. Thus, the digital divide is showing up, with the poor getting deprived of education. This, over time, will result in a deeper social divide and greater inequality.

Parents have had to play an important role in motivating their children at home to attend classes via the Internet. So the parents' own literacy level, motivation and availability has become crucial. Poor families have found it difficult to find the time to do all this, since they have to go out to work. Even many middle-class families, where both spouses work, have faced difficulty. That is why in the West it is being argued that if the economy is to unlock, schools have to open so that children can go there during the day, freeing parents from the duty of taking care of them so that they can go to work.

In education, henceforth, the public sector will have to play a more important role. With a large number of workers losing their incomes, their children will not be able to go to private schools, where the fees are higher. That will be true for many middle-class families as well. Many will have to consider sending their children to government schools rather than to private ones that they were attending till now.

In higher education, a lot of private institutions have mushroomed over the past thirty years. To make a profit (indirectly) they charge high fees. Even in public-sector institutions there has been a proliferation of 'paying' courses. An impoverished population will not be able to afford to send their children to these institutions, so enrolment and, in turn, profits will drop, and some of them may close down or will have to charge even higher fees. Overall, demand will shift towards public-sector institutions and the government will have to be ready to increase the budget for public education.

As society unlocked, holding classes with physical distancing became an issue. Online classes, as argued above, made the deprived sections lose out due to lack of electricity and wireless infrastructure. So this infrastructure will have to be provided by the public sector to make it freely available. Better-trained teachers will be required to teach in new ways and will have to be paid more than other competing jobs. This will be feasible only if society prioritizes education more than it has done till now.

For the new mode of teaching, course content will have to be compressed and explained better so it can hold students' interest. The young have a short attention span and within that time the teacher has to get an idea across to them. Unfortunately, most teaching in the country, at all levels, is of poor quality, with children expected to learn by rote and mechanically pass exams. That is why most students and teachers are opposed in principle to open-book exams. This attitude will have to change in the distance-learning mode via the Internet. Good teaching is all about getting across the basics to the students and then expecting them to develop an interest in learning about the concepts further. Education will require a rethink. The National Education Policy 2020 was announced on 29 July 2020, but it did not factor in the concerns thrown up by COVID-19, as discussed above.

In brief, this sector has seen a decline in its contribution to the GDP, and technology has been playing a greater role. But this will have to confront the issue of the technology divide that aggravates inequality between the haves and the have-nots. The new normal will require much better teaching and for the public sector to play a much greater role. Perhaps the time has come to go for neighbourhood schools and other such innovations.

## The New Normal

There is no one industry or service. They are all different, with their own requirements in the present situation. There are labour-intensive sectors and capital-intensive ones. Those that are considerably automated have different requirements than the ones that are labour-intensive, where people also work in close physical proximity to each other. The meat industry everywhere has faced rising infections—such as in Germany and the US. The automobile sector has many robots in their factories, and yet, for many operations it needs workers.

The greater the use of robots and artificial intelligence (AI), the lesser the employment. So, in a pandemic, industries that are more automated can work more easily with physical distancing. It is being suggested that there should be more automation so that in a future pandemic, work need not stop. Similarly, in the services sector too, it is being suggested that there should be more 'work from home' and more use of AI. What would this mean for employment?

There was already a crisis of unemployment in many countries before the pandemic hit. In the post-COVID-19 scenario, if there is to be more automation, unemployment will increase in traditional industries and services as well. In India, there could be a big displacement of the cottage and micro sectors by the growth of big industry. The former employs many times more labour than the latter for a given unit of output. So the shift will result in a huge rise in unemployment. Take the case of the shift to e-commerce from brick-and-mortar retail stores. E-commerce no doubt has given jobs to delivery personnel, warehousing workers and so on. But it also displaces ten times the number of workers in small neighbourhood stores. These workers, being poorly trained, will now have nowhere else to go and will become unemployed.

Due to such trends in the world over the past decade, the idea of a Universal Basic Income (UBI) scheme has been floated. Those who would have earlier scoffed at such a dole now realize that this is the only way demand can be sustained in a modern-day capitalist economy. But this suggestion for such a scheme is a sign of a crisis— that the system cannot generate enough jobs for everyone. It implicitly assumes that people only want money in hand. It is a transactional idea that people are only there to generate demand for businesses. It is being ignored that workers are people with self-esteem. Work gives a worker dignity, which simply handing them cash does not. Such a scheme would result in greater alienation of workers and create its own social and political problems. It would be better to modify systems so that jobs are given priority over investment and technology.

One way or the other, industry and services will not return to how they functioned before the pandemic hit the world. There will be a new normal. Under this, the workers ought to get a living wage so that they are ensured a civilized existence. It is likely to involve arranging a place to live close to the office or the factory (Kumar, 1994), working in sanitary and hygienic conditions and taking care of the health requirements and educational needs of their children. All this will add to the cost of production but not adversely impact growth since demand would be strong.

Practising physical distancing in public transportation will mean that the carrying capacity of the Metro and public buses will fall drastically. So people may go for more personalized transport unless the frequency of public transport is greatly increased. The cost of commute will go up and that is why staying close to the place of work would be important. It would also be environmentally more desirable.

The new normal would also involve redefining of capacity for many businesses, as they will be producing less than earlier. What was called full employment output in the pre-pandemic phase will now be less in the post-pandemic phase. So the resource base of the economy will shrink, costs will rise and, on average, people will have less of material goods but that does not mean that there welfare would decline.

In the new normal, productivity will decline and the standards of living as currently defined would be lower. Unemployment will rise, which means that demand will remain short and growth rates will be hit. Inequality will rise as some sectors automate more and pay their workers higher wages while other sectors pay less, given the excess supply of labour. Owners of technology companies will see their wealth grow as their company's stocks will rise much more than those of others. For instance, shareholders of Amazon, Tesla and Reliance Jio, have seen their wealth soar during the pandemic. The growing inequality and unemployment is likely to lead to an increase in social and political instability and also crime. So society will have to conceive of a new normal that is more equitable and less alienating.

# VI

# What Should the Government Do?

The previous chapters presented the nature and extent of the crisis faced by society due to the COVID-19 pandemic. Every segment of society has been impacted but the worst affected is the unorganized sector. Official data does not fully represent this crisis and the officialdom has tried to downplay its extent. That is why the necessary steps to control the pandemic and its fallout have not been implemented with the urgency that was necessary. Unemployment is acute and the economy is in a deep depression—something that has never been witnessed before. The healthcare situation could not be brought under control quickly enough, but, under pressure, the lockdown restrictions started getting eased even though the number of cases detected and the number of people dying were rising steadily (graphs IV.1.1 and IV.1.2). In the countries that have successfully tackled the pandemic, this easing came after the numbers plateaued or declined substantially. So, as argued earlier, India has had the worst of all worlds.

## State vs Markets

To deal with the current crisis, society needed to pull itself up by the bootstraps. The government needed to intervene massively in three broad areas. First, in giving succour to the poor and the needy; second, in taking care of the healthcare situation; and, finally, in preventing the economy from collapsing. Markets have largely become non-functional and cannot deliver on these fronts. Hence, all sections of society—be it the big businesses or the workers—have been expecting the government to help.

Modern-day economies depend on the markets performing their basic function of exchange of goods and services. As discussed in the previous chapter, when markets fail, as they did during the lockdown, the government has to step in to keep the economy going. Right from the 1970s, there has been much debate on 'state vs markets'—which is better for society? The government was characterized as the 'leviathan' (overgrown and overbearing) and inefficient. A consensus was built that the state ought to retreat in favour of the markets and increasingly, they were favoured.

Margaret Thatcher became the prime minister of the UK in 1979 and Ronald Reagan became the president of the US in 1981. Both of them pushed the ideological agenda of markets. Thatcher talked of TINA (There Is No Alternative) and broke the back of trade unions. This ideological agenda was strengthened by the gradual decline of the Soviet Union since the 1970s and China taking a 180-degree turn in its economic policies. The pendulum swung towards the markets and away from government intervention in the economy. The state has been in retreat. The philosophy became: 'Let the markets prevail' (See Kumar, 2013).

The IMF, the World Bank and other international financial institutions have pushed this agenda. They were accused of propagating a 'one size fits all' solution to the world. The policy package was labelled the 'Washington Consensus' (Williamson, 1989). Doubts were raised about the efficacy of the markets to deliver efficiently during the global financial crisis of 2007–09. During the term of Alan Greenspan, the chair of the Federal Reserve of the

United States from 1987 to 2006, the stock markets boomed—in the late 1990s and the early 2000s. He was considered a god by the markets. His term ended before the global financial crisis impacted the world, towards the end of 2007. He then admitted in 2008 in a congressional hearing that he was wrong and that markets were not self-correcting—the hand of the state was required for the markets to function properly.

As the world economy recovered from the global financial crisis, this lesson was again put aside. And we are now paying for it. The pandemic has again shown us that markets can fail miserably and the government is needed to provide relief to the citizens. As argued in Chapter I, the role of the government needs to be reassessed. The question is: What should the government in India have done to tackle the crisis and what did it do?

## *India Beset by Crisis on Multiple Fronts*

By mid-March, the government realized that a lockdown had become inevitable to control the spread of the disease. Some states started implementing lockdowns in mid-March. The one-day janata curfew organized on Sunday, 22 March, was in preparation for a nationwide lockdown from 25 March. The lockdown was further extended, with some relaxations on 14 April, and then in various phases through May. These were followed by Unlock 1 in June and subsequent phases of unlock after that. Increasingly, more and more activity was permitted (Annexure 01).

As mentioned in Chapter I, a lockdown is not the cure to a disease but serves two important purposes. First, it slows down and, in some cases, halts the spread of the disease in the country and, second, it buys the government time to put in place the healthcare infrastructure needed to meet any eventuality that may arise. But, as discussed in Chapter III, the lockdown administered a big shock to the economy, especially hitting the unorganized sectors that exist on the very edge of survival. Thus, India had to confront two emergencies simultaneously—a health crisis and an economic one.

As argued in Chapter IV, while the lockdown was implemented, the preparation required for it to be a success was missing. Namely there was a need to:

1) Take care of the poor by making essentials available to them wherever they were.
2) Decongest the poor in the cities so that their isolation could become feasible.
3) Initiate a massive programme of testing and contact tracing to slow the spread of the disease.
4) Prepare and create the healthcare infrastructure needed to take care of those who got infected.
5) Prevent potential business failures on a large scale.

A package encapsulating all of this was needed. The government, however, did not put such a package in place and the lockdown was only partially successful. It did help reduce the rate at which the disease spread but it did not control it. As argued in Chapter IV, in India, the pandemic kept spreading; the lockdown had to be partially reimposed in some areas, restrictions could not be eased quickly in large parts of the economy and the revival of the economy became difficult.

The health and the economic emergencies became dire for every section of the population. There was enormous pressure on the government to act so the situation did not spin out of control. The government's own financial situation deteriorated and demands on its resources increased, leading to policy difficulties. In the absence of a clear-cut thought process, there was much confusion in policy. Priorities were not re-evaluated and policymakers acted as if they could continue to do what they had been doing earlier, only a bit more. But, along with other experts—both national and international—they were behind the curve.

*Government Intervention: Steps Undertaken Globally*

The governments in the advanced countries were quick to announce substantial relief packages. They saw that unemployment was shooting up and businesses failing. The US first gave $8.3 billion in early March, followed by a $100-billion emergency aid package in mid-March and a $2-trillion rescue package at the end of March. It provided money to individuals, funds for healthcare facilities and aid to businesses strapped for cash. Subsequently, at the end of April, another $480 billion was sanctioned to help the economy.

The total package amounted to about $2.5 trillion. Individuals earning less than $75,000 were to get $1200 and $500 for each child. Small businesses were to receive money to pay salaries under the Paycheck Protection Program (PPP). So a package of about 15 per cent of the GDP (reduced due to the depression in the economy) covered most sections of the economy and was given directly from the budget. The total deficit in the budget was estimated to climb to about 19 per cent of the GDP. This was in addition to the monetary policy steps announced by the central bank (Federal Reserve System). It provided for liquidity and cuts in interest rates to boost the economy. At the beginning of March, the rate of interest was cut to 0.5 per cent and then to 0 per cent. Liquidity was made available to municipalities and firms.

Japan, by end of April, had announced a programme of $1.1 trillion, of which $452 billion was to come from the budget. Thus, a stimulus of about 10 per cent of the GDP (reduced) was to come from the budget. The UK, in April, announced a rescue package that was 15 per cent of the GDP to support businesses.

Segal and Dylan (2020) report that G20 as a whole, at a virtual meeting on 26 March, committed to spending $5 trillion (7.4 per cent of the 2019 GDP). By the end of April, the figure went up to $6.3 trillion, or 9.3 per cent of the 2019 GDP. Of this, $3.2 trillion (4.8 per cent of the GDP) was to be from the budget. The rest was credit enhancements and tax relief. Segal and Dylan also point out that the response to the economic crisis this time has been far quicker than during the global financial crisis in 2007–09. Further, they also point out that the emerging-market economies have announced a much smaller package than those of developed countries, perhaps due to fiscal constraints.

The packages announced globally consist of the following elements:

1. Increased government expenditures leading to an increased fiscal deficit
2. Loans to existing businesses to tide over these difficult times
3. Loans/grants to businesses to pay at least part of the wages to workers
4. Cash transfers to people who have had to face pay cuts
5. Starting of public works for the unemployed
6. Tax concessions to businesses to boost profits

Let us discuss each of these to understand their content, intent and impact on the economy.

### Increasing Fiscal Deficit

Government expenditures lead to higher demand in the economy. But when revenue is collected to finance the expenditure, it reduces the purchasing power of those paying taxes. An excess of expenditures over revenues of the government is called the fiscal deficit. In other words, fiscal deficit is the situation in which the government spends more than its revenues. So, crudely speaking, demand in the economy increases by the extent of the fiscal deficit (Kalecki, 1971 and Kumar, 1988).

As mentioned in Chapter III, incomes fall drastically during a lockdown, which means tax collections also fall sharply. But expenditures rise to take care of the various needs of businesses, workers and medical expenses. The result is a sharp rise in the fiscal deficit in the budget of the government. For the US, the UK and Japan, the rise in deficit based on increased expenditures is 10–20 per cent of the GDP (Table V.1). This is not counting the likely decline in the revenues due to the decline in incomes. So, for most advanced economies, the rise in the fiscal deficit could be anything between 15–25 per cent of the GDP.

In the post-1980s' world, a high fiscal deficit was frowned upon, since it was supposed to limit the freedom of the private sector and crowd out private investment by pre-empting resources. An arbitrary number, 3 per cent of the GDP, has been fixed to be the right amount of fiscal deficit for an economy. In India, also under the Fiscal Responsibility and Budget Management (FRBM) Act, 2003, this number has been declared to be the target the government should aim for. But the government has seldom achieved it.

In today's conditions, when the lockdown has led to a collapse in demand (Chapter III), most analysts are calling for a high fiscal deficit to boost the economy—to stimulate growth. Even businessmen and those in the finance sector who have traditionally been opposed to raising the fiscal deficit see virtue in now raising it. Kumar (2020i) argues that the massive deficit will neither create inflation nor crowd out private investment under the present circumstances.

## Loans to Existing Businesses

Chapters II and III point out that many small businesses or those that are highly leveraged and have little reserves, begin to fail when they have to shut down during a pandemic. They all have loans on which they have to pay interest and repay the loans they may have taken to set up the business. With no revenue coming in due to closure of the business, these companies lack the funds to either pay interest or any part towards repayment of the loans, and subsequently go into default. This creates a non-performing asset (NPA) for the banks and lending institutions, and this can also result in business failure.

If a large number of businesses collapse, the revival of the economy after a lockdown will be difficult, and may even be impossible. In the current situation, to prevent businesses from collapsing, the governments have announced loan packages to businesses and the central banks have offered additional liquidity. A moratorium on the repayment of loans and interest payment has also been announced so that businesses can pay the money they owe the banks after a certain number of months. The idea is that, by then, the businesses will pick up again and start generating revenue. In India, a six-month moratorium was allowed. But this only postpones the day of reckoning, since the interest will keep mounting. Interest on funds not repaid will also mount. In October, the government, prodded by the Supreme Court, offered to take the burden of the extra interest on the unpaid loan. If a business, when it restarts, makes little profit since demand is low, it will still not have the funds to pay the creditors and will eventually fail. Thus, for such businesses, the day of reckoning is only postponed.

The alternative is that a loan is given to the business by the government, and that is converted into equity when the business restarts. This is a more viable strategy. It is suggested that the equity be sold by the government in a few years, when the business gets going. It is also said that this way, the government also gains a certain premium. But this is going to be a messy situation if the governments have to take care of their investment in millions of businesses.

This scheme may also encourage crony capitalism, with the well-connected cornering a large share of the loans and many others not getting loans even if they are viable. In India, this could result in an increase in fraud.

If businesses collapse in spite of the loan, if demand does not pick up soon, the government will stand to lose the money it invested in these businesses. This is the reason banks are not lending to weak businesses even though liquidity has been pumped into the system to allow liberal lending. The chances are that many weak businesses will fail despite the loans being offered.

## Loans/Grants to Businesses to Pay Workers

Businesses use working capital to pay wages and buy raw material. In a lockdown, as discussed in Chapter III, as work stops, workers are fired or their salaries cut to save on working capital and lower the interest burden. This leads to a decline in demand and a further downturn in the economy. Only the government or companies with large reserves continue to pay full wages. But even these companies find their profits and reserves dwindling due to stoppage of production.

Thus, if workers continue to get some income, even if they are not working, they can buy the essentials of life and prevent demand from falling precipitously. Workers mostly live in rented accommodation and if they don't pay rent, risk becoming homeless, leading to societal breakdown. They may also have to pay instalments for things bought on loans or pay tuition fees for their children. In advanced countries, a lot of people take loans, sometimes several of them, to lead a life beyond their means. Often, they have little savings and a lot of liabilities.

Rental income is important for landlords, or they will not be able to meet their commitments. Similarly, if a large number of people stop paying their monthly instalments, there will be a large number of foreclosures at the same time and many banks and financial institutions could collapse. Thus, a large number of workers losing their incomes at the same time can set off a chain of failures, leading to further collapse in demand. In effect, a part of the payment to the workers is payment to landlords and finance companies.

So, in the developed countries, governments set into motion a programme to pay the businesses to a) keep their workers on the payroll and b) pay them some fraction of the salary, if not the full amount. This comes under the PPP in the US. Since workers remain on their respective payrolls, when businesses restart, labour is available again to begin work. In the US, the provision was that the loans would be written off if the workers were kept on the payrolls.

In India, the problem is worse, as discussed in Chapter II—a large number of workers are in the unorganized sector. During the pandemic they got little relief, with hardly any access to food and no money to pay rent. So they migrated in large numbers back to their villages. Thus, when businesses wanted to restart after the lockdown was eased, there was a shortage of labour in the cities. This slowed down the recovery of the economy, both due to shortage of demand and continuing supply bottlenecks.

This is the reason it was argued earlier that recovery in India would be slower than in the developed world. Further, the point of paying workers' wages (in the advanced countries) even if they were not working was to keep demand from collapsing and help revive the economy faster. But it is argued here that the payment by the government to businesses to pay the workers is a help to businesses also. However, this step has not been taken in India, impeding recovery.

Cash Transfers to Workers Who Lose Incomes

This is similar to the case where businesses pay the workers part of the money they get from the government. However, many workers got fired in spite of the government's help and are no longer on any payroll. These workers also need support. In the US, 44 million—one third of the workers—filed for jobless claims in the first twelve weeks after March.

To provide support to such people, governments transferred money into their bank accounts. This money was inadequate to support them but, along with the other money they could get for being unemployed and the food programme that was initiated, these workers could survive.

So, again, the basic thrust of this programme was to prevent societal breakdown and keep demand from collapsing completely.

In India, poor women were offered Rs 500 per month for three months, along with things such as free gas cylinders for cooking.

Families were offered free foodgrains and lentils. The programme could not cover all the poor but did help out some.

## Starting Public Works for the Unemployed

Another way that the government can give incomes to the unemployed is to start public works during periods of crisis. This is not done in most developed economies. But in India, this has been ongoing for a long time, given the problem of unemployment, especially in rural areas. The National Rural Employment Guarantee Act was passed in 2005. It led to the MGNREGS, under which a poor family could demand work in rural areas and get up to hundred days of work for one member at a predefined wage. This was to supplement the income they earned during the rest of the year.

It is a demand-driven programme, where any worker can ask the local authorities for work. Usually, the work is unskilled, such as work to be done on roads, making check dams or digging pits for rainwater storage.

In India, allocation for such work was increased so that those who had migrated back to the villages could get work under this scheme and earn a basic income. However, many workers who had migrated back were skilled and did not like the idea of doing manual unskilled labour at very low wages.

There has been demand to start a scheme similar to MGNREGS in urban areas as well, since so many workers who lost employment are living with their families in the cities. This problem has been persisting since demonetization, when the unorganized sector was badly hit for the first time (Kumar, 2018). Now the problem has become acute, with even the organized sector retrenching workers.

What kind of work can be allotted under the employment guarantee scheme? Both in the cities and in the villages, infrastructure is woefully weak and in need of upgradation (Kumar, 1994). The unemployed can be set to build this infrastructure. Education, too, requires massive improvement, since it is weak in large swaths of the country, both in the rural and the urban areas. Schools lack buildings, teachers and facilities. Often, classes are overcrowded due to lack of adequate staff. The unemployed can be gainfully employed in construction, teaching, COVID-19-related contact tracing and other similar jobs.

Thus, starting/expanding a public-works programme is a good way of generating both employment and demand to boost the sagging economy. Kings in olden times used to build palaces and forts during droughts. The Bada Imambara in Lucknow has a plaque testifying to this. US president Franklin D. Roosevelt used the New Deal programme, initiated in 1933, to start public works on a large scale to counter the effects of the depression in the US economy. Now, once again, the time has come to initiate massive public works, since the situation is worse than during the 1930s.

## Tax Concessions to Businesses to Boost Profits

Businesses feel that if they are given tax concessions, their profitability will rise and they will invest more. That is not true in the short run and especially when a business is shut down and in losses, there is no question of paying taxes, so any concession on tax will be meaningless. What it would do is to increase the deficit in the budget. That could boost demand. However, usually, this goes with the idea that the budget should be balanced so as not to pre-empt savings from the private sector. Due to such pressures, when tax collection falls, the government also cuts back on its expenditure, which reduces demand. So cutting tax on businesses does not boost demand, especially when the business is shut down or suffering losses, and if the fiscal deficit is maintained at the old level.

Actually, the government's increasing its expenditures is a more viable way of increasing demand. And if this expenditure generates incomes for the poor, the increase in demand would be the maximum, since the poor will spend the entire amount they earn. Even if the tax cut boosts profits, since it goes mostly to the well-off, demand rises but by a little, since they consume only a small percentage of their income. They could invest more and boost demand but, as already argued, in the present circumstances, chances are they will not do that, given that capacity utilization is low. So, overall, the increase in demand will be negligible in the current situation.

Another suggestion is to cut indirect taxes to boost demand. This would result in a decline in prices and it is assumed that consumers would buy more, thereby leading to an increase in demand. But given the uncertainty, demand for discretionary items may hardly rise even if the prices of these goods decline. As far as essentials are concerned, most of them bear no indirect tax, so there can be no cut in their tax rate. The prices of essentials that bear some indirect taxes can be lowered by cutting tax on them. But these are not the goods facing a problem in demand. The well-off sections bought them in large quantities during the lockdown and hoarded them, irrespective of the price, and this can happen again. So the companies producing them will not cut their prices and absorb the tax cut as increased profits. Finally, if nothing else changes, this tax cut will lead to an increase in the fiscal deficit. But, if this is kept unchanged, there will be no increase in overall demand.

In brief, more than a tax cut, if demand has to be increased, the fiscal deficit should be allowed to increase by whichever means. Further, demand will increase the most if this is done via transfers to the unemployed and the poor. Finally, currently, when tax collection is falling drastically, the fiscal deficit has risen in the first four months of the year, to Rs 8 lakh crore while it should technically have been about Rs 2 lakh crore (Table V.2). If a tax cut is implemented, it will rise further and the issue will be how to finance it (Kumar, 2020i).

*How Does a Stimulus Work?*

After being behind the curve (See Chapter IV), the IMF admitted that the world was facing a global recession. Eighty countries asked the IMF for help and the latter signalled its willingness to deploy its entire kitty of $1 trillion to support them. The UNDP predicted trillions of dollars of loss of incomes globally. The G20 put together a stimulus package of $5 trillion by June and the UNDP stated that developing countries need a crisis package of $2.5 trillion—for a total of $7.5 trillion of stimulus. Earlier, the packages announced by the US, Japan and the European Union (EU) were mentioned. But will these stimulus packages help?

What is a stimulus and how does it help an economy revive? As the name suggests, the package of policies called the stimulus is supposed to boost the economy—by a multiple of the amount of government intervention. Can a stimulus do that in the present circumstances?

In the present situation, without a stimulus, the expected loss is much more than the $7.5 trillion being offered globally. But even if the loss is taken to be $7.5 trillion, for the world economy of about $89 trillion in 2019–20, the expected loss would be 8.3 per cent of the global GDP, which would lead the global economy to decline to $81.5 trillion. The question is: If the stimulus does not do what it is expected to in the present circumstances, how much would the world economy contract by?

A stimulus works by boosting any or all of the macro variables such as consumption, investment and external trade. However, three questions arise:

1) How effective can a stimulus be in a lockdown situation?
2) How much stimulus is needed?
3) How would the stimulus be financed?

The Chinese example can help us understand what a stimulus can do. The Chinese were the first to unlock from a rather successful lockdown and could ramp up production when the lockdown was eased. They also had the advantage of being the only country in lockdown when others were not, so their production was not as badly hurt as that of other countries'. Yet, they are putting together a stimulus package of up to 8 per cent of the GDP.

As discussed in Chapter III, the Chinese economy has not recovered quickly back to the pre-pandemic situation, since consumer sentiment has plummeted; private investment will not recover soon and exports cannot rise to pre-pandemic levels, since other economies are down. An increased demand for ventilators, masks and PPEs is a tiny fraction of overall exports from China. Increased government expenditures—the stimulus—cannot compensate for all this.

China will, however, benefit from a collapse of commodity prices (such as a sharp decline in petroleum prices). But the bigger danger at present is deflation due to a collapse in global demand, and that will adversely impact China. So the Chinese example is not very encouraging, in spite of it being currently in the best possible situation for a stimulus to work. Further, when China went into lockdown, it was the only country to do so, in contrast, the rest of the countries were in a lockdown together. So the demand collapse for others is worse than what China faced.

## The Futility of a Stimulus to Businesses during a Lockdown

As discussed earlier, an increase in the fiscal deficit boosts demand. But conservative economists don't like it and argue that international agencies and capital will punish India for increasing its deficit. But what they forget is that all governments globally are allowing the fiscal deficit to increase dramatically (Table V.1), so India will not be singled out and punished by the global financial system (which is itself facing a crisis). If, to reduce the deficit, the currently planned government expenditures are cut, demand will fall. So, for a stimulus, the deficit will have to be allowed to rise.

What businesses understand by stimulus is that money is to be given to them. They don't want more money given to workers and farmers to revive demand, even though that is what is needed. During the lockdown, businesses incurred heavy losses and they want to make up for it.

But the government, giving money to businesses during a lockdown, will not result in restarting of the closed factories and offices. It can only partly cover the losses. This means that economic activity cannot restart with what businesses call a stimulus. They can only survive for a short while. Only if their closure is brief, businesses may restart and slowly overcome their losses.

In a nutshell, it can be said that the global economy is facing the consequence of the stoppage of economic activity due to lockdowns and not the usual business cycle downturn. The following conclusions follow:

1. Using standard fiscal spend to boost demand will not work when businesses are shut.
2. Cutting taxes on profits to boost demand will not work at present since businesses are closed or working at low capacity.
3. The stimulus would be most effective if the incomes of the unemployed and the poor are boosted, who will spend all of it and raise demand in the economy.
4. The limited resources the government has should be used to create public-works programmes to offer employment.
5. Funds should be used to help sustain life at a basic level, but that will require a large relief package for the poor.

The implication of the above is that instead of considering giving to businesses, governments should formulate a larger 'survival' package. The advanced countries are doing something like this and the developing world, especially India, should also follow such an approach. Later in this chapter it is discussed why the stimulus is not working in the Indian economy in spite of the high fiscal deficit.

## The Indian Government's Package: Fiscal and Monetary Policies

As depicted in Chapter IV, from Day 1 of the lockdown, it was clear that the poor would suffer grievously and need government support.

### Initial Package

The government announced a package of Rs 1.7 lakh crore for the poor on 27 March. And as mentioned earlier, this package included giving Rs 500 each to 200 million poor women through the Jan Dhan accounts, free gas cylinders to 8 crore poor families through the Ujjwala Yojana, and grains and lentils though the public distribution system. This package, amounting to 0.8 per cent of the 2019 GDP, was not all new or from the budget. Its fresh budgetary implication was only about half of the sum announced, since the PM Kisan scheme had already been announced in the budget. Funds from the Building and Other Construction Workers' Welfare Cess Fund and the District Mineral Foundation funds were also to be used for relief (Annexures V.1 and V.2).

The government initially asked businesses to not fire workers or cut their wages and salaries, similar to what the US had announced. But the difference is that in the US, businesses were offered money to follow through, while in India, businesses were expected to do so on their own. As discussed in Chapter III, only businesses that had substantial reserves could do this. The matter went to the Supreme Court and this provision was withdrawn. The unorganized sector, the largest employer in the country, could not implement this.

The RBI has announced several monetary policy packages since February. It has cut the repo and the reverse repo rates to lower interest rates in the economy. Banks can borrow from the RBI at the repo rate when they are tight for funds. When the banks have surplus money, they can deposit it with the RBI and earn the reverse repo rate. Further, the RBI injected liquidity into the system by cutting the cash reserve ratio (CRR) and various other means. CRR is the fraction of the deposits that banks get from customers, which they are required to keep with the RBI as a contingency. So, cutting CRR results in banks having more funds to lend to borrowers. The RBI allowed a three-month moratorium on repayment of loans (including EMIs), etc. It attempted to support an already struggling financial system so it did not take a worse beating due to the downturn in the economy.

However, all this was wholly inadequate to deal with the crisis confronting the nation, especially that facing the marginalized sections. Every 1 per cent fall in the GDP means a loss of income of Rs 2 lakh crore—and the loss due to the expected fall in the GDP was expected to be far greater than what was on offer from the government and the RBI.

Further, India has weak governance. Often, policies are announced but not delivered right. For instance, many do not have ration cards at all—such as the tribals, nomadic tribes and the homeless. Others do not have ration cards in the place where they currently reside, such as those who have migrated from their villages to the cities. So these people cannot avail of the free ration offered by the government. Similarly, many may not have operational bank accounts in which the government can transfer money or, again, these accounts may be in their villages and there may be no way to withdraw the money where they reside. So the money sent by the government may not reach many among the poor. There was massive corruption in the distribution of gas cylinders in the past and few refilled their gas cylinders as it turned out to be more expensive than gathering wood. Again, this may be a problem plaguing some recipients. Cooked-food distribution started by state governments and some NGOs did not reach many people, so there were complaints of hunger.

As argued earlier, monetary policy can only play a limited role during a lockdown. When businesses are not working, a lowering of interest rate will not lead to higher investment or demand.

The relief in loan repayment will help businesses survive a little longer. Relief in EMI payments will also help the middle classes. But this postponement of payments does not mean a reduction in the interest burden, which keeps mounting, so the problem is not resolved. What is also necessary is relaxing paperwork in banks to make accounts operational. For instance, with little mobility, how can people complete their KYC, without which their accounts get frozen? Thus, KYC requirements need to be relaxed for the period when mobility is restricted.

Big Package: Is It Big or Relevant?

By the middle of May, the government realized that the situation had turned dire for the poor. The PM addressed the nation on 12 May and announced a seemingly unprecedented Rs 20 lakh crore package (10 per cent of the 2019 GDP) (Annexures V.1 and 2). This raised huge expectations of relief for every section of society. He exhorted that one needed to convert adversity into opportunity and underlined that India had to become more self-sufficient, or 'atma nirbhar'. He referred to workers, farmers, the cottage and small- and medium-sector producers, and the middle classes. He lauded local manufacturing. It seemed that the government was planning to provide for all the marginalized sections. Self-reliance implied that there would be a retreat from globalization. This was not out of line with what many nations had been talking of—reducing their dependence on imports and creating local supply chains.

The PM left it to the finance minister Nirmala Sitharaman to unveil the package, which she did over five detailed press conferences. She first addressed the concerns of the MSME sector, then that of migrant labour, then the farmers, and after that the structural reforms and finally the miscellaneous issues (See Annexure V.1). But she refused to address critical issues, such as the extent of support to the poor from the budget and the government's likely revenue collections.

Right at the end, she gave the consolidated figure for the total package as Rs 20.97 lakh crore. The budgetary support to the marginalized sections was only Rs 2 lakh crore, or 1 per cent of the 2019-20 GDP (Annexure V.2). The rest was all going to be credit, to be given for a variety of purposes. The package also counted the earlier RBI announcements on enhancing liquidity and lending, which was stated to amount to Rs 9 lakh crore. In some cases of credit offered, the government is to be the guarantor of loans from banks. So, there would be a budgetary implication later on, only if there is default at some later date.

The expected allocations to the three aspects of the crisis facing the nation—the unemployed slipping below the poverty line; the creation of a massive healthcare infrastructure; and the need to boost demand to prevent business failures—received marginal support. The marginalized were in desperate need to be reassured that the country cared about them—that would have reduced their frustration and alienation. This was an opportunity for the government to show that society is a 'caring' one.

The ongoing pandemic has highlighted the need for a strong and efficient public sector to deal with a national crisis. But the package proposes to dismantle the public sector further via allowing the entry of the private sector into areas of operation of the former, structural changes, disinvestment, mergers and so on. This will reduce the capacity of the government to provide succour in case of any future calamity. Another contradiction in the government's position was that it expected to attract more foreign capital. But how does that square with talk of self-reliance?

The finance ministry announced a number of policies such as change in the definitions of MSME, changes in APMC and the Essential Commodities Act, 1955, along with changes in the IBC and Companies Act. The government argued that these steps would lead to more investment in the economy. But all this addresses the situation in the long run and not the immediate demand crisis.

## Package: Supply Side Rather than Demand Enhancing

The package is largely focused on the supply side. It offers concessions to businesses so they can revive their animal spirits to invest more. But when much of the economy is stalled, can there be supply-side response? Further, how can activity resume if demand remains short, given that the package has a very small component to help increase it immediately?

The PM's exhortation to turn adversity into opportunity seemed to be addressed to businesses. But that did not address the immediate requirement of taking care of migrants and mitigating the distress of the poor. The PM's faith that the private sector would invest more when its profits were down was misplaced. Only the public sector can invest in adverse circumstances. So the supply-side package will not spur more investment or production when demand is down. The example of the behaviour of private-sector hospitals during the pandemic is before us. They mostly withdrew, leaving the burden of healthcare to the public sector.

A whole range of policies in the package were only a repeat of announcements made in past budgets, such as help for fisheries and milk production; a package for potatoes, onions and tomatoes; and aircraft maintenance. Clearly, these are long- and medium-term issues, or they would have been implemented earlier. Further, when the airline industry is in a deep crisis, many companies are likely to fail and with no immediate revival in sight, how is creating a hub for maintenance in India an immediate priority? It is also unclear how policies announced regarding space and atomic energy are linked to the immediate crisis. Why spend energy on these matters when there is need for singular focus on the immediate crisis?

### Changes Suggested for Agriculture and Labour

Which sector of the Indian economy does not have a problem? Some policy changes are needed for each of them. But there is a right time for making such changes. It is often said that big changes can be pushed through during a crisis. The economic crisis of 1989–91, which was used to bring into effect the pro-business New Economic Policy starting June 1991, is an example (Kumar, 2013).

The government has pushed through certain reforms during this period that it was trying to ever since it came to power in 2014. However, it was not able to do so because of a strong Opposition. Now, due to the COVID-19 pandemic, the Opposition has been silenced and the government can push any policy, since it has a majority in the Lok Sabha and can more or less get it in the Rajya Sabha too. The current crisis has only made it easier for the government. The government has wanted big changes in agriculture, land and labour, but is this the right time or the right thing to do now, given the grave crisis we all face?

It is not that a lack of changes in these areas has held up economic growth in the past decade. India achieved an almost 9 per cent rate of growth between 2004 and 2008, before the rate fell due to the global financial crisis. This was achieved with the existing land, labour and agriculture situation in the country. The reason for the recent decline in the rate of growth has to do with growing inequality, policy shocks and shortage of demand (Kumar, 2018, and Kumar, 2019a).

What are the problems faced by agriculture? Most are small and marginal farmers, with little land and a small amount of production. The average size of a farm has dropped from 1.15 hectares in 2010–11 to 1.08 hectares in 2015–16, as families have been subdivided. In 2015–16, there were 126 million small and marginal farmers owning less than 2 hectares of land—they constituted 86.2 per cent of all farmers in India. It is difficult for the government to reach out to most of them. These farmers own an average of 0.6 hectares of land and produce little surplus for the market.

The main problem faced by the small farmers is lack of capital and technology. They are usually indebted to local moneylenders and traders, who advance them funds for carrying on cultivation.

The condition usually is that the farmers sell their produce to these lenders when the crop is harvested. Invariably these indebted farmers receive a price less than that in the market. So they are always short of capital and have to keep borrowing. They do not have the staying power of well-off farmers, who can bide their time for higher prices, especially during the lean season.

Every region has an APMC, which establishes a place the farmers can sell their produce in. It is regulated by law and is supposed to help the farmers get a better price than if they dealt directly with traders. But there have been problems with the APMC's functioning and small farmers still get a lower price than they should. So many have been advocating that the APMC be done away with, so farmers can get a better price.

The big corporate houses that have entered the retailing of fruits and vegetables via their retail stores or through direct delivery to customers have been wanting to have a free hand for procuring their supplies. Resultantly, now the APMC has been diluted and the farmers can sell directly to anyone and not have to go through the APMC. But which small farmer can do so? The big corporates will find it difficult to deal with a large number of small farmers and are also likely to buy from traders, who will act as aggregators. Thus, the hold of the traders over the farmers is not going to weaken through this change. In fact, one more margin will get added. It stands to reason why the big corporates would pay more when they can get the goods at a lower price and increase their profits. No wonder that farmers are protesting vehemently.

The other big problem related to agriculture is that it is dependent on rains. Production can fluctuate, and it does—a lot. Often, there is either a shortage or a glut in the market. This makes the prices of the commodities fluctuate. Sometimes the price rise is large and that leads to consumer unrest. This has happened in the case of onions and tomatoes. When the price collapses due to a glut, the farmers' incomes collapse too and there is again a crisis. The price fluctuation is high in commodities that are perishable and where safe storage facility is inadequate. The price fluctuation is often aggravated by speculation by traders and black marketeers, among others. A small shortage can turn big by holding back stocks of that commodity. For instance, a 25 per cent shortfall in production of onions can be used to trigger prices to rise by several hundred per cent.

The government has a scheme of procurement, stock holding and public distribution to moderate price fluctuations but this is only applicable to a limited number of agricultural produce. To control the speculative rise in prices of some major sensitive commodities, the government could invoke the Essential Commodities Act. Once invoked, it limits stock-holding by anyone, especially traders. Under the Act, exports of produce can be restricted to meet internal demand first. But that makes India an unreliable exporter, which affects future exports. The rich farmers also see this as limiting their incomes through control of prices. This Act is being diluted now so that it can only be used in extreme situations. The benefit of this dilution will largely accrue to traders and not to small farmers or consumers.

If there was adequate infrastructure to store commodities during a glut, which could then be released when there was a shortfall, the problem would largely be taken care of. Thus, there is need for cold storages and agro processing, and the package announced encourages such investment by making provision for credit to anyone wanting to invest.

But the question is whether such investment will take place now. It has been talked about for a long time but not enough has happened. Even if it does, it will not be immediate. So, at best, it is a long-term proposition. In these times, when incomes are declining and investment has more or less frozen, one cannot expect much investment to take place under the schemes announced.

Finally, the current problem of lack of demand and a decline in prices of food items received by farmers is an immediate one. Produce should have been procured from rural areas and marketed in the urban areas, so that prices in both the rural and urban areas could have been stabilized. An extended procurement and public distribution is needed right away but is nowhere in sight.

In brief, there is no immediate succour that small and medium farmers can expect. They are too small to be able to delink from traders and market their produce on their own. Further, can marketing of produce take place without any regulation of trade? In fact, this would help traders and corporates wanting to enter the agriculture trade to exploit the situation even more. Finally, are these steps needed now when a big crisis faces agriculture?

Chapters II and IV have presented the acute crisis that labour in India faces—not only now but even before the pandemic hit. Workers have been increasingly marginalized and are now getting further alienated because neither the state nor their employers have taken care of their basic needs. To rub salt on their wounds, many state governments are changing labour laws through ordinance, which essentially means working conditions are deteriorating and hours of work are increasing. These steps can only widen disparities and lead to a further fall in demand over time, which will make it even more difficult for businesses to restart work soon.

In a nutshell, what needs to be done immediately is not being given due importance, while long-term changes, adverse both for the marginalized sections in agriculture and for labour, are being pushed through. The Opposition has not been able to raise its voice against such changes—it has possibly not even thought about it. These steps are hardly the stimulus the economy needs.

*. . . But Resources Are Short*

Growth Projections

In spite of easing of the lockdown since mid-April, production did not recover immediately to pre-pandemic levels. That should not have been expected either, as discussed in Chapter III. Further, at various times, the disease has flared up in the major metros such as Mumbai,

Delhi, Chennai, Bengaluru, Hyderabad and Ahmedabad. Since these are the centres of production and trade in the country, periodic or extended lockdowns in these places means that economic revival can only be slow. Further, states such as, Kerala and Telangana have had to institute fresh restrictions on movements due to outbreak of the disease thus slowing the normalization process.

Table IV.3 shows that during the lockdown, the economy could at best produce 25 per cent of the output. That means that compared to production in April 2019, production in April 2020 was down by 75 per cent.

Starting from this low in April, Graph III.1 shows various possibilities assuming linear progression to September using data presented in Table IV.3 and then to the pre-pandemic levels:

1. If the economy recovers in four months to pre-pandemic levels and then grows at the pre-pandemic rate. The average rate of growth for 2020–21 would be -12 per cent. So the GDP of Rs 204 lakh crore will go down to Rs 180 lakh crore in 2020–21.
2. If the economy starts to recover in May and progresses to the pre-pandemic level in ten months, the average rate of growth for 2020–21 will be -28.79 per cent. So, the GDP of Rs 204 lakh crore will reduce to Rs 145 lakh crore in 2020–21.
3. If the economy starts recovery in May and progresses to the pre-pandemic level in sixteen months, the average rate of growth for 2020–21 will be -33.13 per cent. So, the GDP of Rs 204 lakh crore will be reduced to Rs 136.4 lakh crore in 2020–21.
4. If the economy starts recovery in May and progresses to the pre-pandemic level in twenty-two months, the average rate of growth for 2020–21 will be -35.58 per cent. So the GDP of Rs 204 lakh crore will be down to Rs 131.4 lakh crore in 2020—21.

All evidence is that the economy is recovering slowly since many sectors are hardly working (Annexure IV.2). Assume that the economy is following the second scenario and recovering to the

January 2020 state by March 2021. This is also an optimistic guess, since many analysts are predicting recovery over two years.

## Likely Revenue of the Government

The government collects revenue from incomes, production, consumption and other sources (See Kumar, 2019a) via direct taxes, indirect taxes and non-tax revenues. For example, income tax and corporation tax are direct taxes while GST and customs are indirect taxes. Non-tax revenue includes dividend from PSUs and proceeds from auction of spectrum and so on. Both the states and the Centre collect different taxes but the latter collects most of them. The Centre passes 42 per cent of the taxes it collects to the states.

When incomes drop, direct tax collection drops. Most of the direct tax is collected from the organized sector, since incomes in the unorganized sector are largely below the taxable limit. Businesses were shut for months on end and even when they restarted, they worked at way below their capacity. So most businesses will show a loss for the year or, at best, a greatly reduced profit. Only some businesses producing essentials such as FMCG and medical supplies will show profit, since they continued to produce even during the lockdown. But they are a small proportion of overall business in the country. Further, the corporation tax rate was drastically reduced in 2019 and that means that businesses will pay a lower per cent of their profits as tax this year, compared to 2019–20.

Given that both business income and the tax rate they pay will decline in 2020–21, tax collections from businesses will drop sharply.

Many workers and managers from the organized sector were laid off or their salaries and wages reduced. This process is ongoing, since many businesses are running into losses and retrenching workers. Those who are retired and dependent on interest incomes from savings in banks or from investment in the stock markets also find their incomes declining and will pay less tax. Finally, rents have been falling due to business losses and failures. Many tenants have shifted to properties charging lower rent and landlords who realize they will not get new tenants have reduced rents. Many small businesses also pay income tax and that will also decline as a large number of them are failing. Thus, except for the public sector and government employees, incomes elsewhere will be much less than last year and hence income tax collection will also fall sharply.

The direct tax collection last year was around 5.5 per cent of the GDP. If the GDP drops by approximately 29 per cent, given the situation described in the previous paragraphs, direct tax collection is likely to drop to about 4 per cent of the GDP. The reason is that all the sources of direct taxes will decline sharply.

The biggest source of tax is indirect taxes collected on production and consumption. There is the GST and tax on petroleum goods and alcohol for human consumption. When production and sales decline, collection from these taxes fall. However, the government has been helped by the extra tax it is collecting on petroleum products.

Crude oil prices dropped sharply in global markets due to a collapse in demand. The benefit of this decline in input price should have been passed on to consumers by lowering the prices of petrol and diesel. Instead, the government increased the prices of these goods. The benefit of lower crude oil prices was collected as extra taxes. The increase in taxes would have led to an increase in revenue of Rs 1.6 lakh crore at the level of consumption in 2019–20. But if the economy is down, transportation and use of energy for other purposes will all be down, so consumption of these items will be less than in 2019–20 and revenue collection will also be less. But given the tension on the borders, the defence forces are consuming more energy. Given these several factors simultaneously working in opposite directions, more will be collected. Last year the collection by the Centre was Rs 2.5 lakh crore, and this year it could be Rs 3 lakh crore.

GST collections will be considerably less than last year. The reason is that GST rates are higher on non-essential goods and services and zero on essential goods. Sin goods pay 28 per cent plus a cess that can be 15 per cent, so aerated drinks and luxury cars pay 43 per cent tax, while non-essential goods are at 28 and 18 per cent. Most services are at 18 per cent. Production of all these has fallen drastically so tax collections from these items has been much less than last year. Most production is of essential goods and they bear no tax or a low rate of tax (5 and 12 per cent). In effect, production of items that pay a high tax rate has fallen drastically while production of items that pay no tax or low tax has been maintained. So the average rate of tax collection has fallen drastically. Finally, since imports have been down substantially, the collection of IGST has fallen proportionately. Also customs duty collections on imports have fallen.

Indirect taxes collect 10.5 per cent of the GDP but due to reduced production and sales and decline in imports, this ratio is likely to fall sharply. If the GDP declines by 29 per cent, this ratio will fall substantially and is likely to be about 8 per cent of the GDP. It would have fallen even more but for the increased collections from petroleum products.

Thus, the total tax collection as per cent of the GDP will fall from 16–12 per cent in 2020–21.

The implication for the states will be serious. They get 42 per cent of the taxes collected by the Centre, and that will fall because the Centre will collect less. Their own tax collection will fall due to the decline in the tax/GDP ratio. So, they will be doubly hit.

The non-tax revenue will also fall by a similar proportion since that is also linked to economic activity. It consists of interest receipts, dividends and profits and auction of various things like spectrum. Given the state of the economy all these items will also yield much less revenue.

Government was expecting a lot of funds from disinvestment. With the uncertainty in the stock markets and with businesses suffering losses, there will be limited capacity in the private sector to buy PSU shares. The big ticket disinvestment is of LIC. But given that insurance is likely to suffer a loss due to increased claims, it is unlikely that the government would be able to push through this sale. Similarly, disinvestment of Air India at a time when many airlines will be failing seems difficult. Same for the Oil sector PSU sale. The petroleum sector is passing through difficult times with demand declining. Disinvestment at this stage will not fetch a good price. So, some of it is likely to be postponed.

Last year the Centre and the states together collected taxes which were 16 per cent of the Rs 204 lakh crore GDP or about Rs 32 lakh crore. Now of the lower amount of GDP of Rs 145 lakh crore, only 12 per cent will be collected, that is Rs 17.4 lakh crore. So, there will be a fall in tax revenue by about Rs 14.6 lakh crore. If disinvestment and non-tax revenue also decline to half of what is planned, there would be another shortfall of Rs 2.5 lakh crore in revenue.

In brief, if the GDP falls by 29 per cent over last year, the budget of the Centre and the states will see a revenue shortfall of about Rs 17 lakh crore. This would be 11.7 per cent of the GDP for 2020–21. Most other analysts when giving their estimates are not factoring a decline in the GDP or a decline in the tax/GDP ratio.

## Fiscal Deficit Shoots Up

The budget would have to be redone since it was planned with an assumed growth of 10 per cent (Budget at a Glance, 2020–21). All expenditures were also accordingly planned. They consist of the committed expenditures like interest payments, defence, police, post and telegraph, railways and salaries. These are hard to cut. The new proposed expenditures can be cut. Like, on public investment. But then the demand shortage in the economy will only aggravate.

If no expenditures are cut in the budget then the deficit in the budget will expand by the extent of shortfall in revenue. That is, the fiscal deficit will rise by 11.7 per cent of the GDP.

The fiscal deficit of the public sector as a whole (Centre, states and the public sector) was already running at 10 per cent of the

GDP of 2020-21, that is Rs 22.5 lakh crore. Of the lower GDP of Rs 145 lakh crore it amounts to 15.5 per cent.

In other words, without any change in expenditures committed in the budget, the fiscal deficit would rise to 27.2 per cent of the GDP due to lower revenue collections. This is unprecedented. So, planned expenditures will have to be curtailed. Of course, the less essential items such as travel and meetings can be greatly curtailed but that will not save much.

Even if the government does not provide for the COVID-19-related expenditures mentioned in Chapters I and III, the Fiscal Deficit of 27.2 per cent is huge. But the surprise is that in spite of this large stimulus, the economy is still going to contract by 29 per cent. This raises several issues. First, why is this so? Second, if this stimulus is not working then what can be done? Third, where to find the resources to fund such a huge deficit?

Out of the fiscal deficit of 27.2 per cent, the decline in taxes will not provide a stimulus (Kumar, 2010i). So the stimulus will only be 15.5 per cent, which is large by historical standards but not enough to prevent the economy from contracting because the decline in private consumption and investment is greater than this. Table V.3 presents data on these items. If private investment falls by 75 per cent (investment will only occur in primary sector, industries producing essentials and public sector) for the year and the balance of the fall in the GDP is due to decline in consumption as shown in Table V.3, the drop in demand would be 29 per cent of the GDP, greater than the Fiscal Deficit and much greater than the stimulus. Hence the economy will continue to decline.

In brief, the unprecedented fiscal stimulus would not work in spite of its large magnitude. The automatic stabilizer, as it is called, will be inadequate because of the fall in private demand.

The above deficit is for the year as a whole but in the initial months of lockdown and after it is eased when economic activity is very low, the deficit would be much larger since tax collection would be much less. Table V.2 shows that for the Centre alone, the fiscal deficit is at 11.3 per cent, assuming a drop in the GDP of 10 per cent only. Taking the deficit of the Centre, states and other public sectors, and assuming a drop in the GDP of 29 per cent, the deficit would be much larger, as depicted in the previous paragraph.

Most analysts do not see the GDP and revenue collection falling by as much as suggested above. They see the GDP falling only by around 10 per cent (Table IV.2) and do not factor in the fall in government revenue. So, they only ask for an increase in the fiscal deficit by a few per cent, around 5 per cent at a maximum, to act as a stimulus. They calculate everything on a GDP of Rs 204 lakh crore achieved in 2019–20. Even if it declines by 5 per cent, it would fall to Rs 194 lakh crore. The tax revenue in the budget for 2020–21 was calculated on the basis of a growth of 10 per cent. But with a growth of -5 per cent, there would be a turnaround of 15 per cent in budgetary figures. If the revenue (tax plus non-tax) is short by only 15 per cent, compared to the 2020–21 figures, it would be Rs 6 lakh crore. So the fiscal deficit of 10 per cent for 2020–21— i.e., Rs 22.5 lakh crore—would become Rs 28.5 lakh crore or 14.7 per cent of the GDP. This is already much more than what some experts are asking for (5 per cent).

What can be done? Additional expenditures on dealing with the pandemic—health costs, testing, support to the poor, etc., must be undertaken, and that would raise the deficit further. How much will be required?

If 200 million workers initially lost work, and assuming that they support three others, about 800 million people slipped below the poverty line. They will have to be provided for at a minimum level. If they are given half the World Bank extreme poverty line income ($1.9 per person per day at Rs 75 to the dollar) for a year, that will require Rs 20.4 lakh crore. Assume that subsidies and the allocation for MGNREGS (about Rs 4 lakh crore) can be included in this, the additional amount required would be Rs 16 lakh crore. Add to this Rs 1 lakh crore additional for COVID-related health expenditures and Rs 3 lakh crore to support small businesses. The total comes to

Rs 20 lakh crore of additional expenditures above what was planned in the budget or 13.8 per cent of the GDP of 2020–21.

Thus, the deficit will further shoot up to 41 per cent (27.2 + 13.8) of the GDP if other expenditures are not cut. Two things follow from this.

First, there will be no option but to go solely for a 'survival' package to support the poor and the unemployed and keep small businesses from collapsing. There will be no funds to give a stimulus to businesses, such as their demand for reduction in GST rates. If that is done, even less resources will be collected and even funding the survival package will not be possible. Giving money to businesses will deliver only when they are in a position to restart, otherwise fiscal space will be exhausted. As already argued, it would be better to give money to the unemployed.

Conservative economists argue that a high fiscal deficit is bad and would be frowned upon by international credit-rating agencies. But why should it matter, given that globally all economies are going for a massive increase in fiscal deficit, as discussed earlier in this chapter (Table V.1). Global finance will itself face a headwind and not be able to punish any of the nations for raising their fiscal deficit. This deficit would also not be inflationary, since the economy would be in depression with a fall in demand and prices would tend to decline rather than rise. As discussed in chapters III and IV, the problem will be the likelihood of deflation.

## Financing the Impossible Deficit

### Budget Needs Reformulation

How will such a huge deficit, 41 per cent of the GDP, be financed? There will be no option but to cut government expenditures. Given that neither will revenue be what is projected in the budget for 2020–21, nor will the expenditures be what they were estimated to be, the budget needs to be redrawn immediately, cutting expenditures drastically.

Salaries in the public sector will have to be cut when 80 crore people have slipped below the poverty line due to a fall in incomes and agriculturists also face a drop in incomes, so that 94 per cent of the workforce faces a reduction in income. Then the remaining 6 per cent will have to also take a cut in their incomes, including public-sector employees, who make up two-third of this. Capital budget of the government will also have to be drastically pruned to save funds for the survival package. Big projects that are capital-intensive and can be delayed could be postponed temporarily and the money saved allotted to creating employment under rural and urban employment-guarantee schemes.

Tax expenditures to the well-off sections of the population, which amount to a few per cent of the GDP, will have to be curtailed. This is the opposite of the demand for reduction in the GST rates or cuts in direct taxes. All these proposals together may save 7 per cent of the GDP. There will still be 34 per cent to finance.

Wealth Tax Will Not Work

Can there be a levy on the wealth of well-off sections? This tax was abolished in India in the 2016–17 budget. Given the huge inequality in society, levying this tax at this juncture seems to be eminently sensible. IANS (2020) reports that the top 1 per cent in India holds 42.5 per cent and the top 10 per cent hold 72.3 per cent of the country's wealth. This is largely based on stock market valuations and white declared incomes. Going by these estimates, the top 1 per cent would have about Rs 300 lakh crore of wealth and the top 10 per cent about Rs 500 lakh crore of wealth. If a 1 per cent tax is levied on the wealth of the top 1 per cent, the government would get Rs 3 lakh crore (2 per cent of the GDP). This would still be inadequate to finance the deficit, though.

However, even this would be difficult, since the wealth of the well-off will also decline drastically. The stock markets have been down (except in the case of some companies) and property prices have also fallen as businesses fail and vacate property. Many of those who have lost employment have also moved to properties with lower rents, so rents have also fallen and property prices have declined correspondingly. The stock markets have risen due to expectation of a quick rebound in the economy, which is unlikely to last, and as the company reports come, the prices of most stocks will fall. Thus, much less than Rs 3 lakh crore will get collected from wealth tax.

Further, a tax on wealth would have to be paid from the current income of the property owners, which has also declined drastically as profits and rents have fallen. A wealth tax will further lower the returns on property, which means their prices will fall further. As incomes of the propertied fall, their investment in the economy will also fall due to the wealth effect, as discussed earlier.

In brief, a wealth tax in the present depressed conditions could lead to a sharp decline in wealth and investment, while yielding very little tax revenue. While I have been a proponent of a full-fledged wealth tax since the 1980s (See Kumar, 1994), this is not the right time for it.

## Borrowings to Gallop

The only option for the government is to increase borrowings. For doing so, it could float long-term bonds carrying a low interest rate and get wealth holders to subscribe to it. In times of uncertainty, people go liquid. So funds are being shifted out of other investments to deposits in banks, especially PSU banks. At the same time, banks are finding that demand for credit is low because of the decline in production and investment. This has meant that banks have been parking their huge excess liquidity with the RBI to earn a return at reverse repo rate. The RBI should lower the reverse repo rate further (it has been doing so for sometime) and the government should float the bonds at just above the reverse repo rate. This will encourage banks to subscribe to these bonds, since they will get a higher return than they would by depositing funds in the RBI. Most corporates will have little funds to subscribe, since most of them would be dissaving and trying to stay liquid to continue operations while they operate at low capacity utilization. Only those producing essentials and working at near full capacity would have the surpluses to invest in these bonds.

It has also been suggested that temples and other religious institutions have huge wealth and could be asked to donate to the kitty. Could they subscribe to the bonds? A lot of the wealth of these institutions may be in the form of property, gold and jewellery. These assets would have to be monetized by selling, leasing, renting or mortgaging, and that would not be easy in the depressed property markets. What they have as fixed deposits in banks may be used but that may not be very large. In fact, many supposedly rich temples complained of liquidity issues during the lockdown as their income fell because people could not visit them or donate to them. They even complained that they were not able to pay their workers and priests, implying a weak liquidity position.

The government would have to lower the return offered in small savings schemes, such as post office savings, public provident fund and so on, and also reduce the tax concessions offered on these investments. This would help lower the interest burden on the budget as well as diversion of funds to these schemes rather than to the low-interest bonds.

## The Resource Base of the Economy Will Shrink

The constraint on how much can be borrowed by the government will be the savings in the economy. As already argued in Chapter III:

1. Incomes will fall for most economic agents.
2. The capacity of the economy will fall, so the resource base will be narrower than earlier.
3. There will be dissaving in the economy.

It was argued that when incomes fall, savings also fall, even if people save the same proportion of their income (called savings propensity). But when incomes fall drastically, this behaviour changes. Those who lose employment have no income and their consumption equals the support they get from the government and their past savings, if they have any. Thus, their savings propensity becomes zero (Kumar, 2020i).

For those who remain employed but face pay cuts, consumption is confined to essentials only. Depending on the cut and the income they still draw, their savings also fall. For those who are well-off in spite of the pandemic but uncertain about the future, savings will go up, since they will curtail discretionary expenditures. This set of people is a small percentage of the total employment. The property owners whose incomes also fall due to the downturn in business also cut their expenditure due to the wealth effect, but on the whole are likely to save less. As discussed in Chapter III, businesses mostly dissave, especially those that fail. Considering everything, the savings rate in the economy would decline.

Since incomes decline, a fall in the savings rate also would lead to a sharp drop in the total savings.

The fall in the savings rate should mean that the multiplier in the economy will rise. It should lead to a higher level of output. But, as already discussed, the investment rate will fall dramatically. Further, with business failures taking place and capacity redefined, existing capital would be destroyed/become dysfunctional so that there would be negative investment. So, in the net, investment in the economy will fall drastically and may even turn negative. That is why, in spite of the higher multiplier, the level of output will fall rather than rise.

The point is that the resource base of the economy will be down, with a drastic decline in output, investment and savings. So the government will find it difficult to raise large amounts of resources and any attempt to boost the economy will be limited by the economy's available resource base.

## Monetization of the Deficit

As a last resort, there is always the possibility of getting the central bank to print more currency. In other words, the deficit is monetized. The RBI will have to lend to the government to cover the shortfall in the resources in the budget, by buying the government bonds.

This will increase the currency with the public but money supply will not rise much, since the public will hold more cash and the leakage from the circulation of money will rise. Therefore, the money multiplier will fall sharply and money supply will not rise. The velocity of transactions will also fall, since money will circulate slower with the downturn in the economy and decline in economic activity. That is why releasing more money/liquidity is not a solution when economic activity is down. It shows that money is not a resource in itself—it only helps circulate incomes (Chapter II) if they are generated.

Thus, the financial sector will also see a lot of changes. People will hold more liquidity, interest rates will go down quite a bit, demand for credit from business will be down, there will be a lot more of government borrowing from all sections and so on. In spite of the sharp increase in liquidity, prices will not go up because demand will still be short.

### Conclusion

To sum up, markets fail due to lockdowns and extensive government intervention in the economy is required. A stimulus is suggested, since it is supposed to act as a catalyst to boost the economy. Globally, various kinds of stimuli are being tried but, for India, only the one that transfers resources to the poor will be successful in boosting demand and reviving the economy. The various packages announced by the government and the RBI are more long- and medium-term measures and immediate relief needed by the poor is a small component of the total package announced, even though this would have been the most effective. No wonder, among the major world economies, India is the most impacted due to the pandemic.

Finally, what should the government have done? What are the resources needed and why does the budget need to be redrawn? It has been argued that the fiscal deficit is already very high but, still, the automatic stabilizer is not delivering. The resource base of the economy has dwindled due to the new normal for the economy and savings have sharply fallen. As a result, the government will not be able to finance the deficit by borrowing from the savers and the deficit will have to be monetized. This will have implications for the financial sector.

What emerges is that while the developed capitalist economies may pull through quicker, India will recover gradually due to the existence of the large unorganized sector, which will find it difficult to revive. And also because government policies are unable to impact this sector. The lesson is that the past neglect of this sector and of labour is costly for the economy. All in all, the situation is pretty dire and the sooner the government takes the right corrective steps, the better.

# VII

# Conclusion

## Unfair Polity: Its High Cost and Lessons for the Future

The SARS-CoV-2 virus hit the world in December 2019. What started as a medical emergency quickly turned into an economic emergency too. Both these crises are still evolving, since the behaviour of the virus has not yet been well understood. In the context of the economy, it is difficult to understand how it behaves when both supply and demand freeze. The pandemic, the lockdown and the impact of the two are a developing story and their contours are now clearer. This book presents the impact of these two interrelated developments on Indian society and how it will be impacted in the coming times based on projecting what is now evident.

### Need for Data and Prompt Action

The experts and the officialdom have been behind the curve, as usual. When the economy was tanking during the lockdown, they were talking of a slow growth of 1.9 per cent during 2020–21, and then, a little later, they said it would decline by 4.5 per cent. They clearly wanted to present an optimistic picture but that is only delusional and confuses all private economic actors and policymakers. They sense that things are going grossly wrong but act as if they aren't too bad. This leads to incorrect action on many fronts.

The incorrect assessment of individual experts, business associations, banks and rating agencies is not as damaging to the system as the erroneous announcement by the policymakers. Individual actors act on the signals coming from the policymakers, which can have systemic consequences. When it turns out that the policymakers were wrong in their prognosis, economic actors suffer. This dents the former's credibility and, as a result, their pronouncements in the future will be taken less seriously, making them less effective and creating difficulties for governance.

For instance, if policymakers act as if the situation is not too bad, the tough steps needed will not be taken and the problem will deteriorate. That could be why the government did not go for a big package to boost the incomes of those who had lost employment and fallen below the poverty line, and, instead, went for supply-side measures. Therefore, instead of the short-run demand-revival plan, the government decided to go for medium- and long-term policy changes. The 'survival' package (Kumar, 2020c) that was required was not implemented and time was lost for urgently dealing with both the pandemic and the economic crisis.

## Growing Crisis in India

The situation in India in September 2020 was far grimmer than in March since it has had the worst of all worlds. As mentioned in Chapter I, lockdown was needed but was not properly implemented. It had to be relaxed prematurely under pressure from businesses. Resultantly, the number of cases rose rapidly and in many places, for a time, overwhelmed the medical system. The lockdown has had to be reimposed in many places where the case count rose sharply, like, in Bengaluru and Chennai. This slowed the economic revival and created a situation wherein both the economic and health crisis continued with little respite. By September, India became the country with the highest number of daily infections, its economy in doldrums and society in crisis.

As mentioned in Chapter III, the situation now is worse than in a war or during the global financial crisis of 2007–09. This is an unprecedented situation, as nothing like this has been faced by the modern-day economy. So the situation has to be treated as such. Unfortunately, this urgency has not been shown by the Indian government. The government, in fact, has been carrying on business as usual. As mentioned in chapters III and V, since the GDP has fallen sharply during and post the lockdown, tax revenue during the year will also fall sharply. Expenditure priorities will have to be revamped to take care of the additional health expenditures and the needs of the large number of people who have lost incomes. Thus, the projections in the budget presented on 1 February 2020 have become redundant and the budget needs to be redrawn immediately. Delay is proving to be costly.

Chapters II and IV point out that the pandemic has exposed the continued marginalization of a vast majority of Indians working in the unorganized sector of the economy, and the neglect they face from policymakers. The pandemic and the economic downturn have impacted them the hardest. Not that the organized sector has not been hit hard. However, they have the savings to take care of themselves for some time. The unorganized sector lives on the edge of survival, with little or no savings. A short shutdown of the economy, therefore, has led to a deep crisis in their lives. This makes the Indian situation unlike that of the advanced economies and its recovery will be slower than theirs. The pain will continue for a much longer time in India than in the advanced countries.

It may appear from time to time that the economy is recovering and the Ministry of Finance has repeatedly said that green shoots are emerging. Green shoots only means that some revival is taking place and that is not a surprise since unlock means that more business activity is allowed. As shown in Annexure IV.2, some sectors like Pharma, IT and FMCG will obviously do well while others like hotels and travel will continue to flounder. So a holistic view of recovery will have to be taken. The pandemic and lockdown have led to very weak consumer and business confidence, which will make the recovery slow (Graph III.1).

The neglect of the unorganized sector is also reflected in the official data. The data for the non-agriculture unorganized sector is collected only once in five years, called the reference years. In between these reference years, the data of the organized sector and ratios estimated in the reference years are used to estimate the unorganized sector (Kumar, 2018). So the organized sector becomes a proxy for the unorganized sector; and there is no independent estimate of the unorganized sector. Ever since the shock of demonetization in 2016, this method does not hold as the two sectors have diverged. Consequently, the organized sector cannot be taken as the proxy for the unorganized sector—it has to be estimated independently.

This problem has again cropped up. Official agencies are using organized-sector data, except for the agricultural sector (GoI, 2020d). Further, the official document admits that much of the organized-sector data was not available and even in the case of agriculture, for certain commodities, the targets of production were taken as the production. The non-agriculture unorganized sector completely shut down during the lockdown and had hardly revived even as the lockdown was eased. This is due to the problems of the lack of demand, inadequacy of working capital and supply bottlenecks. Thus, overall GDP growth is far less than projected by official agencies. Foreign agencies such as the IMF do not collect data independently and base their analysis on the official data, and, therefore, end up more or less replicating the same errors.

## The Health Aspect

This book outlines the nature of the health and economic crises facing India and highlights the links between the two. It also analyses the lessons that can be learnt from the experience of other major countries, such as China and the US.

Viruses are nothing new. Every few years, one or another appears. What makes SARS-CoV-2 different is that it is virulent and spreads rapidly. It does not kill a high percentage of those infected (unlike Ebola), but if it infects a lot of people, even a small percentage dying adds up to a large number. It is therefore extremely important that its spread is contained. Since it is a new virus, most of us don't have the antibodies to kill it, and the disease spreads in the body. That is why a medicine and/or a vaccine is required. But this is not easy, in spite of all the scientific progress mankind has made.

The spread of the disease has to be checked, so that the existing medical system does not get overwhelmed. If the disease continues to spread unabated, it will surely lead to societal breakdown. In countries such as Italy, the systems were overwhelmed and for a short while, a choice had to be made between who would be allowed to live and who would be left to die. To avoid such a situation, a lockdown becomes necessary. If people do not come in contact with each other, the spread of the disease slows down.

The earlier the lockdown is implemented, the better for a nation. But it has to be strictly implemented for it to work. This is the lesson from China, the US and other European countries. It is also necessary to do large-scale testing and contact tracing. That is, one needs to find out who is infected and who has been in contact with that person. Without these two, the disease will continue to spread. These two things become even more important when the lockdown is eased.

This book argues that India has failed on the above-mentioned fronts. First, the lockdown was delayed and then suddenly implemented, catching people unawares. This unplanned move caused panic among people. Second, while the lockdown did slow down the spread of the disease, since it was not implemented properly, the spread continued. In March, India was at the bottom of the list of countries with the number of cases, but, by July, it had become one of the top three nations. Third, neither did India have enough testing capability, nor did it undertake adequate contact tracing, meaning the spread of the disease could not be controlled. Fourth, the time the lockdown bought the government was not properly utilized to ramp up medical facilities in the country. As a result, many parts of the country witnessed a breakdown of the medical infrastructure. Finally, the lockdown had to be prematurely eased under pressure from businesses. As the disease spread, in major parts of the country, the lockdown had to be reimposed in these parts and overall business suffered again.

What was implicit in the easing of the lockdown as a choice between 'life and livelihood' was that it was acceptable for many people to die. But how many deaths can society accept in a short time? It was said that sooner or later, everyone would get infected and that there would be 'herd' immunity. But if huge numbers get infected quickly, a large number would have to be hospitalized and many millions would die. Not only would the elderly with comorbidities die, many younger people would die, even though their proportion would be less than that of the elderly.

Some have argued that too much should not be made of COVID-19, since many more people die annually due to other diseases such as tuberculosis. Chapter I however, points out that this is not a valid comparison.

Experts have been discovering new aspects of the disease and its cure. Heat has not slowed its spread, nor has BCG inoculation. Protocols about how to deal with it have kept changing—for example, the use of masks outdoors and the safe distance to maintain between people. The 3-foot rule became a 6-foot one. Now, in fact, it is suspected that it can spread through the air and, therefore, greater caution is required.

The pandemic has highlighted the weaknesses of the health infrastructure in many countries. Investment in health has been inadequate and privatization has raised costs. This has been detrimental to the fight against the pandemic. To address this issue, Spain quickly nationalized its private hospitals. The pandemic has required individuals to isolate themselves, and this has brought about a host of social problems. Isolation has also brought about psychological problems and violence within families. In the US, the poorer sections have had a greater incidence of the disease.

It has been argued in this book that it is better to preserve life first and then livelihood. This would have been feasible in India if the government had put its entire effort into a 'survival' package. Since this was not done, the lockdown failed and then the argument followed that it had to be eased so at least livelihood could be preserved. The country has lost on both counts—life and livelihood.

## Lockdown: Brutal but Half-Hearted

The survival package was spelt out by me in March and is explained in the book. Its elements include providing essentials to people wherever they are, so that they do not need to move around; decongesting people living in congested areas; ramping up the healthcare infrastructure, including testing; and, finally, protecting small and marginal businesses from collapsing. This was eminently doable, since the country had huge stocks of foodgrains and other essentials were also being produced. It required planning and implementation, but India has shown that it is weak when it comes to planning and implementation.

Countries that delayed a lockdown or implemented it half-heartedly have seen the disease spread and people die in large numbers. Examples of a delay in lockdown or its non-observance or a laxity in implementation are UK, Brazil and parts of the US. In India, the lockdown was delayed and its implementation patchy. Therefore, it has had to be reimposed in many parts and the country has not been able to reap the full benefit of the lockdown.

To ease a lockdown, massive testing and contact tracing are required to prevent the disease from spreading. In India, testing has no doubt been ramped up compared to March, but going by per million of the population, it is one of the lowest in the world (Graph 06). As a result, post Unlock 1, starting 1 June, the number of infections detected rose rapidly in India.

As mentioned in Chapter I, a lockdown is not a cure to the disease but only a means to slow its spread so that a) the healthcare system is not overwhelmed and b) the government can obtain time to ramp up the healthcare infrastructure and testing. The disease will remain a concern until a vaccine and/or a medicine is discovered. However, historical experience shows that it can take years to get either of these.

Once again, those in charge of the country have shown that they care little about the unorganized sector and the poor. If for the sake of business, more of them have to die, so be it. The policy makers did not consider protecting their lives even if businesses ran at losses for some more time. The tragedy is that it need not have gone that way, since both life and livelihood can be preserved, as China has shown.

## The Economic Implications of a Lockdown

In a lockdown, because people cannot move around, production and sales come to a halt, except for essentials such as food, utilities and medical services. Consumption of energy declines and pollution levels drop sharply. During the current crisis, a large number of people lost their jobs and even those who did not, could not go to work or worked from home. It is argued in this book that work declined more than what is signified by loss of employment and the GDP fell drastically, compared to last year.

The book explains why a modern-day economy is more susceptible to failure during a lockdown. It is due to the extensive division of labour, growing specialization and rising concentration of production. This stretches across the globe and no nation is now self-sufficient. This is globalization—disruption in any part of the world affects others. It started from China in January and, thereafter, spread across the world as one after the other all the large economies went into lockdowns.

Long supply chains require more trade, transportation, storage and finance. Consequently, a lot of working capital is needed and interest has to be paid on it. When production and sales stop, servicing the working capital becomes difficult; costs mount and businesses begin to fail since revenue is not generated to service these costs. To save on costs, businesses stop paying wages and retrench workers. This impacts demand, and businesses further decline. Many businesses that were already in trouble prior to the pandemic are failing and need support from the government. The financial sector also begins to face problems as businesses fail, and defaults on loans take place.

The kind of globalization that has been going on since the mid-1970s has led to very high levels of inequality within nations, and that has led to both the weakening of labour and a shortage of demand. The impact of these trends was highlighted by the lockdown as a lot of workers became jobless and small businesses declined. The world economy is now paying a heavy price for this kind of globalization and mutual global interdependence.

## Lockdown, Unorganized Sector, Employment and Demand

India has faced a bigger challenge because it has both a very large unorganized sector where incomes are low and a very high degree of inequality. The poor have little resilience to deal with adversity. These problems are a result of the model of development and globalization adopted in India and the growth of the black economy since Independence (Kumar, 2013). The unorganized sector in India employs 94 per cent of the workforce and produces 45 per cent of the output.

The book points out that the non-agriculture component of the unorganized sector completely shut down during the lockdown and about 200 million people lost employment, including the self-employed. Most of the micro-sector units closed down and are unlikely to revive because they have little working capital, which got exhausted quickly when they shut down. Most of these people fell below the poverty line and did not have the savings to buy even the essentials. Many did not get any of the announced support from the government and decided to migrate back to the villages they came from to work in the cities. There were the disturbing sights of millions of people walking hundreds of kilometres in intense heat with little food and water, their belongings on their heads and children in tow. The police beat them up and transporters cheated them, but they had no option.

Many workers in the organized sector, who get paid better and have greater security of tenure, lost employment or faced cuts in wages and salaries. Businessmen lost profits and their incomes also declined. Landlords lost rental income as tenants were reluctant to pay rent or wanted rent to be reduced. Farmers lost incomes as the price of their produce declined, quite sharply in the case of perishables. Thus, a vast majority of people lost incomes in the economy.

The loss of incomes impacted consumer demand in the economy. Due to uncertainty, people mostly bought essentials, and demand for non-essentials fell. Many industries such as tourism, airlines, hotels, restaurants, autos, taxis and entertainment completely shut down, since physical distancing was not possible.

As many businesses shut down and the prospect of opening up became bleak, investment also dropped sharply. This reduced demand further. Since most of the countries in the world faced the same problem, exports dropped sharply too. This further dented demand.

*Growth Possibilities*

During the lockdown, only essential production could take place and this was less than 25 per cent of the activity in pre-pandemic months. That is assuming agriculture, other essential consumer goods and utilities worked unhindered. Much of the government also shut down, except for the police and the administration. But for the medical field, most services stopped working or worked at low capacity in industries, such as the media, transport and trade.

The book points out that as the lockdown was eased, some activity revived but most could not. Many businesses could not even reopen until June, such as malls and restaurants. Even those businesses that could open faced low demand and could not get back to full production. Some analysts had suggested that the economy would rebound immediately on opening and, therefore, recovery would be 'V-shaped'. But an economy is not like a rubber ball, which bounces back immediately when thrown to the ground. Every section of the population suffered under the lockdown, which essentially means that there were costs, which, in turn, created irreversibility. People and businesses who face adversity change their behaviour and actions. The implication is that the fall and the rise are not symmetric and the rise will not be as sharp as the fall.

Given the change in consumer behaviour due to the fall in incomes and the decline in new investment, demand will not be back to where it was before the pandemic hit the economy. Taking this into account, the book argues that at an optimistic guess, recovery to the pre-pandemic state of the economy will take at least a year. Even then it will not return to the situation of, say, January 2020, but to a new normal. This would be so even if a vaccine comes out by end of 2020 or a medicine is discovered.

Starting with a drop of 75 per cent in the GDP during the lockdown in April 2020, it may be inferred optimistically that the rate of growth in 2020–21 will be -29 per cent. Some argue that the rate of growth will be -4.5 per cent. They need to show how the economy will start growing at 15 per cent over last year's level starting July 2020, to achieve this rate of growth.

Even before the pandemic hit India, the economy was not performing well, with the rate of growth falling every quarter since the last quarter of 2017–18. This was due to the decline in demand, following the shocks to the economy since 2016—first when the demonetization was brought into effect so suddenly in 2016, then the implementation of the GST in 2017 and finally the NBFC crisis in 2018. So a recovery has to overcome the impact of the lockdown and the earlier problems.

## Facing a Dire Situation on Many Fronts

As mentioned so many times earlier, what was required was a quick and thorough lockdown and then its rapid easing. The book argues that India failed on both these counts because of its prevailing social structure. Most workers do not earn a living wage and live in abysmal conditions, especially in the cities. They live in crowded conditions, with little possibility of isolation. They have little of savings, so they buy their necessities daily. Simply put, their condition of living requires them to move around.

The book points out that for a successful lockdown, early action was needed before the disease could have spread, but India delayed this. A 'survival package' for workers and businesses was also needed. It is undoubtedly difficult to implement this but given the situation, it had to be taken up on a war footing. The entire administration and political set-up needed to just focus on this and nothing else. Such a package was not implemented, which led to the lockdown failing to control the spread of the disease. This essentially implies that India has been one of the most affected countries in the world.

Businesses wanting to open up were not wrong, because the lockdown was not working for them—the disease was spreading and workers were not getting work. But, instead of applying pressure for premature opening up, they needed to apply pressure to see that the lockdown was properly implemented (as in New York City and China), so they could open up safely. The lesson from other countries is that a premature easing of the lockdown leads to the disease spreading like wildfire.

India has had the worst of all worlds, with more lockdowns, and there is continuing adverse impact on health, the economy and workers. The lesson has not yet been learnt that India is unable to cope with the current pandemic because of the adverse living conditions of the majority of its people. Now the labour laws are being diluted, which will ensure a further worsening of the workers' living conditions. This will ensure that when the next pandemic strikes, the country will flounder again. The tragedy is that India is today headed towards societal breakdown for the short-term gains of just some sections of society. But it appears that a basic rethink of any current ruling ideology always comes at a heavy cost—social, political and economic.

## Demand for a Stimulus

Governments the world over have recognized the huge impact of the lockdown on wages, profits and the growth of the economy. All economies have entered depression, with consumer and business confidence deeply dented. Markets have failed and cannot lift the economy back on its feet. The only option left is for the government to step in and provide support to everyone and prevent the economy from collapsing further. All over the world, governments are doing just that. They are boosting expenditures to increase demand, and this is leading to unprecedented levels of fiscal deficit in their budgets.

Businesses have been demanding funds to cover their losses. But when businesses are stalled, offering more credit or cutting interest rates will not work. Tax cuts will also not work when most businesses will be running at a loss.

This book points out that of the various steps governments are taking, the best way to increase demand is to give money to the unemployed and those facing pay cuts. Funding the 'survival package' described above will boost demand. In India, MGNREGS, the rural employment scheme, can be used to give incomes to the unemployed migrants. So it needs to be funded much more than what has currently been done. A similar scheme for the urban unemployed also needs to be initiated.

Unfortunately, the Indian government's package to counter the downturn in the economy has been inadequate compared to what needs to be done. Most of it is based on supply-side policies and offering credit, but these act in the medium and long term and do not take care of the immediate need of boosting demand. The government needs to change tack. MGNREGS is possibly not being funded adequately so as to ensure that the migrants return to the cities when businesses revive. Businesses have been saying that they will face a shortage of labour due to migration and will not be able to restart fully. This is a poor strategy, since without an increase in demand, most businesses will work at much below full capacity and won't need many more workers. Thus, the workers returning to the cities would be further frustrated.

*The Question of Resources*

It is estimated that the survival package will require an additional Rs 20 lakh crore; over and above the current allocations. If other expenditures are retained at the level decided earlier, the fiscal deficit will shoot up to unprecedented levels, 41 per cent of the GDP for 2020–21. Assuming that such a survival package is implemented, how would it be financed?

It has been argued that if the GDP falls by about 30 per cent in the year, government's revenue will fall by a much larger percentage. Given the structure of revenues, the tax/GDP will fall from 16 per cent last year to about 12 per cent. Even if the survival package is not funded, the fiscal deficit will become 27.2 per cent of the GDP in 2020–21. Other analysts do not anticipate such a large deficit because they use the higher GDP of 2019–20 to do the calculation. They also do not calculate the shortfall in tax collection or recalculate the fiscal deficit in the budget, since the assumptions of the budget will not hold.

It is further argued that in spite of such a huge stimulus, the economy will decline by 30 per cent, to Rs 145 lakh crore. The reason is that the fall in demand due to private consumption and investment (30 per cent of the GDP) will be more than the stimulus provided by the fiscal deficit. The entire fiscal deficit of 27.2 per cent will not act as the stimulus—only 15.5 per cent will. If the survival package of Rs 20 lakh crore is implemented, the fiscal deficit will rise by another 13.8 per cent of the GDP to 41 per cent of the GDP. This would then equal the fall in private demand and help maintain demand in the economy.

It is argued in this book that because of a fall in incomes, there will be dissaving and the savings rate will fall. This will raise the value of the multiplier in the economy. But the investment rate will also fall and due to business failures, it would be close to zero, if not negative. Exports will decline due to the global decline and so will imports. Thus, most sources of demand will be down and fiscal deficit will be the only one that can help raise demand.

A fiscal deficit of 27.2 per cent or 41 per cent of the GDP would be unprecedented. The question would be how to finance it. It is argued that in the present situation, raising taxes would not be feasible, not even through wealth tax. So one option would be to cut government expenditures, including cuts in salaries of government employees. It was argued that when 800 million Indians have fallen below the poverty line and the resource base of the country has shrunk drastically, by Rs 60 lakh crore, others cannot continue to earn what they were getting earlier. Capital expenditures would have to be postponed this year. But none of this would be enough.

It is argued that government would have to borrow by floating long-term bonds bearing a low interest rate, just above the reverse repo rate. The banks and the wealthy could buy these bonds since they would be safe. To lower the rates, the RBI would have to cut interest rates further.

The balance of the deficit would have to be monetized, with the RBI lending directly to the government by buying its bonds. This would no doubt increase currency in circulation but in times of depression, when the velocity of circulation, money multiplier and transactions will all decline, this kind of monetization should not create a problem of excessive liquidity and inflation. The problem is likely to be deflation due to a fall in commodity prices and wages.

It is argued that as businesses fail, the stressed financial sector would be under greater stress and its balance sheet would deteriorate. So both the government and the RBI would have to see that business failure is minimized but, in spite of that, the financial sector is likely to be impacted and would need appropriate support.

Capacity of the economy, its potential to produce, would have to be redefined due to the need for physical distancing. The resource base of the economy would be less than before the pandemic. So, in spite of the higher fiscal deficit, much less will be produced. There will be a need for a new way of thinking about macroeconomics (Kumar, 2020i). At present, only the short run can be anticipated and corrective steps taken, but since there is huge uncertainty, governments will have to take policy steps, as discussed in this book, anticipating the worst in the long run.

## The New Normal

Globally, societies are facing a deep crisis due to the pandemic. There will be a new normal in the way the economy and society will function. There will be big changes in much of production, travel, retailing, tourism and entertainment. Physical distancing will have to be maintained, and that would mean redefining capacity. There would be a trend towards more automation and use of robots. The move towards e-commerce has accelerated and this will continue. The trend towards electronic transactions will accelerate as people avoid using cash.

Labour-intensive industries will see the biggest changes and as they start using more machines and automation, unemployment will aggravate. Before the pandemic hit the world, this was already creating large-scale social problems in many countries. The unemployed were blaming migration for their woes and turning against migrants. Right-wing politicians were exploiting this fear in many countries and accentuating pre-existing divides. Globalization was being increasingly blamed for the problems faced by many sections of the population, and pressures were building up to reassess it. As the crisis deepens due to rising inequality and a lack of employment opportunities, the political and social divide being witnessed globally over the past decade will accentuate.

Globalization was seen as the cause of shift of jobs in traditional industries, such as textiles and steel, to the less-developed economies with their low-wage labour. The US was putting pressure on its industries for reducing trade and getting it to shift its factories back home to generate employment there. This trend will strengthen across nations as they have realized during the pandemic that long supply chains can get disrupted and lead to dislocation of production. So, globally, trade is likely to decline, with more home production taking place. India's Atmanirbhar Bharat programme is also along these lines.

The developing countries will have to fight harder for markets and, in the process, cut wages. That can only aggravate the inequalities and, in a vicious cycle, create further social and economic problems.

Vaccines and medicines that may be discovered in due course are likely to be expensive and first available in the advanced countries. Thus, the advanced countries are likely to recover before the poorer nations and be able to normalize their economies faster. This will be another source of the growing inequality and global discord. The WHO has a programme for making vaccines available to the poorer nations also, but how successful that would be remains to be seen.

## Contradictory Trends: Which Way Do the Winds Blow?

There will be contradictory trends between what needs to be done and what is being done. The pandemic has shown that there is need for more equity in society, but is that likely, given the trends mentioned above? There will be the need to provide employment to all, but is that feasible with growing automation?

The success of the fight against the disease depends on the cooperation of the population with the authorities. For this, transparency is crucial. If people do not believe in the authorities, they will not comply with the restrictions, as has been the case with lockdown in many countries. Further, the disease is a social phenomenon and if people are alienated, they will not care about others and the disease will spread faster. For instance, if people do not wear a mask in public, the spread will accelerate, such as happened in Brazil and the south and west of US.

As already argued, the disease will come under control when it is globally, not just locally, eliminated. It does not respect boundaries or the status of individuals. We have lived for long with viruses in our bodies, which just do not disappear and can assert themselves at some point of time, such as, say, chicken pox, herpes and HIV. These have been studied over decades and it is known that they can break out in painful episodes and can effect different organs of the body.

We do not know much about the new coronavirus. If one is lucky, it might be a mild attack but it is not known who will get a strong attack and lose their life. Even a younger person or a child can be that unlucky one (though the probability is less), but no one can predict who exactly will be affected and how by the virus. Even with herd immunity, there will be plenty of people who will get a strong attack. Also, those who have got cured have been found to be susceptible to being infected again, since it seems that immunity lasts for only a limited period of time.

So being socially responsible is crucial—everyone needs to take the necessary precautions so the disease does not spread. Those who are refusing to do so are not only putting their own lives at risk but those of others around them who are more vulnerable. In the US and Brazil, there have been campaigns against the wearing of masks on the plea that it is against their fundamental rights. Such people are putting individuals over society.

A basic lesson from the pandemic is that societies that are better organized and where the population has faith in the leadership have been better able to tackle the crisis, such as the Scandinavian countries, South Korea, Taiwan and Japan. These are also the countries that have greater equity, better public services and less alienation. In such societies, public commitment to the wider good is greater and their capacity to mobilize stronger. This is the reason they have been able to deal with the crisis much better than others.

Where people are alienated, do not trust the leadership and suspect a motive in what it suggests, the lockdown has not worked. This has hurt efforts in India. When the lockdown started being eased in May and the case load was still low, many said that the government was fooling the people and there was no crisis. The sceptics also said that this was not a disease to be worried about, since other diseases caused many more deaths. So they saw a motive in the government's steps, namely a bid to grab greater power.

In India, due to the treatment meted out to the migrant workers and the failure of the healthcare system, it is unlikely that these people will trust the system and, in turn, social compliance will suffer. It will be everyone for themselves. More equity is needed for better social cohesion but, as argued above, disparities are likely to increase across sectors, more so due to an increase in unemployment. The position of labour, which was already weakening due to the global mobility of capital, will weaken further as automation occurs. Many states in India, using the pandemic as an excuse, have changed labour laws, which will make the situation even more inequitable. This is the opposite of what is needed.

There is need for greater autonomy of local bodies and the states, so they can react quickly to the developing crisis in their jurisdiction. But the dominance of the Central authority has increased even more now due to the pandemic and its consequences. As argued in Chapter V, the resource shortage is acute and this is impacting the states more than the Centre, which has greater freedom to raise resources. So the states are becoming more dependent on the Centre, which is not good for a diverse country such as India.

In brief, there are contradictory tendencies visible today between what needs to be done and what is being done. While the need is for greater transparency and democratization, the trend is towards using diktats and strong policing by invoking the Disaster Management Act. Those in power need to be accountable for better policies and their implementation, and for that, a strong Opposition is needed. But today, the Opposition is demoralized because the Disaster Management Act limits the individual's rights. In many cases where there has been spontaneous protest, the government has disallowed it and taken action.

## Post-Pandemic Society and Economy

Society will have to learn from the experience of dealing with this pandemic, which has devastated large numbers of people and brought many nations to the brink of collapse. Societies have to be able to respond rapidly to any threat. This requires reform both at the societal and the scientific levels.

Expenditures on R&D need to be enhanced, so that the virus monitoring mechanism is boosted and threats can be detected early. Since this has to be a global effort, a coordinating agency such as the WHO needs to be greatly strengthened. To deal with the medical emergency, if it arises, healthcare infrastructure in India needs to be enhanced.

People need to be better prepared to deal with a crisis. They need to be resilient to withstand shocks. This requires people to have productive employment, a living wage and savings to survive such shocks. This would also reduce migration of the dispossessed to concentrated urban agglomerates, which are becoming unmanageable. The need is for decentralized urbanization, with closer participation of people and greater commitment to society.

The level of education has to be improved, so people can better understand their situation and not live in confusion. This will help nations respond better to any crisis. Those with little knowledge of science are likely to be open to dogmas and superstition. So education will have to play an important role. In India, education is largely by rote and that prevents students from getting a real understanding of what they study. For this, there need to be better teachers, with courses focusing on the basics. Teachers have to be given greater dignity in society. A policy of neighbourhood schools is needed, so that all children get the same opportunity.

Along with education, the standard of other public services has to be far better than what it currently is, such as clean water, sewage and sanitation. Housing has to be affordable and close to people's respective places of work, at least for a majority. The Internet has to be treated as part of public goods so education can reach the poor too. Kumar (1994) presented an alternative economic and social package that consisted of the above-mentioned features and showed that it is achievable within the resource base of the Indian economy - it showed that the 'desirable is feasible'.

The difference between the welfare of society and growth of the economy has to be understood. Growth in the past fifty years has been dichotomizing, with those at the top of the income ladder cornering most of the gains from growth and technological advancements. The huge inequality that has followed has resulted in economic problems and also the big political and social challenges discussed above. The associated consumerism on which the present models of growth are based has led to environmental destruction. It is a major contributor to climate change and a reduction in biological diversity. It is leading to human-animal conflict, which is a likely cause of the present pandemic (as it is believed that the virus originated from the Wuhan wet market in China). Consumerism is also widening the divide between the rich and the poor.

So growth has come at the expense of increasing health problems and rising social and political tensions in society. Consumerism has led to a tremendous waste of resources. It is like digging holes and filling holes, where there is activity without any productivity. We produce and throw away things (such as clothes and food), leading to pollution, both during production and disposal of waste. This is sustained by high-pressure advertising, which propagates wasteful lifestyles. It was shown in Bowles, et al (1984) that, in 1980, 50 per cent of the production in the US was a waste. Kumar (2006) showed that 25 per cent of production in India was a waste. Thus, the present level of welfare can be obtained by society as a whole, with much less production and, consequently, much less pollution.

As argued above, due to changes in production necessitated by the pandemic, costs will rise everywhere and production will be lesser than what it was earlier. The resource base of society will contract and there will be less available for everyone. At present, the thinking is that if consumption declines, welfare will be less. But if societies realize the value of equity and environmental consciousness, consumerism will decline without welfare being affected. So, post the pandemic, humankind will have to rethink many of the current basic features of life—consumerism, trade, inequality and protection of the environment.

*Rethinking the Development Paradigm*

The pandemic has brought out the vulnerability of humankind. The way we led our lives changed completely from the beginning of 2020. Nature has highlighted our vulnerability right at the cellular level, in spite of our tremendous scientific progress. It is a call to be better prepared, since another pandemic may come in due course, which may be even more deadly and give us much less time. Our scientific advances, which give us a better understanding of everything from subatomic particles to the vast expanses of the universe, are still inadequate when it comes to understanding the human body and the diseases that may afflict it.

We need to adopt the precautionary principle—whatever can go wrong will go wrong—so one has to be careful about what one does. Society has to develop a long-term perspective rather than the increasingly short-run perspective it has been adopting. This is necessary at the societal, scientific and technological levels (See Kumar, 2013). Many things that can be delayed until we understand their consequences better must not be pushed for narrow profits. This is especially true of technology, whose ethical aspects are not immediately clear. Often, greed overrides ethical concerns. So technology needs to be guided by society.

This requires a strengthening of society by making governance structures accountable. Today, vested interests control the levers of power. In India, they control both the ruling party and the Opposition. This is the case in most countries, and that leads to the truncation of democracy across the world. No wonder poverty persists, inequality grows and alienation takes its toll. With the present-day technology, there can be enough production, so that everyone gets a living wage and no one needs to live on the margins of survival. This may require shorter work weeks, so everyone can be employed and there is better distribution of resources among everyone. The shortcut of a Universal Basic Income is not desirable, since work gives dignity to people.

Time and again, those at the helm of the nation's governance have treated the unorganized sector and farming as residual. The unorganized sector is a consequence of the policies being pursued and attempts to formalize it are damaging it further. The GST has been detrimental to it and needs to be revamped (Kumar, 2019b). The change in the definition of MSME during the pandemic again highlights that this sector is a residual for policymakers. This mindset of those in power has to change.

Gandhi suggested development from below, so that everyone could be included in society. The pandemic has made it clear that this is what is needed for the long-term survival of society. His focus on non-violence is crucial—it has to encompass individuals, countries and nature. War, of course, involves violence and must stop. This will also stop the research on biological and chemical weapons, which can go out of control and is ethically repugnant. Violence against each other and against nature needs to stop. Exploitation of others and of nature is violence, and consumerism leads to violence. While Gandhi did not have answers to all human and social matters for all times, his thoughts can be a starting point for building a society with a long-term perspective and better survival capabilities.

The COVID-19 pandemic has brought forth an unprecedented crisis in society. It also presents an opportunity to reform society for a better future. It depends on humankind's foresight whether it grabs the opportunity or lets it go to waste, as has happened so many times in the past. If the crisis is viewed in narrow terms, it will result in a worsening of the situation in future, while, if it is viewed in a broader human and global perspective, it can raise humankind to new heights of harmonious existence. India, which has been the hardest hit, needs to introspect the most on this crisis, to be able to chalk out a better future for itself.

# Epilogue

## Post-Script: Uncertainty Persists

The economic and medical aspects of the coronavirus's impact keep throwing up surprises. The picture changed rapidly across countries earlier and now again, since mid-October. Till then, India had the largest number of daily cases but then, suddenly, cases exploded in the US (it had 5 lakh cases in the last week of October) and much of Europe.

Restrictions on businesses and night-time curfews were imposed in much of Europe. Businesses that were already fragile due to the first set of lockdowns are struggling to survive another. In the US, the medical system in some of the states is nearing capacity. Consequently, major world economies that had started to recover from the lows of March–April have been adversely impacted. The world over, stock markets, including in India, reacted negatively to these developments.

The Indian scenario has been confusing both on the health and economic fronts. Reports are that the number of tests has been reduced to show a lower daily case count. But this is risky, since it means that testing and tracing cannot be carried out, which will then result in an explosion of cases. Doing this just before the winter months, when cases are expected to rise, is dangerous, especially in north India, where pollution levels rise and major festivals are celebrated which leads to people moving around much more.

## Medical Aspects

In India, the daily count had peaked in September. October saw big declines in infections and deaths, but that does not mean that the country is over the hump. In the end of October, there were more than 45,000 cases a day. This implies a reduction in cases but not that the first round is over.

In India, there are persistent reports that deaths are not getting fully reported and testing has been slowed down. With reduced testing, contact tracing slows down and the disease can spread rapidly. This is the lesson from various countries. Those countries that have taken all kinds of precautions have done well, while those that have delayed or relaxed controls prematurely have suffered.

Populations are fatigued with having to stay indoors for so long. Many have resisted a curb on their movements and defied authorities. If compliance is not voluntary, it has been seen that policies become less effective for everyone and aggravate the spread of the disease. More drastic measures then become necessary, leading to people becoming more depressed and sometimes to social unrest, which creates further difficulties. In India, this has been visible during festivals. For instance, Pongal and political protests in Kerala led to the rapid spread of the disease there, whereas until July, it had been an example of how to control the disease. Durga Pujo, Diwali and other such festivals are also a cause for worry, since people shopped in large numbers and many did not maintain social distancing.

The news about medicines and production of antibodies in infected humans is mixed. Remdesivir was supposed to be a good medicine in advanced cases but some studies now indicate that it does not reduce mortality. Similarly, there is mixed news about the efficacy of the convalescent plasma therapy. So some of the promising remedies in severe cases are now off the table. Similarly, studies are showing that antibodies in those who had earlier been infected may not last for more than a few months. Finally, according to some studies, those who were asymptomatic earlier can get severely infected later on. In other words, no one is safe, even if infected earlier, and everyone needs to take the same precautions, whether earlier infected by the virus or not.

The good news is that doctors have learnt a lot about how to deal with the disease and death rates have fallen drastically, compared to early days. Research suggests that Indians are less vulnerable, since they live in largely unhygienic conditions and have higher immunity. But Indians die within fewer days of hospitalization than people in the advanced countries. There are many factors underlying this and one of them is the low expenditure on health—India's health budget per capita is the fourth lowest in the world.

Further, the development of vaccines is proceeding at a steady pace and these may be available soon. But to vaccinate the vulnerable may take months, so it could be midsummer before the vaccine begins to reach the population at large. The results from the third-stage trials will help determine the effectiveness of the vaccines—what proportion of the population will benefit from it and how long the immunity will last. Thus, it will be midsummer 2021 before some normalization can be expected.

In brief, while our understanding of the disease has evolved enormously, the challenge of the coronavirus persists and we cannot lower our guard until mid-2021. Partial or total lockdowns may still be necessary and recovery can falter any time. Countries have to be prepared for that.

## Lockdown and the Economy

A lockdown is a voluntary stoppage of economic activity, outside the house, in the market. That hits both demand and supply, and makes production difficult. This especially impacts the unorganized sector and small-scale production. Unfortunately, there is little data for these sectors in India, since it is collected once in five years. One has to rely on alternative sources and make assumptions on what is happening in these sectors. Or one can just ignore it, as most officialdom and experts do.

Since August, there has been repeated mention of green shoots. But what does it mean? Things are better than they were in March–April but it does not imply recovery to where the economy was in December 2019, before the pandemic hit the world. In the July–September quarter, the US economy has grown at a record annual rate of 33.1 per cent, after it had declined by 31.4 per cent in the previous quarter. But that means it is still 3 per cent below its level last year.

The economy will do better as it opens up; more economic activity will occur. In India, due to pent-up demand and festivals, more shopping has occurred and demand has risen. But the worry is that increased demand will not last beyond the festivals, especially given that many businesses have failed and unemployment not only continues to be high but is likely to increase. With such uncertainty, the improvements in consumer sentiment and investor confidence are likely to again decline, reversing the improvements in the economy.

In the case of the US economy data is available from Yelp, a website for feedback on businesses. Sundaram (2020) reported on 31 August that 163,735 small businesses had closed; out of these, 97,966 had permanently closed. Initially, in March, 180,000 small business had reported closure. Since March, restaurants, bars and nightlife venues have been hit the hardest, with 32,109 restaurants closed, as of 31 August. Retail also saw a large increase in permanent closures. Yelp also reports 'a correlation between states with a high number of closures and states with a high unemployment rate'. Further, large cities have reported higher closures and businesses in trouble. Los Angeles and New York have reported the highest number of closures.

In India, the media is persistently reporting large youth unemployment and growing dissatisfaction. Farmers are reporting receiving a price below the MSP and, consequently, seeing a drop in incomes in spite of bumper rabi and kharif harvests. Twenty per cent of small businesses are unable to pay their EMIs and many more are seeking an extension on their moratorium; so many micro-sector units are facing a crisis.

## Positive News

It is not all gloom and doom, though. As already mentioned in the book, certain sectors of the economy will do well and actually benefit from the pandemic. In October, the Ministry of Finance reported the following high-frequency data, signifying operations close to their level in February 2020:

1. CMIE reporting unemployment rate at 6.7 per cent in September, compared to 7.8 per cent in February.
2. Electricity demand in September 8 per cent higher than in February.
3. GST e-way bills in September at the same level as in February.
4. GST collections in September 2020 at 10 per cent higher than last year.
5. Diesel and petrol demand close to February levels.
6. Steel consumption in September 1 per cent above February level.
7. Auto-sector sales at February level and higher than last year.
8. Tractor sales 37 per cent higher in August, compared to February.
9. FMCG sector shows robust growth.
10. E-commerce doing much better this festive season than last year.

## The Good News Not Yet So Good

IHS Markit India Manufacturing Purchasing Managers' Index (PMI) rose to 58.9 in October. It was 56.8 in September, 52 in August and 27.4 in April. This indicates increased activity in the manufacturing sector. But it is a month-to-month comparison. So it indicates increased activity in October, compared to September, which was better than in August and so on. But from April to July, there was continuous contraction compared to March 2020. So, in October and September, there was growth over a very low base of July, but not over August or September 2019. One can conclude that activity is still way below February 2020 level.

The unemployment situation remains grim, with many in the organized sector still without work and with those still in employment having faced salary cuts. With continued high demand for work under MGNREGS and reports of workers who have returned to cities not able to get work, it is clear that many industries, especially in the services sector, are still not able to offer work. Uncertainty about work continues due to the threat of a second wave of the coronavirus attack.

The increase in sales in the auto sector has very specific underlying factors—pent-up demand for months and need for private transport, given the safety requirement and lack of public transport. It cannot last, given that unemployment among the salaried and professionals remains large. Demand was also higher due to need to replace fifteen-year-old vehicles. Actually, retail sales of Bajaj Auto and Hero in September were still 3 per cent below the last year's level. Deliveries to dealers were higher for stocking purposes. So retail demand is yet to pick up for two-wheelers.

GST data hides the fact that companies were in trouble. Larger units were given time to file returns until end of June and smaller ones until end of September. So there was bunching of payments in September, and that is what the October data represents. When major contributors to GST, such as airlines, tourism, hotels and restaurants, textiles and leather goods, were still operating way below capacity in September and contributing little to GST, the reason for high collection of GST in October can only be due to bunching.

The increase in petrol consumption is due to greater use of personal vehicles, given the paucity of public transport. Higher diesel consumption partly reflects the massive requirements of defence forces at the borders due to disturbed conditions since May and use in agriculture. Commercial-vehicle sales have remained low, signifying a lack of confidence in the transport sector that demand increase will last. So increase in petrol and diesel consumption does not signify that production in the economy has reached February 2020 level.

## The Not-So-Good News

Most of the good news has special factors behind it. But there is plenty of other news that points to the economy being still some way off from its February 2020 level. A few of these factors are listed below:

Macro Aspects

1. As pointed out above, employment is yet to recover to the earlier levels, and this is crucial for revival of demand and increase in output to the pre-pandemic levels.
2. Incomes of many have dropped sharply due to unemployment and cuts in wage and salary. Further, surveys reveal that 80 per cent of households will not be able to bear the cost of COVID-19 treatment of a family member and will slip into poverty. So demand will remain short.
3. Index of industrial production [IIP] is still below last year's levels.
4. Core-sector contraction continues in spite of a low base last year.
5. Currency with public has increased beyond the level before demonetization. This signifies continuing uncertainty and people going liquid.
6. Consumer confidence remains low for the present due to continuing uncertainty.
7. Business sentiment also remains low, which implies that investment will not revive soon.
8. Investment remains depressed. Without it recovering, growth will not revive.

9.  Total tax collections and non-tax revenues are far below the target for 2020–21.
10. Fiscal deficit of the Centre reached 115 per cent of the target in September itself. This is in spite of the compression of expenditures. It is 11 per cent of the GDP for this period. Add to that the fiscal deficit for the states and off-balance sheet items and it will be around 20 per cent.
11. Stock market indices have risen but uncertainty persists.

Sectoral Aspects

1.  Many brick-and-mortar retail stores report lower sales, despite the festive season.
2.  One in five small businesses are reported to be unable to pay their EMIs.
3.  The education sector has not been able to recover to the February state. Reopening of schools and colleges is proving difficult. Many private institutions have closed down or are on the verge of closing down. Admissions and start of new session are delayed.
4.  The health sector has not been able to perform routine functions, with many patients keeping away due to fear of contracting the coronavirus.
5.  Real estate sales in Gurgaon and many towns are still weak.
6.  Hotels, restaurants, travel and tourism are far below their level of operation in February 2020.
7.  Religious places reopening has been delayed and devotees visiting them are fewer.
8.  Media and advertising are not yet back to February 2020 levels.
9.  Book sales are reported to be way below the levels in February 2020.
10. Businesses closures are being reported from time to time.

## Political Aspects

Political turmoil is growing, which is diverting attention from the urgent task of dealing with the pandemic and its consequences.

1. Farm protests are taking place across the country on the issue of the new farm bills.
2. Trade unions are protesting against the changes being introduced in labour laws.
3. Employees are protesting against privatization in railways, insurance, defence production units and other PSUs.
4. The youth is protesting against unemployment and cuts in jobs.

Consequently, in the Bihar elections, a strong anti-incumbency is being witnessed in spite of a divided opposition and the strong appeal of the prime minister.

# Acknowledgements

I would like to acknowledge the discussions I have had with my former colleagues and research students, which have helped me formulate my ideas over the past few months. I would particularly like to mention Professor Ritu Priya Mehrotra, Professor Saumen Chattopadhyay, Prafulla Prusty and Sunil Dharan. Discussions with Ajay Vir Jakhar were useful for understanding the impact on agriculture. Anushruti Singh and Kartik Kant helped with data work and I am grateful to them. I would also like to thank Bharat Krishak Samaj and IndiaSpend for help with some data.

I would like to acknowledge the interaction with participants of the various webinars I have delivered since April since they helped me sharpen my arguments presented here. I have also had some interaction with business people who gave me feedback on what was going on in their sector. Finally, I would like to acknowledge the inputs from friends in HDFC and ICRA for giving their perceptions about the state of the economy. These interactions were helpful in formulating my views about the economic impact of the pandemic.

I would like to thank Manish Kumar, the commissioning editor at Penguin Random House India, for pursuing me since April to write this book. He has had much to contribute to the final shape of the book through his comments and encouragement. I would also like to thank the copy editor Ujjaini Dasgupta for the very meticulous and hard work of rapidly editing the manuscript and making it more readable.

Finally, I would like to acknowledge the support of my wife Neerja and son Nakul, who, in these difficult times, took on the extra burden of taking care of everything in the house while I was busy putting this book together.

# Annexures

## Annexure 01.

Economic Activities Allowed/Eased Under Each of the Unlock Phases (Based on Office Orders of Ministry of Home Affairs)

### Unlock 1

Ministry of Home Affairs Office Order Dated 30 May 2020

1. The following activities will be allowed with effect from 8 June 2020
   (i) Religious places/places of worship for public.
   (ii) Hotels, restaurants and other hospitality services.
   (iii) Shopping malls.

2. Night curfew
   (iv) Movement of individuals shall remain strictly prohibited between 9 p.m. to 5 a.m. throughout the country, except for essential activities.

3. Lockdown Limited to Containment Zones Unrestricted Movement of Persons and Goods
   (i) There shall be no restriction on inter-state and intra-state movement of persons and goods. No separate permission/approval/e-permit will be required for such movements.
   (ii) However, if a state/UT, based on reasons of public health and its assessment of the situation, proposes to regulate movement

of persons, it will give wide publicity in advance regarding the restrictions to be placed on such movement, and the related procedures to be followed.

(iii) Movement by passenger trains and Shramik special trains; domestic passenger air travel; movement of Indian Nationals stranded outside the country and of specified persons to travel abroad; evacuation of foreign nationals; and sign-on and sign-off of Indian seafarers will continue to be regulated as per SOPs issued.

4. No state/UT shall stop the movement of any type of goods/cargo for cross land-border trade under Treaties with neighbouring countries.

5. Gatherings: Large public gatherings/congregations continue to remain prohibited.
Marriage-related gatherings: Number of guests not to exceed 50.
Funeral/last rites-related gatherings: Number of persons not to exceed 20.

## Unlock 2
Ministry of Home Affairs Office Order Dated 29 June 2020:

1. Activities permitted during Unlock 2 outside containment zones:
In areas outside containment zones, all activities will be permitted, except the following:

(i) Schools, colleges, educational and coaching institutions will remain closed till 31 July 2020. Online/distance learning shall continue to be permitted and shall be encouraged.
Training institutions of the Central and State Governments will be allowed to function from 15 July 2020, for which Standard Operating Procedure (SOP) will be issued by the Department of Personnel & Training (DoPT).

(ii) International air travel of passengers, except as permitted by MHA.

(iii) Metro rail.

(iv) Cinema halls, gymnasiums, swimming pools, entertainment parks, theatres, bars, auditoriums, assembly halls and similar places.

(v) Social/political/sports/entertainment/academic/cultural/religious functions and other large congregations.

Dates for restarting the above activities may be decided separately and necessary SOPs shall be issued for ensuring social distancing and to contain the spread of COVID-19.

Domestic flights and passenger trains have already been allowed in a limited manner. Their operations will be further expanded in a calibrated manner.

2. Night curfew

Movement of individuals shall remain strictly prohibited between 10 p.m. to 5 a.m. throughout the country, except for essential activities, including operation of industrial units in multiple shifts, movement of persons and goods on national and state highways, loading and unloading of cargo and travel of persons to their destinations after disembarking from buses, trains and airplanes. Local authorities shall issue orders, in the entire area of their jurisdiction, under appropriate provisions of law, such as under Section 144 of CrPC, and ensure strict compliance.

3. Lockdown limited to Containment Zones.

Lockdown shall continue to remain in force in the containment zones till 31 July 2020.

4. States/UTs, based on their assessment of the situation, may prohibit certain activities outside the containment zones, or impose such restrictions as deemed necessary.

However, there shall be no restriction on inter-state and intra-state movement of persons and goods including those for cross land-border trade under treaties with neighbouring countries. No separate permission/approval/e-permit will be required for such movements.

5. Movement of persons with SOPs.

Movement by passenger trains and Shramik special trains; domestic passenger air travel; movement of Indian nationals stranded outside the country and of specified persons to travel abroad; evacuation of foreign nationals; and sign-on and sign-off of Indian seafarers will continue to be regulated as per SOPs issued.

## Unlock 3

Ministry of Home Affairs Office Order Dated 29 July 2020.

1. Activities permitted during Unlock 3 outside containment zones.

In areas outside the Containment Zones, all activities will be permitted, except the following:

(i) Schools, colleges, educational and coaching institutions will remain closed till 31 August 2020. Online/distance learning shall continue to be permitted and shall be encouraged.

(ii) Cinema halls, swimming pools, entertainment parks, theatres, bars, auditoriums, assembly halls and similar places.

Yoga institutes and gymnasiums will be allowed to function from 5 August 2020, for which standard operating procedure (SOP) will be issued by the Ministry of Health & Family Welfare (MoHFW).

(iii) International air travel of passengers, except as permitted by MHA.

(iv) Metro Rail.

(v) Social/political/sports/entertainment/academic/cultural/religious functions and other large congregations.

Dates for restarting the above activities may be decided separately and necessary SOPs shall be issued for ensuring social distancing and to contain the spread of COVID-19.

2. Independence Day functions

Independence Day functions at national, state, district, subdivisional, municipal and panchayat levels and 'at home' functions, wherever held, will be allowed with social distancing and by following other health protocols, for e.g. wearing of masks. In this regard, instructions issued vide MHA letter no 2/5/2020-public dated 21 July 2020 shall be followed.

3. Lockdown limited to containment zones.

Lockdown shall continue to remain in force in the containment zones till 31 August 2020.

4. States/UTs, based on their assessment of the situation, may prohibit certain activities outside the containment zones, or impose such restrictions as deemed necessary.

However, there shall be no restriction on inter-state and intra-state movement of persons and goods, including those for cross land-border trade under treaties with neighbouring countries. No separate permission/approval/e-permit will be required for such movements.

(i) Movement of persons with SOPs.

Movement by passenger trains and Shramik special trains; domestic passenger air travel; movement of Indian nationals stranded outside the country and of specified persons to travel abroad; evacuation of foreign nationals; and sign-on and sign-off of Indian seafarers will continue to be regulated as per SOPs issued.

## Unlock 4

Ministry of Home Affairs Office Order Dated 29 August 2020.

1. Activities permitted during Unlock 4 outside containment zones.
   In areas outside the Containment Zones, all activities will be permitted, except the following:
   (i) Schools, colleges, educational and coaching institutions will continue to remain closed for students and regular class activity up to 30 September 2020. However, following will be permitted:
   a. Online/distance learning shall continue to be permitted and shall be encouraged.
   b. States/UTs may permit up to 50 per cent of teaching and non-teaching staff to be called to the schools at a time for online teaching/telecounselling and related work, in areas outside containment zones only, with effect from 21 September 2020, for which SOP will be issued by the MoHFW.
   c. Students of classes 9 to 12 may be permitted to visit their schools, in areas outside the containment zones only, on voluntary basis, for taking guidance from their teachers. This will be subject to written consent of their parents/guardians and will be permitted with effect from 21 September 2020 for which, SOP will be issued by MoHFW.
   d. Skill or entrepreneurship training will be permitted in National Skill Training Institutes, Industrial Training Institutes (ITIs), short term training centres registered with National Skill Development Corporation or State Skill Development Missions or other Ministries of Government of India or state governments.
   National Institute for Entrepreneurship and Small Business Development (NIESBUD), Indian Institute of Entrepreneurship (IIE) and their training providers will also be permitted.
   These will be permitted with effect from 21 September 2020, for which SOP will be issued by MoHFW.
   e. Higher education institutions only for research scholars (PhD) and post-graduate students of technical and professional programmes requiring laboratory/experimental works. These will be permitted by the Department of Higher Education (DHE) in consultation with MHA, based on the assessment of the situation, and keeping in view incidence of COVID-19 in the states/UTs.
   (ii) Metro rail will be allowed to operate with effect from 7 September 2020 in a graded manner, by the Ministry of Housing and Urban

Affairs (MOHUA)/Ministry of Railways (MOR), in consultation with MHA. In this regard, SOP will be issued by MOHUA.

(iii) Social/academic/sports/entertainment/cultural/religious/political functions and other congregations with a ceiling of 100 persons will be permitted with effect from 21 September 2020, with mandatory wearing of face masks, social distancing, provision for thermal scanning and hand wash or sanitizer.

However, marriage-related gatherings with number of guests not exceeding 50 and funeral/last rites-related gatherings with number of persons not exceeding 20 will continue to be allowed up to 20 September 2020, after which the ceiling of 100 persons will apply.

(iv) Cinema halls, swimming pools, entertainment parks, theatres and similar places will remain closed. However, open-air theatres will be permitted to open with effect from 21 September 2020.

(v) International air travel of passengers, except as permitted by MHA.

2. Lockdown limited to containment zones.

(i) Lockdown shall remain in force in the containment zones until 30 September 2020.

3. State/UT governments shall not impose any local lockdown (state/district/subdivision/city level), outside the containment zones, without prior consultation with the Central government.

4. No restriction on inter-state and intra-state movement.
There shall be no restriction on inter-state and intra-state movement of persons and goods, including those for cross land-border trade under treaties with neighbouring countries. No separate permission/approval/e-permit will be required for such movements.

5. Movement of persons with SOPs.
Movement by passenger trains; domestic passenger air travel; movement of persons on Vande Bharat and Air Transport Bubble flights; and sign-on and sign-off of Indian seafarers will continue to be regulated as per SOPs issued.

## Unlock 5
Ministry of Home Affairs Office Order Dated 30 September 2020.

1. Activities permitted outside the containment zones.

   In areas outside the containment zones, all activities will be permitted, except the following:

   (i) State/UT governments may take a decision in respect of reopening of schools and coaching institutions, after 15 October 2020, in a graded manner. The decision shall be taken in consultation with the respective school/institution management, based on their assessment of the situation, and subject to the following conditions:

   a. Online/distance learning shall continue to be the preferred mode of teaching and shall be encouraged.

   b. Where schools are conducting online classes, and some students prefer to attend online classes rather than physically attend school, they may be permitted to do so.

   c. Students may attend schools/institutions only with the written consent of parents.

   d. Attendance must not be enforced and must depend entirely on parental consent.

   e. States/UTs will prepare their own SOP regarding health and safety precautions for reopening of schools/institutions based on the SOP to be issued by Department of School Education and Literacy (DoSEL), Ministry of Education, Government of India, keeping local requirements in view.

   f. Schools, which are allowed to open, will have to mandatorily follow the SOP to be issued by Education Departments of States/UTs prepared as above.

   (ii) Department of Higher Education (DHE), Ministry of Education may take a decision on the timing of the opening of colleges/higher education institutions, in consultation with Ministry of Home Affairs (MHA), based on the assessment of the situation. Online/distance learning shall continue to be the preferred mode of teaching and shall be encouraged.

   However, higher education institutions only for research scholars (PhD) and post-graduate students in science and technology stream requiring laboratory/experimental works will be permitted to open from 15 October 2020, as under:

   a. For centrally funded higher education institutions, the head of the institution will satisfy herself/himself that there is a genuine requirement of research scholars (PhD) and post-graduate students in science and technology stream for laboratory/experimental works.

b.   For all other higher education institutions, e.g. state universities, private universities etc., they may open only for research scholars (PhD) and postgraduate students in science and technology stream requiring laboratory/experimental works as per decision to be taken by the respective state/UT governments.

(iii) Swimming pools being used for training of sportspersons will be permitted to open with effect from 15 October 2020, for which the SOP will be issued by Ministry of Youth Affairs & Sports (MoYA&S).

(iv) Cinemas/theatres/multiplexes will be permitted to open with up to 50 per cent of their seating capacity, in areas outside the containment zones only, with effect from 15 October 2020, for which SOP will be issued by Ministry of Information & Broadcasting.

(v) Entertainment parks and similar places will be permitted to open with effect from 15 October 2020, for which the SOP will be issued by Ministry of Health & Family Welfare (MoHFW).

(vi) Business to Business (B2B) exhibitions will be permitted to open in areas outside the containment zones only, with effect from 15 October 2020, for which SOP will be issued by the Department of Commerce.

(vii) Social/academic/sports/entertainment/cultural/religious/political functions and other congregations have already been permitted with a ceiling of 100 persons, outside containment zones only. Such gatherings beyond the limit of 100 persons may be permitted, outside containment zones, by state/UT governments only after 15 October 2020, and subject to the following conditions:

a.   In closed spaces, a maximum of 50 per cent of the hall capacity will be allowed, with a ceiling of 200 persons. Wearing of face masks, maintaining social distancing, provision for thermal scanning and use of hand wash or sanitizer will be mandatory.

b.   In open spaces, keeping the size of the ground/space in view, and with strict observance of social distancing, mandatory wearing of face masks, provision for thermal scanning and hand wash or sanitizer.

State/UT governments will issue detailed SOPs, to regulate such gatherings and strictly enforce the same.

(viii) International air travel of passengers, except as permitted by MHA.

3. **Lockdown limited to containment zones**
   Lockdown shall remain in force in the Containment Zones till 31 October 2020.

4. State/UT governments shall not impose any local lockdown (state/district/subdivision/city level), outside the containment zones, without prior consultation with the Central government.

5. **No restriction on inter-state and intra-state movement**
   There shall be no restriction on inter-state and intra-state movement of persons and goods, including those for cross land-border trade under treaties with neighbouring countries. No separate permission/approval/e-permit will be required for such movements.

6. **Movement of persons with SOPs**
   Movement by passenger trains; domestic passenger air travel; movement of persons on Vande Bharat and Air Transport Bubble flights; and sign-on and sign-off of Indian seafarers will continue to be regulated as per SOPs issued.

## Annexure III.1

Major US Media Companies Laying Off and/or Cutting Salaries
(Up to End of May)

1. American Media
2. Boston Herald
3. Bustle Digital Group
4. BuzzFeed
5. Conde Nast
6. CQ Roll Call
7. Culture Trip
8. Financial Times
9. Fortune
10. Fox Corp
11. Gannett
12. G/O Media
13. Group Nine Media
14. Guardian UG Media Group
15. Lee Enterprises
16. Los Angeles Times
17. McClatchy
18. Meredith
19. New York Post
20. NPR
21. Playboy
22. Protocol
23. Quartz
24. San Diego Magazine
25. Sports Illustrated
26. Telegraph Media Group
27. The Atlantic
28. The Dallas Morning News
29. The Hill
30. The Plain Dealer
31. The Tampa Bay Times
32. The Times-Picayune and The Advocate
33. Tribune Publishing
34. Univision
35. Valence Media
36. ViacomCBS
37. Vice
38. Vox Media
39. *W* Magazine

Source: Kirsch (2020)
(Last updated 29 May 2020)

## Annexure III.2
Companies (Globally) in Trouble or Closing Down
(Up to Mid-June)

### Airlines & Transportation
1. Air Canada
2. Air New Zealand
3. Avis Car Rental
4. Boeing
5. Enterprise Holdings
6. Flight Centre
7. Helloworld Travel
8. Hertz
9. Lyft
10. Norwegian Air
11. Scandinavian Airlines
12. Stena Line
13. Transat AT
14. TripAdvisor
15. ZipCar

### Airports
1. Prospect
2. Concession Vendors Global Miami Joint Venture
3. Airport Concessions Group
4. OTG
5. Philadelphia International Airport
6. Orlando International Airport
7. Baltimore-Washington International Thurgood Marshall Airport.

### Arts, Culture & Entertainment
1. International Alliance of Theatrical Stage Employees estimated 120,000 jobs eliminated
2. 20th Century Fox
3. Alley Theatre
4. Caesars Entertainment Corp.
5. California Academy of Sciences
6. Christie Lights
7. Cineplex Inc.
8. Circuit of the Americas
9. Cirque du Soleil
10. Talent agency Endeavor
11. Karla Otto
12. Krupp Group
13. Massachusetts Museum of Contemporary Art
14. Norman Rockwell Museum
15. Hancock Shaker Village
16. McCarter Theater
17. Metro-Goldwyn-Mayer Studios
18. Metropolitan Museum of Art
19. Museum of Modern Art
20. Mystic Seaport Museum
21. Hollywood talent agency Paradigm
22. PR Consulting
23. Science Museum of Minnesota
24. Sequel
25. SkyCity Entertainment

26. South By Southwest
27. Spring
28. TeamSanJose
29. Whitney Museum
30. Upright Citizens Brigade
31. ViacomCBS

**Education**
1. Boston University
2. Kent State University
3. Sacramento City Unified School District
4. The New School
5. University of Colorado at Boulder

**Finance**
1. Cantor Fitzgerald
2. Meridian Capital Group

**Government**
Local governments in Michigan

**Healthcare**
1. Cookeville Regional Medical Centre
2. Beaumont Health

**Hotels**
1. Carmel Valley Ranch
2. Carlyle and Plaza Hotels
3. Claremont Hotel Properties
4. Eden Roc Hotels
5. Four Seasons
6. Gaylord Rockies Resort & Convention Centre
7. Great Wolf Lodge
8. Kimpton Hotel Aventi

9. Ian Schrager-owned Public
10. Las Alcobas Resort & Spa
11. Marriott International
12. McMenamins
13. MGM Resorts
14. Oglebay Resort and Conference Centre
15. Oyo Hotels
16. Palace Hotel
17. Pebblebrook Hotel Trust
18. Redcape Hotel Group
19. RIU Plaza Fisherman's Wharf
20. Sage Hospitality Group
21. Scandic
22. Sydell Hotels
23. President Trump's hotels
24. Warwick Rittenhouse Square Hotel
25. Westin Boston Waterfront
26. Ventana Big Sur

**Industry**
MBI Energy Services

**Manufacturing & Logistics**
1. Arconic
2. Delta Sky
3. General Electric
4. General Motors
5. Marsh Plating Corp
6. Mitchell Plastics
7. Schafer Woodworks Inc.
8. Tilden Mining Co.
9. Wayzata Home Products

**Real Estate**
Trump Organization

## Restaurants & Dining

1. Aqimero
2. Ritz-Carlton hotel
3. Bon Appetit Management Company
4. Burgerville
5. Cameron Mitchell Restaurants
6. Compass Coffee
7. Danny Meyer's Union Square Hospitality Group
8. Dyn365
9. Earl's Restaurants, Inc.
10. Eatwell DC
11. Founders Brewing Co
12. Friendly's
13. HMSHost
14. JuiceLand
15. Landry's Inc.
16. Levy's Premium Foodservice
17. Punch Bowl Social
18. Shake Shack
19. Trump National Doral
20. Vesta Food Service

## Retail

1. B8ta
2. Cultivate
3. Destination XL
4. DSW
5. Myer Holdings
6. Paper Source
7. Primark
8. Sephora
9. Laura Ashley
10. McNally Jackson
11. Mountain Equipment Co-op
12. Simon Property Group

13. Tuft & Needle
14. Under Armour

## Silicon Valley & Technology

1. Airbnb
2. Bird
3. Carta
4. ClassPass
5. Compass
6. ConsenSys
7. D2iQ
8. DataRobot
9. Envoy
10. Eventbrite
11. Everlane
12. ezCater
13. Eight Sleep
14. Triplebyte
15. The Guild
16. Cabin
17. GetAround
18. Groupon
19. Iris Nova
20. KeepTruckin
21. Knotel
22. Komodo Health
23. Leafly
24. Lola
25. Magic Leap
26. Modsy
27. Opendoor
28. Overtime
29. PerkSpot
30. Pivot3
31. Rent The Runway
32. Remote Year
33. RigUp
34. Rover
35. ShowPad
36. Sonder

37. SpotHero
38. Textio
39. Thumbtack
40. TripActions
41. Uber
42. VSCO
43. Wonderschool
44. Yelp
45. ZipRecruiter
46. Zeus Living

**Sports & Fitness**
1. Utah Jazz
2. CorePower Yoga
3. Golden Gate Parks
4. The WWE
5. XFL

**Likely to Cut Back Employment**
1. Delta Airlines
2. American Airlines
3. United Airlines

**Utilities**
Dish

**Elsewhere**
1. Boston's Tea Party Ships & Museum
2. Old Town Trolley Cars
3. Central Ohio's YMCA
4. Fitler Club
5. Greater Philadelphia YMCA
6. Lucky Chances Casino
7. California Grand Casino
8. National Rifle Association
9. Oneida Nation
10. Tombstone, Arizona
11. The Wing

Source: Voytko (2020) (accessed on 25 June 2020)

## Annexure IV.1

List of Companies in India That Have Laid Off Employees or Enforced Salary Cuts

1. Ola
2. ShareChat
3. WeWork
4. Swiggy
5. Zomato
6. Uber
7. Reliance Industries
8. Oyo Rooms
9. *The Times of India*
10. The Quint
11. News Nation Network
12. *The Indian Express*
13. Curefit
14. Livspace
15. MakeMyTrip
16. BookMyShow
17. CarDekho

A NASSCOM survey reported that 70 per cent of start-ups had less than three months of cash. It was reported that many of them planned to retrench and/or cut salaries.

Sources: Medhi (2020) and Scroll Staff (2020)

## Annexure IV.2

News of Working of Indian Economy and Sectors April-July 2020

General

### Industrial Production

1.  TNN. (2020b). April data: Mining at -27.4%, manufacturing at -64.3%, electricity at -22.6, Capital foods at -92% and consumer durables at -95.7%.

2.  TNN. (2020c). May 2020 compared to May 2019.
    NSO only released index numbers as a majority of the industrial sector establishments were not operating since the end of March.
    IIP contracted 34.7%. Manufacturing at -39.3%, Capital Goods -64.3%, Consumer Durables -68.5%, Mining -21% and Electricity -15.4%.

3.  FICCI-Dhruva Advisors Industry Survey.
    June 2020 Report: 30% firms operating at 70% plus capacity utilisation, 45% of firms expect capacity utilisation to be above 70% in the near term.

4.  Pant, S. (2020). Industries look at January to return to full production.

5.  ET Bureau. (2020a).
    Automobiles at 65-80% of June last year.
    Physical Retail at 67% of pre pandemic.
    Real Estate at 67% of pre pandemic.
    Restaurants at 20% of pre pandemic.
    FMCG Sales picked up; Mainly for food and hygiene goods. Demand for non-essentials low.
    Ecommerce 80-90% of pre pandemic.
    Power: Low demand from industrial states.
    Contracted 24% in April, 15.2% in May and 12.5% in 3 weeks of June.
    Hospitality 15% occupancy in May. For the year, max 35% occupancy.
    Petroleum: Decline of 45.7% in April and 23.2% in May and some increase in June.
    Railway freight improved in May by 26% over April.
    Toll collection Rs 8.25 crore April, Rs 36.84 crore May and Rs 49.8 crore in 3 weeks of June.

6. RBI Risk Assessment Report
   (Part of the Financial Stability Report, Issue no. 21. July 2020)

   % of respondents said chances of recovery in next 6 months are bleak

   | | |
   |---|---|
   | Tourism and Hospitality | 90 |
   | Aviation | 85 |
   | MSMEs | 60 |
   | Automobiles | 50 |
   | Construction and Real Estate | 50 |

7. Reports of Companies for June 2020 quarter
   Shinde, R and S. Kadam. (2020). Sample of 176 companies including, sectors doing well; BFSI, FMCG and IT (67 companies):
   9.2% drop in net sales and 8.5% drop in net profits year on year
   Excluding these sectors, aggregate sales fell 36% and net profit declined 61%.

8. PMI Services
   The IHS Markit Data: April 5.4, May 12.6 and June 33.7.
   In June, 59% reported no change in output, 4% registered growth and 37% recorded a reduction.
   Employment across services fell in June.
   New Orders fell sharply in June.

9. PMI Manufacturing
   The IHS Markit Data: Jan 55.3, April 27.4, May 30.8 and June 47.2.

10. Core Sector Growth
    Ministry of Commerce and Industry: Drop in April of 37%. In May it was 23.4%.
    Fertilizer saw an increase of 7.5%.
    Steel dropped -78.7% in April and -48.4% in May
    Cement dropped -85.3% in April and -22.2% in May.
    Electricity saw a drop of -23% in April and -15.5% in May.

Saini, M. (2020). *Power* consumption rate was 2,488 million units per day last year during April to June and 1,120 million units this year in the same period.
Most industries are working at 50% and only one shift.
ACC saw volumes fall 33%.
JSW Steel saw 25% fall in shipments.

11. Foreign Trade
    Ministry of Commerce and Industry: Growth in dollar terms—
    Merchandise Exports -60.28%, Imports -58.65%, Trade balance
    -$6.76 billion
    Services Exports -2.54%, Imports -6.37% Balance +$6.93 billion
    Overall trade balance +$0.16 billion

12. Inflation
    MOSPI gives the inflation data. It could not be collected in April due
    to lockdown. Hence it was imputed.
    Consumption basket has changed so the inflation data needs to be
    redone.
    WPI inflation was negative in April and May; in June it was -1.8% but
    food inflation was 2.04%.
    CPI inflation rate stood at 6.09 per cent in June and food inflation at
    7.87 per cent.
    Big divergence has occurred between WPI and CPI.

13. Budgetary Nos.
    Data from Ministry of Finance
    Fiscal Deficit
    May end FD was at 58.6% of the BE. Expenditure–Revenue was
    Rs 4.66 lakh crore
    *Tax collection*
    Direct tax compared to last year: June quarter down 31% and
    Corporation tax down 79%.
    GST Collection April Rs 28,309 crore, May Rs 62,009 crore and June
    Rs 90,917 crore.
    GST collection usually rises sharply in March and April (See Graph V.1)
    but this year due to COVID 19, payment was allowed to be postponed
    up to 24 June. So tax from March was postponed to June.

14. Employment
    Indian Express, 4 June, Azim Premji University study showed that
    about half the workers lost employment in Bihar, Jharkhand, Madhya
    Pradesh and Odisha.
    Odisha 67%, Jharkhand 58%, Madhya Pradesh 48% and Bihar 46%.
    Casual workers worse hit. Bihar 80%, Jharkhand 76%, Madhya Pradesh 65%.
    Half did not get money under Jan Dhan and 20% did not get rations
    in Bihar and Jharkhand.

Sectors

**Manufacturing**

1.  Automobiles and Ancillaries
    In June, Factory output was at 45–50% of previous year
    Bajaj Auto revenues fell 60%
    Tractor sales in June 12% higher than last year
    Maruti Suzuki India Limited: Sales down by 81% in Q1. Net Loss
    Rs 249 crore compared to Profits of Rs 1436 crore. April sales and
    production were zero. Quarterly loss in 15 years.

2.  Textiles
    Jha and Narasimhan (2020).
    Companies like Century Textiles, Gokaldas Exports, Filatex and several
    medium and small units in Karnataka, Ludhiana and Tiruppur regions
    have started operations at 25 per cent capacity.
    'We are eyeing Diwali as the possible opportunity for restoration . . .
    Financial year 2020-21 could be a washout for textile players,' Dalmia said.
    Getting adequate manpower to ramp up production is one of the major
    challenges.
    '. . . Retail sales are expected to be at half for the next three months,
    hence with 40-50 per cent business, many factories will find it difficult
    to remain viable. There are about 75,000-80,000 units across the
    country . . .'

3.  Leather Goods
    PTI (2020b). Leather goods exporters are likely to suffer a 40-50
    percent decline.
    'Importers from the US, UK, France, Italy, Spain and Germany have
    either cancelled contracts or put them on hold . . .'
    In West Bengal, some tanneries and leather manufacturing units
    in Bantala are operational for the last two weeks, but with skeletal
    workforce.

4.  FMCG (from company reports for Q1)
    Britannia says it is operating at full capacity
    Hindustan Unilever sales down 7%
    Nestle India's domestic sales rose 2.55 per cent to Rs 2907.74 crore
    in April–June quarter as against Rs 2835.37 crore a year ago. Exports
    declined 9.32 per cent to Rs 133.71 crore as against Rs 147.46 crore

in the corresponding quarter last year. During April–June, there was over two-fold jump in sales from e-commerce; 'out of home' sector performance was subdued.

5.  Capital Goods
    L&T: 80% workforce back in June.

6.  Pharmaceuticals
    GlaxoSmithKline Pharmaceuticals. In May operating at about 70 per cent of normative manufacturing levels and are hopeful to improve this in the coming days. The company said it has seen a slowdown in sales across some of its therapeutic areas during the first quarter mainly from deferment of vaccination at clinics and slowdown in the non-essential portfolio.

## Services

1.  Education
    Institutions closed—only limited Internet education going on. Syllabi truncated.
    Exams postponed, entrance exams for new session postponed, sessions delayed.
    Temporary and ad hoc teachers not renewed. Private institutions fired teachers.
    Coaching institutions impacted.
    Shift in enrolment from private to government institutions.

2.  Health
    For private institutions, profit on COVID related work but other work declined drastically.
    OPDs closed for a while. Optional, elective and non-essential procedures postponed.
    Patients not coming due to fear of contracting disease.
    Accidents declined.
    Lucrative business of patients from other countries stopped.

3.  Real Estate
    The Hindu. (2020). Home sales in 8 cities declined 54% from year earlier period.
    59,538 units sold and new home launches declined to 60,489 units.
    Office space deals fell 37% y-o-y.

4. Religious Places
   Kumar, Anuj. (2020). Daily donations are down from Rs 6–7 lakh to nil.
   Impacted tourism, travel, hotels and so on in the entire region.

5. Hotels and Restaurants
   ITC Q1 results: Hotels closed during the period.

6. Legal Practice
   According to Justice Chandrachud in the *Indian Express*, 24 July 2020: 18,03,327 cases filed all India and 7,90,112 disposed off.
   Chhibber, M. (2020). In the month of April, 82,725 cases were filed in India's courts, while 35,169 cases were disposed of. Compare this to 2019, when the average number of cases filed per month was around 14 lakh (total number of cases 1.70 crore), while the average number disposed of per month was 13.25 lakh (total number of cases 1.59 crore).
   The decline had begun in March, as the total number of cases filed was 8.8 lakh, and the cases disposed of figure stood at 6.2 lakh. The average for the first four months of 2020, thus, has come down to 39 lakh (an average of 9.75 lakh cases per month), while the disposal rate has fallen sharply to around 8.32 lakh cases per month, with a total of 33.33 lakh cases.

7. Transport

a) *Airlines*
   The Hindu special correspondent (2020).
   In June, airlines were flying 30% of the routes and had an occupancy of 55%.
   Average daily passengers were at 70,000 daily compared to 4 lakh in June 2019.
   Indigo Q1 results show sharp losses.
   Salaries cut and workers retrenched in July.

b) *Railways*
   Nag. (2020). "Every day, Indian Railways ran over 13,000 passenger train services and over 8,000 freight train services. The 100% punctuality record, on the other hand, was achieved when just 230 passenger trains were running along with around 3,000 loaded freight trains and 2,200 empty trains."

c)  *Bus Ridership*
    Tiwari, S. (2020). Ridership in Haryana roadways dropped from 292.4 lakh in February to 3 lakh in May. For Gurgaon depot, only 5% ridership was recorded; only 10–15% routes were functioning.

8.  E-Way Bills
    January 56.9 million, April 8.6 million, May 25.4 million, June 39.3 million.

9.  Media
    Advertising slowed down, Paper size reduced, Journalists fired and salaries cut.
    Physical copies sales dropped due to fear of spread from surface.

10. Sports and Entertainment
    Stopped under lockdown till July end.

## Annexure V.1

Package Announced by the Finance Ministry in May 2020: Some Key Aspects

Total announcement: Rs 20.97 lakh crore. Of this, the RBI is to provide Rs 9 lakh crore.

### Loans and Credit to Various Sections

1. Rs 3 lakh crore of collateral-free loans to the MSME sector. Banks to get guarantee for credit, interest due for four years and no principal repayment for twelve months.
2. Liquidity for NBFCs and their AA or less grade paper to be bought—guarantee given.
3. Rental housing scheme for workers.
4. Shishu loans (up to Rs 50,000) Rs 1.62 crore of loan. 2 per cent interest subvention.
5. Housing for lowest of middle class. Scheme started in 2017 extended to 2021. Credit linked subsidy scheme. Rs 70,000 crore. PPP model with concessionaires.
6. Tribals, Kisan credit card scheme new enrolment and post-harvest work for small and marginal farmers—credit of Rs 30,000 crore from NABARD.
7. Rs 1 lakh crore for farm gate infrastructure and Rs 10,000 crore for food enterprises.
8. Schemes for fisheries, milk animal disease, herbal cultivation, honeybee-keeping and operation greens for TOP.
9. Support to state governments Ways and Means advance by RBI increased. Net borrowing ceiling raised to 5 per cent—linked to conditionalities.

### Laws, Rules/Provisions for Changes

1. Definition of MSME changed. Almost everything will be treated as micro sector.
2. Workers: Minimum wage and a national floor wage.
3. National portability of ration cards via Aadhaar—67 crore beneficiaries.
4. Essential Commodities Act 1955 to be given up.
5. APMC to be given up—farmers can sell anywhere.

6. Legal framework to reduce uncertainty for farmers and traders.
7. Structural reform (entry of private sector strengthened) in coal, minerals, defence production, FDI in defence production raised, civil aviation, power distribution in UTs, social infrastructure projects (hospitals) and in space and atomic energy.
8. Health and education steps. These are long-term steps and not linked to COVID-19.
9. IBC and Companies Act changes.
10. PSE all sectors to be opened to private sector—strategic to be defined, others privatized. At least one PSU and not more than 4 units. Privatization and mergers planned.

**Funds Allotted Directly**

1. MGNREGS raised by an additional Rs 40,000 crore.
2. Earlier PM Kisan scheme now counted Rs 17,380 crore.
3. Use of Building and other Construction Workers' Welfare Cess Fund: Rs 31,000 crore.
4. Use of District Mineral Foundation funds: Rs 35,925 crore.
5. Free grains to 9 crore workers for two months—even to those without ration cards.
6. EPF support for three months and contribution reduced for three months: Rs 9250 crore.
7. Street vendors: Rs 5000 crore for loans up to Rs 10,000 per vendor.
8. Funding for fishermen: Rs 20,000 crore.
9. Formalization of micro food enterprises: Rs 10,000 crore.
10. Viability gap funding for social infrastructure: Rs 8100 crore.

## Annexure V.2
Fiscal Implication of the Packages Announced by the Government of India

### 26 March 2020
Finance Minister Nirmala Sitharaman announces the Pradhan Mantri Garib Kalyan Yojana.
Size of the package: Rs 1.7 lakh crore (0.85 per cent of the GDP).
* Front-loading of PM Kisan funds: Rs 17,380 crore.
* Building and Other Construction Workers' Welfare Cess Fund: Rs 31,000 crore.
* District Mineral Foundation funds: Rs 35,925 crore.
Additional fiscal cost: Rs 85,695 crore (0.43 per cent of the GDP).

### 27 March 2020
Liquidity injection by the RBI.
Size: Rs 3.74 lakh crore (1.8 per cent of the GDP).
* Targeted Long-Term Repo Operations (TLTRO): Rs 1,00,000 crore.
* CRR cut by 100 basis points to 3 per cent: Rs 1,37,000 crore.
* Accommodation under Marginal Standing Facility hiked from 2 per cent of SLR to 3 per cent: Rs 1,37,000 crore.
Fiscal cost: 0

### 17 April 2020
Liquidity injection by the RBI.
Size: 0.5 per cent of the GDP.
* TLTRO 2.0: Rs 50,000 crore.
* Refinance of SIDBI, NABARD and NHB: Rs 50,000 crore.
Fiscal cost: 0

### 27 April 2020
Special Liquidity Facility for MFs: Rs 50,000 crore.
Size: 0.25 per cent of the GDP.
Fiscal cost to Central government: 0

### 12 May 2020
PM Narendra Modi announces the Rs 20 lakh crore AtmaNirbhar package, says size is 10 per cent of the GDP, including announcements made by the RBI and the finance ministry earlier.

## 13 May 2020

*Tranche 1 of the AtmaNirbhar package*

Size: Rs 5.94 lakh crore (2.97 per cent of the GDP).

* Collateral-free automatic loans to MSMEs, 100 per cent credit guarantee cover to banks and NBFCs: Rs 3 lakh crore.
* Subordinate debt to stressed MSMEs: Rs 20,000 crore.
* Equity infusion for MSMEs: Rs 50,000 crore.
* EPF support for three months: Rs 2,500 crore.
* EPF contribution reduced for three months: Rs 6,750 crore.
* Liquidity scheme for NBFCs/HFCs/MFIs: Rs 30,000 crore.
* Partial Credit Guarantee Scheme 2.0 for NBFCs, first 20 per cent loss borne by govt: Rs 45,000 crore.
* Liquidity injection by REC and PFC: Rs 90,000 crore.
* 25 per cent reduction in TDS/TCS rate: Rs 50,000 crore.

Fiscal cost: Rs 25,500 crore (0.13 per cent of the GDP).

## 14 May 2020

*Tranche 2*

Size: Rs 3.10 lakh crore (1.55 per cent of the GDP).

* Free foodgrain supply to migrants for two months: Rs 3,500 crore.
* Interest subvention of 2 per cent for prompt-payees of Mudra-Shishu loans: Rs 1,500 crore.
* Special liquidity scheme to provide Rs 10,000 working capital to 50 lakh street vendors: Rs 5,000 crore.
* Credit-linked subsidy scheme for middle-income families: Rs 6–18 lakh a year.
* Additional emergency working capital funding for farmers through NABARD: Rs 30,000 crore.
* Concessional credit to 2.5 crore farmers through Kisan credit cards: Rs 2 lakh crore.

Fiscal cost: Rs 5,000 crore (0.025 per cent of the GDP).

## 15 May 2020

*Tranche 3*

Size: Rs 1.5 lakh crore (0.75 per cent of the GDP).

* Financing facility for agri-infra projects: Rs 1,00,000 crore.
* Scheme for formalization of micro food enterprises: Rs 10,000 crore.
* Funding for fishermen: Rs 20,000 crore.
* Animal husbandry infrastructure development fund to be set up: Rs 15,000 crore.

Policy reforms:
* Essential Commodities Act to be amended to 'deregulate' agricultural foodstuffs and allow clamping of stock limits on these only under 'very exceptional circumstances'.
* Formulation of a central law that will not bind farmers to sell crop only to licensed traders in the APMC mandis.
Fiscal cost: Rs 30,000 crore (0.15 per cent of the GDP).

## 16 May 2020
*Tranche 4*
Size: Rs 8100 crore (0.04 per cent of the GDP).
* Defence FDI hiked from 49 per cent to 74 per cent.
* Viability gap funding (VGP) for social infrastructure.
Fiscal cost: Rs 8100 crore for VGP (0.04 per cent of the GDP).

## 17 May 2020
*Tranche 5*
* New policy for public-sector enterprises (PSEs), strategic sectors to be notified, in which there will be at least one, but not more than four, PSEs in addition to private players.
* Limit of state borrowings increased from 3 per cent to 5 per cent of the GSDP.
* MGNREGA gets additional Rs 40,000 crore.
Fiscal cost: Rs 40,000 crore (0.2 per cent of the GDP).

Source: Express News Service, 'The Rs 20-lakh crore package announced by FM Sitharaman', *Indian Express*, 18 May 2020, https://indianexpress.com/article/business/economy/nirmala-sitharaman-economic-relief-package-coronavirus-lockdown-6415253/ (accessed on 19 May 2020).

# Tables

**Table 01**

Quarterly Growth Rate of GDP at Market Prices 2017–20
(Announced Initially and Later Corrected)

|  | Initial | Corrected |
|---|---|---|
| 2017–18 Q1 | 6 | 6 |
| Q2 | 6.8 | 6.8 |
| Q3 | 7.7 | 7.7 |
| Q4 | 8.1 | 8.1 |
| 2018–19 Q1 | 8 | 7.1 |
| Q2 | 7 | 6.2 |
| Q3 | 6.6 | 5.6 |
| Q4 | 5.8 | 5.7 |
| 2019–20 Q1 | 5 | 5.2 |
| Q2 | 4.4 | |
| Q3 | 4.1 | |
| Q4 | 3.1 | |
| 2020—21Q1 | -24.9 | |

Source: RBI (2019), Monetary Policy Report, October and GoI (2020) http://
www.mospi.gov.in/sites/default/files/press_release/PRESS%20NOTE%20PE%20
and%20Q4%20estimates%20of%20GDP.pdf (accessed on 17 September 2020)

**Table I.1**
Health Infrastructure for Select Countries, Per 1,000 People

|    | Country | Physicians | Hospital Beds | Nurses and Midwives |
|----|---------|-----------|--------------|--------------------|
| 1  | Brazil | 2.2 | 2.2 | 10.1 |
| 2  | China | 2 | 4.2 | 2.7 |
| 3  | France | 3.3 | 6.5 | 11.5 |
| 4  | Germany | 4.2 | 8.3 | 13.2 |
| 5  | India | 0.9 | 0.7 | 1.7 |
| 6  | Iran | 1.6 | 1.5 | 2.6 |
| 7  | Italy | 4 | 3.4 | 5.7 |
| 8  | Japan | 2.4 | 13.4 | 12.2 |
| 9  | Korea, Republic of | 2.4 | 11.5 | 7.3 |
| 10 | Russia | 4 | 8.2 | 8.5 |
| 11 | South Africa | 0.9 | 2.8 | 1.3 |
| 12 | Spain | 3.9 | 3 | 5.7 |
| 13 | Sweden | 4 | 2.6 | 11.8 |
| 14 | UK | 2.8 | 2.8 | 8.2 |
| 15 | US | 2.6 | 2.9 | 14.5 |
| 16 | Vietnam | 0.8 | 2.6 | 1.4 |
| 17 | Euro Area | 3.9 | 6.2 | 9.8 |
| 18 | Low-Income Countries | 0.3 | 0.8 | 1.4 |

Source: World Bank
https://data.worlddbank.org/indicator/SH.MED.PHYS.ZS
Note: Data is for most recent years—2016, 2017 and 2018

**Table II.1**

Per Cent Share in GDP for Select Countries, 2019

|         | Agriculture | Industry | Services |
|---------|-------------|----------|----------|
| Brazil  | 4.44        | 17.92    | 63.25    |
| China   | 7.11        | 38.97    | 53.92    |
| Germany | 0.82        | 26.82    | 62.39    |
| India*  | 15.96       | 24.88    | 49.88    |
| Japan   | 1.24        | 29.07    | 69.31    |
| Russia  | 3.45        | 32.17    | 54.07    |
| US      | 0.92        | 18.21    | 77.37    |

Source: Proportions of economic sectors in the gross domestic product (GDP) in selected countries in 2019
https://www.statista.com/statistics/264653/proportions-of-economic-sectors-in-gross-domestic-product-gdp-in-selected-countries/ (accessed on 25 September 2020)

Note: In India, sectors are defined differently than in this table, but they are used for consistency with other countries' data.

**Table IV.1**

Number of Days for Cases to Rise by a Factor of Ten in India

| Cases | Number of Days | Total Reported Cases |
|-------|----------------|----------------------|
| 1k    | 60             | 1,024                |
| 10k   | 76             | 10,815               |
| 100k  | 111            | 1,01,139             |
| 1M    | 170            | 10,03,832            |

Source: Data Compiled by IndiaSpend from Ministry of Health & Family Welfare

**Table IV.2**
Annual Growth Projected for 2020–21 for India by Different Agencies

| Agency | Growth | Month | Growth | Month | Growth | Month | Growth | Month | Growth | Month |
|---|---|---|---|---|---|---|---|---|---|---|
| IMF | 5.8%. | January | 1.9%. | May | -4.50% | June | -10.30% | October | | |
| Fitch Ratings | 2% | 3 April | 1.8% | 20 April | 0.80% | 23 April | -5% | June | -10.50% | September |
| CII | -0.2% for April–June | | | | | | | | | |
| | 1.5% to -0.9% in May | | | | | | | | | |
| Goldman | -11.80% | earlier | -14.80% | September | | | | | | |
| India Ratings & Research | -5.30% | earlier | -11.80% | September | | | | | | |
| State Bank of India | -6.80% | earlier | -10.90% | September | | | | | | |

Source: Various Newspapers

**Table IV.3**
NAS Sectors Production during and after Lockdown

| Sector | Weight in GVA | Contribution in April | | Post lockdown, June | | Post lockdown, September | |
|---|---|---|---|---|---|---|---|
| | | Contribution of sector to GVA | Note | Contribution of sector to GVA | Note | Contribution of sector to GVA | Note |
| 1 Agriculture, forestry and fishing | 14.9 | 11 | Agri price collapse and no forestry and fishing | 12 | Agri farm prices weak and forestry and fishing revive | 14 | Demand strengthens |
| 2 Mining and quarrying | 3 | 0 | No activity | 1 | Activity begins | 2 | Activity improves |
| 3 Manufacturing | 18 | 1 | Only essential items | 3 | Some non-essential items revive | 10 | Demand for non-essential items rises |
| 4 Electricity, gas, water supply and other utility services | 2.2 | 1.5 | Energy consumption down at least 30% | 2 | Energy consumption increases | 2 | Utilities pick up |
| 5 Construction | 8 | 0 | No activity | 2 | Activity starts | 4 | Activity improves |

| | | | April | | June | | September |
|---|---|---|---|---|---|---|---|
| 6 | Trade, repair, hotels and restaurants | 12.6 | 2 | Only essential trade | 4 | Trade increases but little of hotels and restaurants | 8 | Trade improves but little of hotels and restaurants |
| 7 | Transport, storage, etc. | 6.5 | 1 | Some communication | 3 | Transport and storage start | 5 | Transport and storage further improves |
| 8 | Financial services | 6 | 2 | Limited services | 3 | Services increase | 5 | Services improve |
| 9 | Real estate, etc. | 15.9 | 2 | Only ownership of dwellings | 4 | Activity starts | 11 | Activity improves |
| 10 | Public admin. and defence | 5.6 | 3.5 | Limited essential services | 4 | Services increase | 5 | Services improve further |
| 11 | Other services | 7.2 | 1 | Limited services | 2 | More services | 4 | More services pick up |
| | **Total** | 100 | 25 | | 40 | | 70 | |

Source: NAS 2019. p. 23. data for 2017–18

Note: GVA at Constant 2011–12 prices

April: It is assumed that the entire unorganized sector, 31% of GDP stopped working during lockdown. About 25% of organized sector worked.

June: It is assumed that the entire unorganized sector, 31% of GDP remains shut post lockdown

So, of the organized sector, 55% of GDP, 28% of GDP works. Or, 50% of organized sector worked

September: It is assumed that half the unorganized sector,16% of GDP starts work

So, of the organized sector, 55% of GDP, 40% of GDP works. About 75% of organized sector worked

**Table IV.4**

Daily Arrival of Fruits and Vegetables (in Tonnes) in Azadpur Mandi, Delhi, April–May 2017–2020

| | Month & Year | Fruits | Vegetables | Total |
|---|---|---|---|---|
| 1 | April 2017 | 197146.20 | 178814.40 | 375960.60 |
| 2 | 1–9 May 2017 | 63706.04 | 51435.03 | 115141.06 |
| 3 | April 2018 | 156612.50 | 181286.90 | 337899.40 |
| 4 | 1–9 May 2018 | 50708.80 | 53606.03 | 104314.83 |
| 5 | April 2019 | 172302.20 | 167762.40 | 340064.60 |
| 6 | 1–9 May 2019 | 55132.00 | 48066.10 | 103198.10 |
| 7 | April 2020 | 81046.40 | 112119.90 | 193166.30 |
| 8 | 1–9 May 2020 | 36362.30 | 22492.70 | 58855.00 |
| 9 | Percentage decrease in April 2020 arrival in comparison to April 2017 | 58.89 | 37.30 | 48.62 |
| 10 | Percentage decrease in May 2020 arrival in comparison to May 2017 | 42.92 | 56.27 | 48.88 |
| 11 | Percentage decrease in April 2020 arrival in comparison to April 2018 | 48.25 | 38.15 | 42.83 |
| 12 | Percentage decrease in May 2020 arrival in comparison to May 2018 | 28.29 | 58.04 | 43.58 |
| 13 | Percentage decrease in April 2020 arrival in comparison to April 2019 | 52.96 | 33.17 | 43.20 |
| 14 | Percentage decrease in May 2020 arrival in comparison to May 2019 | 34.05 | 53.20 | 42.97 |

Source: Bharat Krishak Samaj

**Table IV.5**

Total Arrival of Fruits and Vegetables (in Quintals) in Punjab Mandis

| Sr. No | | 2019 | 2020 |
|---|---|---|---|
| 1 | March | 2855987 | 2138476 |
| 2 | April | 2340239 | 1186569 |
| 3 | May | 2437975 | 547174 (Data available for only 13 districts) |
| | Total | 7634201 | 3872219 |

Source: Compiled by Bharat Krishak Samaj

Note: Total Number of Districts in Punjab is 22

**Table IV.6**

Kharif MSP vs Market Price of Major Crops for FY 2019–20 and 2020–21 (in Rs/Quintal)

| No | Crops | MSP FY 19–20 | MSP FY 20–21 | Market Price (April 2020) |
|---|---|---|---|---|
| 1 | Maize | 1760 | 1,850 | 1000 |
| 2 | Tur (Arhar) | 5800 | 6,000 | 5200 |
| 3 | Sunflower Seed | 5650 | 5,885 | 3800 |
| 4 | Soya Bean (Yellow) | 3710 | 3,880 | 3500 |
| 5 | Niger Seed | 5490 | 6,695 | 4600 |
| 6 | Cotton (Med. Staple) | 5255 | 5,515 | 4000 |
| 7 | Cotton (Long Staple) | 5550 | 5,825 | 4200 |

Source: Compiled by Bharat Krishak Samaj

**Table IV.7**

Amount of Loans in Some Sectors Stressed by the Pandemic

72% of the banking-sector debt is to industry

Least-impacted sectors: Pharma, telecom, IT, FMCG, brokerage services, agri and food processing, sugar and fertilizer.

Most impacted sectors: Tourism, hotels, restaurants, construction, real estate, aviation, shipping, media and entertainment.

**(Rs lakh crore)**

| Sectors | Newly Stressed | Stressed from Before | Total Stressed |
|---|---|---|---|
| Corporate sector debt | 15.52 | 22.2 | 37.72 |
| Retail trade and wholesale trade | 5.42 | | |
| Roads sector | 1.94 | | |
| Textile sector | 1.89 | | |
| Engineering | 1.18 | | |
| Petroleum & coal production | 0.73 | | |
| Ports | 0.64 | | |
| Cements | 0.57 | | |
| Chemicals | 0.54 | | |
| Hotels & restaurants | 0.46 | | |

Source: Mathew and Verma. (2020).

https://indianexpress.com/article/explained/explained-what-rbi-expert-panel-has-recommended-for-one-time-loan-recast-6591195/ (accessed on 12 September 2020)

**Table V.1**

Increased Government Expenditures in Select Countries and IMF Data on Fiscal Deficit

| Country | Additional expenditure planned as % of GDP | Fiscal Deficit as % of GDP (IMF data) 2020 | |
|---|---|---|---|
| | June | April | October |
| Brazil | 11.8 | -9.3 | -16.8 |
| China | 7 | -11.2 | -11.9 |
| France | 5 | -9.2 | -10.8 |
| Germany | 8.9 | -5.5 | -8.2 |
| India | 6.9 | -7.4 | -13.1 |
| Indonesia | 4.4 | -5 | -6.3 |
| Japan | 21.1 | -7.1 | -14.2 |
| Russia | 3.4 | -4.8 | -5.3 |
| USA | 13.2 | -15.4 | -18.7 |

Source: Value of COVID-19 fiscal stimulus packages in G20 countries as of June 2020, as a share of GDP
https://www.statista.com/statistics/1107572/covid-19-value-g20-stimulus-packages-share-gdp/ (accessed on 31 July 2020)

IMF data from IMF Fiscal Monitor

**Table V.2**

GDP (Official) and Centre's Fiscal Deficit for April–July 2020
(In lakh crore at current prices)

| | | |
|---|---|---|
| GDP (official) for Q1 2021 | 38.08 | |
| GDP estimated for July 2020 | 16.2 | 1/9 of GDP for balance of year assuming 10% fall in GDP |
| Current GDP for Q1 + July | 54.28 | |
| Fiscal Deficit for April to July at Expected GDP for this period | 8.2% | |
| % of actual GDP for this period | 11.33% | |

Source: Government Press Note and News Papers

Note: GDP for April to July would be 1/3 of Rs 225 lakh crore (expected) or Rs 75 lakh crore.

So, Rs 6.15 lakh crore of deficit would be 8.2%.

Rs 6.15 lakh crore of Rs 54.28 lakh crore is 11.33%

## Table V.3

GDP and its Macro Aggregates at Current Prices for 2017–18 and Calculation for 2020–21

| Variable | Amount in Rs Crore in 2017–18 | % of GDP | GDP 2020–21 % | | |
|---|---|---|---|---|---|
| | | | drop by | net | new share |
| GDP | 170,95,005 | 100 | 29.0 | 71.0 | 100 |
| Pvt. Final Consumption | 100,83,121 | 58.98 | 8.75 | 50.2 | 70.7 |
| Gross Capital Formation | 50,70,703 | 29.66 | 20.25 | 9.4 | 13.2 |
| Govt. Total Exp. | 21,89,892 | 12.8 | 12.8 | 18.0 | |
| Govt. Cap. Formation | 4,53,579 | 2.65 | 2.65 | 3.7 | |
| Subsidy | 3,51,614 | 2.05 | 2.05 | 2.9 | |
| Current Transfers | 5,16,152 | 3.02 | 3.02 | 4.3 | |
| Salaries, etc. | 5,85,722 | 3.43 | 3.43 | 4.8 | |

Source: NAS, 2019 and Own Calculations.

Note: Gross Capital formation includes government capital formation
So, when adding up this has to be taken out of government total expenditure
Capital formation will be in select sectors which are near full capacity such as FMCG & Medical
It is taken to be zero in all other sectors.
If 25% of the economy (as in 2019–20) is working in lockdown that is the share of essentials
The private investment of 27%, will drop to 25% of the 2019-2020 value or to 6.75%, that is, a drop by 20.25%.
Private final consumption will also drop due to fall in incomes. It will be the difference between the GDP and the capital formation in the new situation.

# Graphs

**Graph 01**

Daily Confirmed New Cases (7-Day Moving Average)
Outbreak evolution for US, India, Brazil, UK, Italy and France from
February to October

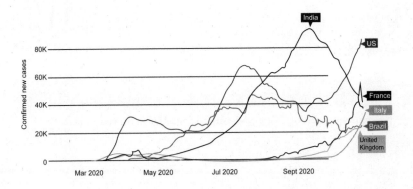

Source: Johns Hopkins University of Medicine, Coronavirus Resource Centre
https://coronavirus.jhu.edu/data/new-cases (accessed on 2 November 2020)

## Graph 02

Quarterly Growth Rates of Select Major Economies 2020

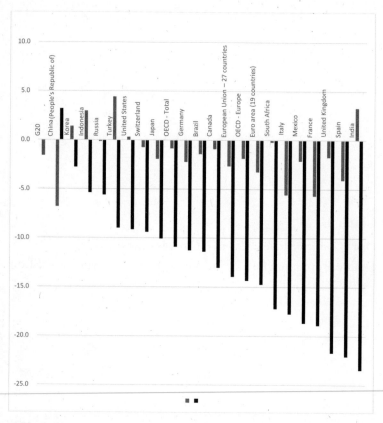

Data extracted on 12 September 2020, 06:23 UTC (GMT) from OECD.Stat

Source: https://stats.oecd.org/index.aspx?queryid=350#

## Graph 03

Quarterly Growth Rates (Year on Year) of Indian Economy, from 2012 to 2021 Q1

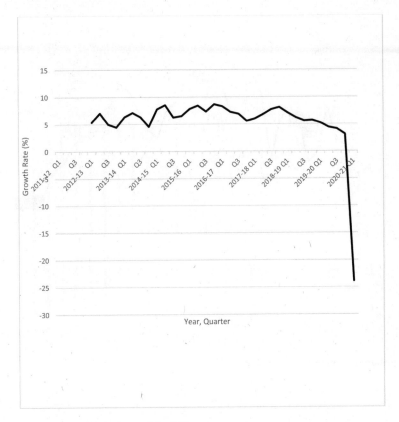

Source: Economic Survey and the RBI

## Graph 04

Quarterly Growth Rates (Year on Year) of Indian Economy, from 2012 to 2020 Q4 and Their Trend

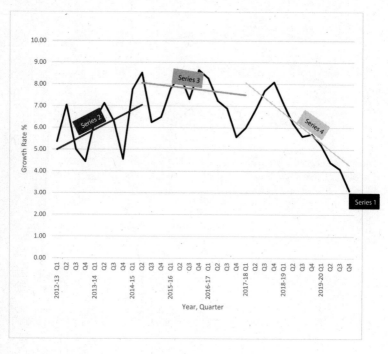

Source: Economic Survey and the RBI

## Graph 05

Quarterly GDP Growth Rate (Initial and Corrected) 2017-20

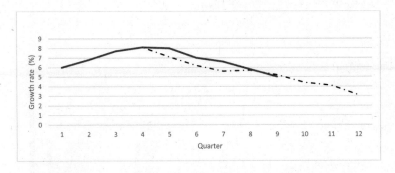

Source: RBI (2019), Monetary Policy Report, October and GoI (2020)
http://www.mospi.gov.in/sites/default/files/press_release/PRESS%20NOTE%20
PE%20and%20Q4%20estimates%20of%20GDP.pdf (accessed on 17 September
2020)

## Graph 06

Tests per Hundred Thousand People in Select Countries on 1 August 2020.

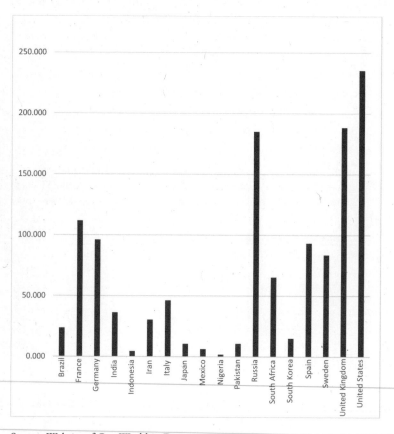

Source: Website of Our World in Data
https://ourworldindata.org/grapher/daily-tests-per-thousand-people-smoothed-7-day?time=2020-03-16 (accessed on 6 August 2020)

## Graph I.1.1

Infections in Case of Select Countries from March to Mid-July

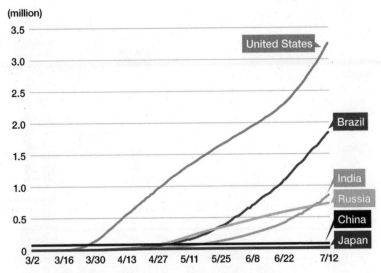

Created by *Nippon.com* based on data from the Ministry of Health, Labor, and Welfare. Dates are for MHLW announcements.

Source: Coronavirus Cases by Country. https://www.nippon.com/en/japan-data/h00673/ (accessed on 31 July 2020)

## Graph I.1.2

Infections in Case of Select Countries from March to Mid-June

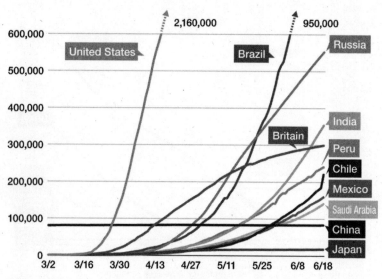

Created by *Nippon.com* based on data from the Ministry of Health, Labor, and Welfare. Dates are for MHLW announcements.

Source: Coronavirus Cases by Country. https://www.nippon.com/en/japan-data/h00673/ (accessed on 31 July 2020)

## Graph I.1.3

Infections in Case of Select Countries from March to Mid-May

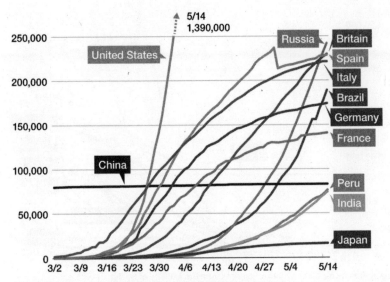

Created by *Nippon.com* based on data from the Ministry of Health, Labor, and Welfare. Dates are for MHLW announcements.

Source: Coronavirus Cases by Country. https://www.nippon.com/en/japan-data/ h00673/ (accessed on 31 July 2020)

## Graph I.1.4

Infections in Case of Select Countries from March to Mid-April

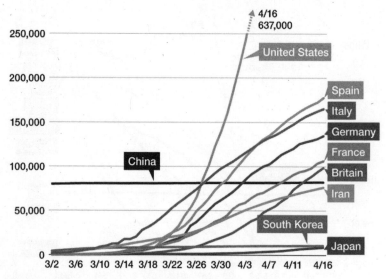

Created by *Nippon.com* based on data from the Ministry of Health, Labor, and Welfare. Dates are for MHLW announcements.

Source: Coronavirus Cases by Country. https://www.nippon.com/en/japan-data/h00673/. (accessed on 31 July 2020)

## Graph I.1.5

Infections in Case of Select Countries from the Beginning of March to mid-March

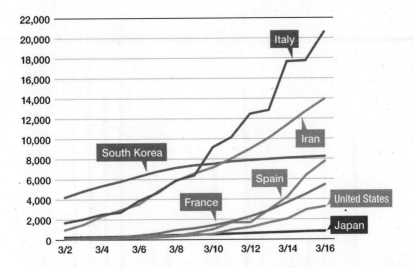

Dates are for Ministry of Health, Labor, and Welfare announcements.

Source: Coronavirus Cases by Country. https://www.nippon.com/en/japan-data/h00673/. (accessed on 31 July 2020)

## Graph I.2

Total Confirmed Deaths/Million up to 5 August 2020

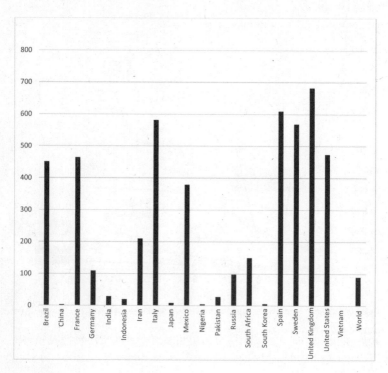

Source: Website: Our World in Data
https://ourworldindata.org/grapher/total-daily-covid-deaths-per-million   (accessed
on 6 August 2020)

## Graph III.1

Rates of Growth of the Indian Economy in FY 2020–21, compared to 2019–20

Under Different Assumptions about Recovery

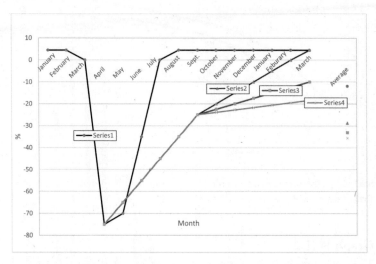

Note: In March, just before the lockdown, growth is 0%; in April at -75% and in May at -70% compared to January 2020.

During recovery, it is assumed that there is a steady rise.

Assumptions underlying the different trajectories and the average rate of growth in 2020–21.

| | |
|---|---|
| Series 1: V shaped Recovery after 2 months and back to January 2020 in 4 months. | Av: -12% |
| Series 2: U shaped Recovery after 2 months and back to January 2020 in 10 months. | Av: -28.79% |
| Series 3: U shaped Recovery after 2 months and back to January 2020 in 16 months. | Av: -33.13% |
| Series 4: U shaped Recovery after 2 months and back to January 2020 in 22 months. | Av: -35.58% |

## Graph IV.1.1

COVID-19 Cases Reported from 1 March to July End

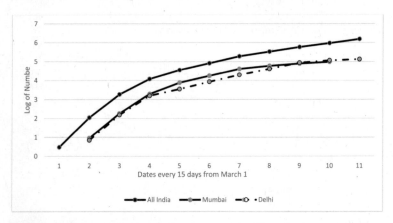

Sources: Data Compiled by IndiaSpend from Ministry of Health & Family Welfare, Brihanmumbai Municipal Corporation

## Graph IV.1.2

Total Recoveries Reported from 1 March to July End

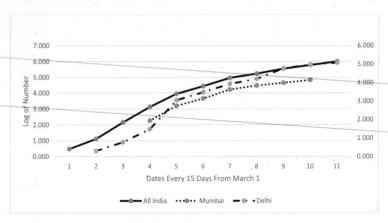

Source: Data Compiled by IndiaSpend from Ministry of Health & Family Welfare, Brihanmumbai Municipal Corporation

## Graph IV.1.3

Deaths Reported from 1 March to July End

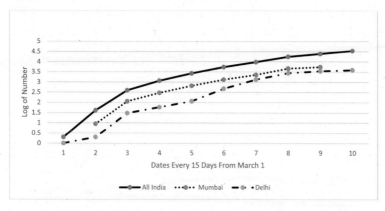

Source: Data Compiled by IndiaSpend from Ministry of Health & Family Welfare,
Brihanmumbai Municipal Corporation

## Graph IV.1.4

Total Cases, Recoveries and Active Cases

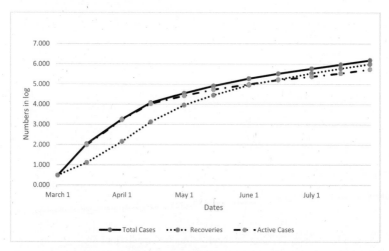

Source: Data Compiled by IndiaSpend from Ministry of Health & Family Welfare,
Brihanmumbai Municipal Corporation

## Graph IV.2

Five-Week Trend of Active Cases in Select States in June–July

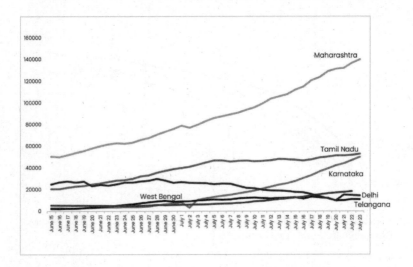

Source: https://covidindia.org/ (accessed on 25 July 2020)

## Graph IV.3

Deaths Per Million on 5 August 2020

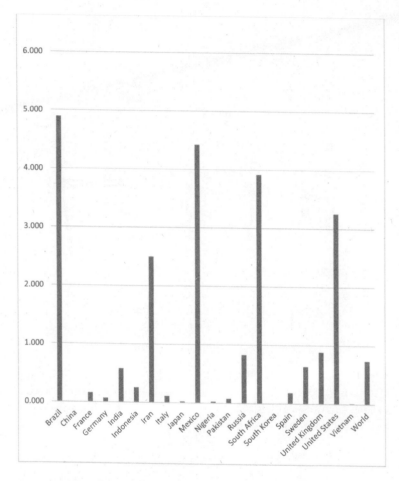

Source: Website: Our World in Data
https://ourworldindata.org/grapher/total-daily-covid-deaths-per-million (accessed on 6 August 2020)

## Graph V.1

GST Monthly Collection 2017–2020

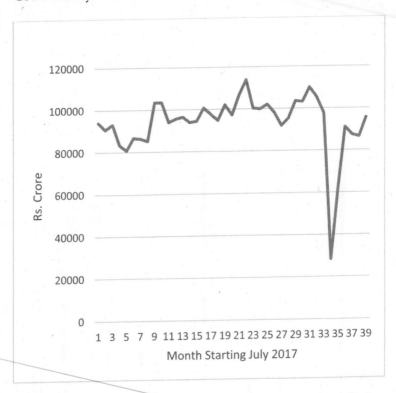

Source: Website GST India Typing. https://gst.indiatyping.com/gst-collection-monthly (accessed on 27 July 2020).
And, Ministry of Finance, Press Release, 1 October 2020

# Bibliography

AFP. (2020). 'Studies see "no benefit" in hydroxychloroquine treatment for Covid-19 patients', France 24 with AFP, 15 May, https://www.france24.com/en/20200515-studies-see-no-benefit-in-hydroxychloroquine-treatment-for-covid-19-patients (accessed on 2 August 2020).

All About History. (2020).'Spanish flu: The deadliest pandemic in history', LiveScience, 12 March, https://www.livescience.com/spanish-flu.html (accessed on 2 August 2020).

Anderson, J., Enrico Bergamini, Sybrand Brekelmans, Aliénor Cameron, Zsolt Darvas, Marta Domínguez Jíménez and Catarina Midões. (2020). 'The fiscal response to the economic fallout from the coronavirus', Bruegel.org, 16 July, https://www.bruegel.org/publications/datasets/covid-national-dataset/ (accessed on 31 July 2020).

BBC. (2020a). 'Coronavirus bailouts: Which country has the most generous deal?', 7 May , https://www.bbc.com/news/business-52450958 (accessed on 4 July 2020).

BBC. (2020b). 'Coronavirus: Chinese economy bounces back into growth', 16 July, https://www.bbc.com/news/business-53399999 (accessed on 3 August 2020).

Bilmes, L.J. (2020).'The Trump administration has made the US less ready for infectious disease outbreaks like coronavirus', The Conversation, 4 February, https://theconversation.com/the-trump-administration-has-made-the-us-less-ready-for-infectious-disease-outbreaks-like-coronavirus-130983 (accessed on 2 August 2020).

Biswas, S. (2020). 'Coronavirus: What India can learn from the deadly 1918 flu', BBC, 18 March, https://www.bbc.com/news/world-asia-india-51904019 (accessed on 2 August 2020).

Bloomberg. (2020). 'Economists are increasingly optimistic about China's economic recovery and GDP growth', *Fortune*, 23 June, https://fortune.com/2020/06/23/china-economy-recovery-2020-gdp-growth-economists/ (accessed on 24 June 2020).

Bowles, S., Gordon, D.M. & Weisskopf, T.E. (1984). *Beyond the Wasteland: A Democratic Alternative to Economic Decline* (London: Verso).

BusinessLine Bureau. (2020). '"On ventilator mode": 20 per cent of traders may shut shop permanently, warns CAIT', *BusinessLine*, 5 May, https://www.thehindubusinessline.com/economy/covid-19-impact-20-per-cent-of-traders-may-shut-shop-permanently-warns-cait/article31509287.ece (accessed on 8 June 2020).

Business Standard. (2020). 'Bigger reforms coming, we'll see a V-shaped recovery: CEA Subramanian', 14 May, https://www.business-standard.com/article/economy-policy/fiscal-stimulus-one-third-of-govt-plans-more-reforms-coming-cea-120051301784_1.html (accessed on 5 June 2020).

Business Today. (2020). 'Coronavirus: CII recommends stimulus package of Rs 15 lakh crore to help MSMEs, poor', 12 May, https://www.businesstoday.in/current/economy-politics/coronavirus-cii-recommends-stimulus-package-of-rs-15-lakh-crore-to-help-msmes-poor/story/403264.html (accessed on 8 June 2020).

CDC. (2020). 'Interim Clinical Guidance for Management of Patients with Confirmed Coronavirus Disease (COVID-19)', 30 June, https://www.cdc.gov/coronavirus/2019-ncov/hcp/clinical-guidance-management-patients.html, (accessed on 2 August 2020).

Centre for Sustainable Employment, Azim Premji University. (2020). 'COVID19: Analysis of Impact and Relief Measures', https://cse.azimpremjiuniversity.edu.in/covid19-analysis-of-impact-and-relief-measures/ (accessed on 4 June 2020).

Chhibber, M. (2020). 'How lockdown has hit judiciary, in numbers—April cases fall to 82k from 14 lakh avg in 2019', *The Print*, 4 May, https://theprint.in/judiciary/how-lockdown-has-hit-judiciary-in-numbers-april-cases-fall-to-82k-from-14-lakh-avg-in-2019/413666/ (accessed on 29 July 2020).

Cunningham, A. (2020). 'Antibodies from former COVID-19 patients could become a medicine', ScienceNewsforStudents, 15 April, https://www.sciencenewsforstudents.org/article/antibodies-covid-19-recovered-patients-treatment (accessed on 16 June 2020).

Davidson, P. (2020). '1.5M more workers file for unemployment even as many Americans return to work amid COVID-19', *USA Today*, 11 June, https://www.usatoday.com/story/money/2020/06/11/jobless-claims-report-another-million-file-unemployment-coronavirus/5338163002/ (accessed on 3 August 2020).

Diamond, J. (1998). *Guns, Germs, and Steel* (London: Vintage).

ENS Economic Bureau. (2020a). 'Unemployment rate soars to 27.11% amid COVID-19 pandemic: CMIE', *The Indian Express*, 6 May, https://indianexpress.com/article/business/unemployment-rate-soars-to-27-11-amid-covid-19-pandemic-cmie-6395714/ (accessed on 8 June 2020).

ENS Economic Bureau. (2020b). 'Amid deteriorating finances, India Inc's credit profile continues to worsen', *The Indian Express*, 13 July, https://indianexpress.com/article/business/amid-deteriorating-finances-india-incs-credit-profile-continues-to-worsen-6502673/ (accessed on 9 November 2020).

ET Bureau. (2020a). 'Green Shoots of Revival Seen', *Economic Times*, 24 June.

ET Bureau. (2020b). 'Core Sector Contraction Slows Down in May', *Economic Times*, 1 July.

Eurostat Statistics Explained. (2020). Weekly death statistics. https://ec.europa.eu/eurostat/statistics-explained/index.php?title=Weekly_death_statistics&stable#Dramatic_rise_in_deaths_in_early_spring (accessed on 10 October 2020).

Express News Service. (2020). 'The Rs 20-lakh crore package announced by FM Sitharaman', *The Indian Express*, 18 May, https://indianexpress.com/article/business/economy/nirmala-sitharaman-economic-relief-package-coronavirus-lockdown-6415253/ (accessed on 19 May 2020).

Gandhi, M. K. (1909). *Hind Swaraj: Or Indian Home Rule* (Ahmedabad: Navajivan Press).

Giattino, C., Hannah Ritchie, Max Roser, Esteban Ortiz-Ospina and Joe Hasell. (2020). Excess mortality during the Coronavirus pandemic

(COVID-19). Our World in Data. 9 October. https://ourworldindata.org/excess-mortality-covid. Accessed 11 October 2020.

GoI, Ministry of Statistics and Programme Implementation, National Statistical Office. (2019). *National Accounts Statistics–2019.*

GoI, Ministry of Finance, Union Budget, (2020a). *Budget at a Glance, 2020–21.*

GoI, Ministry of Statistics & Programme Implementation, National Statistical Office. (2020b). *Press Note on Provisional Estimates of Annual National Income 2019–2020 and Quarterly Estimates of Gross Domestic Product for the Fourth Quarter (Q4) of 2019–2020'*, 29 May, http://www.mospi.gov.in/sites/default/files/press_release/PRESS%20NOTE%20PE%20and%20Q4%20estimates%20of%20GDP.pdf (accessed on 27 June 2020).

GoI, Ministry of Health and Family Welfare, Directorate General of Health Services, Central Bureau of Health Intelligence. (2020c). *National Health Profile 2019*, http://www.cbhidghs.nic.in/showfile.php?lid=1147 (accessed on 11 November 2020).

GoI, Ministry of Statistics & Programme Implementation, National Statistical Office. (2020d). Press Note on Estimates of Gross Domestic Product for The First Quarter (April-June) Of 2020-21. 31 August. http://www.mospi.gov.in/sites/default/files/press_release/PRESS_NOTE-Q1_2020-21.pdf (accessed 31 August, 2020).

Grenfell, R. and T. Drew. (2020). 'Here's why the WHO says a coronavirus vaccine is 18 months away', *The Conversation*, 14 February, https://theconversation.com/heres-why-the-who-says-a-coronavirus-vaccine-is-18-months-away-131213 (accessed on 28 July 2020).

GST India Typing. (2020). 'GST Monthly Collection'. https://gst.indiatyping.com/gst-collection-monthly. (accessed 27 July 2020).

HT Correspondent. (2020). 'Coronavirus update: Rs 500 for 3 months, free cylinders to benefit poor women amid lockdown', *Hindustan Times*, 27 March, https://www.hindustantimes.com/india-news/500-for-3-months-free-cylinders-to-benefit-poor-women/story-kdHIqBtzMSoqmkVFks4OqJ.html (accessed on 5 July 2020).

IANS. (2020). 'India's richest 1% holds over 40% of national wealth: Report', Livemint, 20 January, https://www.livemint.com/news/india/india-s-richest-1-holds-over-40-of-national-wealth-report-11579534691272.html (accessed on 7 July 2020).

Jha, D.K. and T.E. Narasimhan. (2020). 'Coronavirus impact: Textile companies fear FY21 will be a washout', *Business Standard*, 18 May, https://www.business-standard.com/article/companies/coronavirus-impact-textile-companies-fear-fy21-will-be-a-washout-120051601301_1.html (accessed on 30 July 2020).

Kalecki, M. (1971). *Selected Essays on Dynamics of the Capitalist Economy* (Cambridge: Cambridge University Press).

Keynes, J.M. (1936). *The General Theory of Employment, Interest and Money*, 1976 edition (London: Macmillan Press for Royal Economic Society).

Kirsch, N. (2020). 'Tracker: Media Layoffs, Furloughs and Pay Cuts Due to Coronavirus', *Forbes*, 6 April, https://www.forbes.com/sites/noahkirsch/2020/04/06/tracker-media-layoffs-furloughs-and-pay-cuts/#2be32a9652f0 (accessed on 25 June 2020).

Kumar, A. (2020). 'Pandemic leaves Uttarakhand's pilgrimage industry gasping', *The Hindu*, 18 July, https://www.thehindu.com/news/national/other-states/pandemic-chokes-pilgrimage-industry-in-uttarakhand/article32124742.ece (accessed on 11 November 2020).

Kumar, A. (1988). 'Budget 198889: Diminishing Returns of Unchanged Fiscal Policy Regime', *Economic and Political Weekly*, Vol. 23, Issue No. 14–15, 26 March.

-------. (1994). 'Proposals for a Citizens Union Budget for the Nation for 1994–95. An Alternative to the FundBank Dictated Union Budget for 199495', Mimeo. Presented to the Citizens' Committee on 12 February 1994 at Gandhi Peace Foundation, New Delhi. Prepared for the Preparatory Committee for Alternative Economic Policies.

------. (1999). *The Black Economy in India* (New Delhi: Penguin India).

-----. (2006). 'The Flawed Macro Statistics: Overestimated Growth and Underestimated Inflation' in Alternative Survey Group (ed.) *Alternative Economic Survey, India 2005-06: Disempowering Masses*, (New Delhi: Daanish Books), pp. 29–44.

-----. (2009). 'Global Financial Crisis and Government Intervention: Surplus Generation, Gearing Ratio, Asymmetry of Financial Multiplier and Other Considerations', *Accountancy Business and the Public Interest*, Vol. 8, No. 1, 3 February, http://visar.csustan.edu/aaba/aabajourVol8-No1.html (accessed in 2009).

-----. (2013). *The Indian Economy Since Independence: Persisting Colonial Disruption* (New Delhi: Vision Books).

-----. (2018). *Demonetization and the Black Economy* (Gurugram: Penguin Random House India).

-----. (2019a). *Ground Scorching Tax* (Gurugram: Penguin Random House India).

-----. (2019b). 'Finding an Alternative: The Structurally Flawed GST', *Economic and Political Weekly*, Vol. 54, Issue No. 9, 2 March, https://www.epw.in/journal/2019/9/perspectives/structurally-flawed-gst.html (accessed on 11 November 2020).

-----. (2019c). 'The Gathering Storm: The Government in Denial amid a Deepening Economic Crisis', *The Caravan*, 1 November, https://caravanmagazine.in/commentary/government-denial-deepening-economic-crisis (accessed on 11 November 2020).

-----. (2020a). '"Economic uncertainty rises', *The Hindu*, 12 March, https://www.thehindu.com/opinion/op-ed/economic-uncertainty-rises/article31043565.ece?homepage=true#comments_31043565 (accessed on 11 November 2020).

-----. (2020b). 'COVID-19: The World needs to Prepare for an Economic Depression', *The Wire*, 23 March, https://thewire.in/economy/covid-19-world-economic-depression (accessed on 24 March 2020).

-----. (2020c). 'What Can Be Done to Ensure the Wheels Don't Come off the Indian Economy?', *The Wire*, 31 March, https://thewire.in/economy/indian-economy-covid-19-lockdown-policy (accessed on 11 November 2020).

-----. (2020d). 'Impact of COVID-19 and What Needs to Be Done', *Economic and Political Weekly*, Vol. 55, No. 14, 4 April, https://www.epw.in/journal/2020/14/commentary/impact-covid-19-and-what-needs-be-done.html (accessed on 11 November 2020).

-----. (2020e). 'The Pandemic is Changing the Face of Indian Labour', *The Wire*, 9 May, https://thewire.in/economy/covid-19-pandemic-indian-labour (accessed on 9 May 2020).

-----. (2020f). 'COVID 19 Crisis: Understanding the state of economy during and after lockdown', *Economic and Political Weekly*, Vol. 55, Issue No. 19, 9 May, https://www.epw.in/engage/article/covid-19-crisis-understanding-state-economy-during-and-after-lockdown (accessed on 11 November 2020).

-----. (2020g). 'Government's Package Is Not What Is Immediately Needed', *The Mainstream*, Vol. LVIII, No. 24, 30 May, http://mainstreamweekly.net/article9443.html (accessed on 9 June 2020).

-----. (2020h). 'The Pandemic and Lockdown Throws Up More Challenges in Measuring Employment and Work'. *The Wire*. 31 August. https://thewire.in/economy/covid-19-lockdown-employment-job-loss-work-india (accessed on 31 August 2020).

-----. (2020i). 'Macroeconomic Consequences of a Lockdown and Its Policy Implications'. *Economic and Political Weekly*. 26 September. Vol. 55, Issue No. 39.

Mathew, G. and S. Verma. (2020). 'Explained: What RBI expert panel recommends for one-time loan recast'. *The Indian Express*.https://indianexpress.com/article/explained/explained-what-rbi-expert-panel-has-recommended-for-one-time-loan-recast-6591195/ (accessed on 13 September 2020).

Mathur, A. (2020). 'Supreme Court gives relief to employers, says Centre cannot coerce to pay full wages, govt to reply in 4 weeks', *India Today*, 12 June, https://www.indiatoday.in/india/story/supreme-court-gives-relief-to-employers-no-full-payment-of-wages-1688172-2020-06-12 (accessed on 3 August 2020).

Medhi, T. (2020). 'From Ola, Uber to Swiggy, startups lay off employees due to coronavirus', *YourStory*, 7 June, https://yourstory.com/2020/06/ola-uber-swiggy-oyo-startups-lay-off-employees-coronavirus (accessed on 25 June 2020).

Nag, D. (2020). 'No mean feat! How did Indian Railways achieve 100% punctuality of passenger trains? Find out here', *Financial Express*, 3 July, https://www.financialexpress.com/infrastructure/railways/no-mean-feat-how-did-indian-railways-achieve-100-punctuality-of-passenger-trains-find-out-here/2012458/ (accessed on 28 July 2020).

Noronha, G. and D. Sikarwar. (2020). 'GDP will contract in the first quarter: KV Subramanian, CEA', *The Economic Times*, 6 May, https://economictimes.indiatimes.com/news/economy/finance/gdp-will-contract-in-the-first-quarter-kv-subramanian-cea/articleshow/75567696.cms (accessed on 5 August 2020).

Ott, M. (1987). 'The Growing Share of Services in the U.S. Economy-Degeneration or Evolution?', Federal Reserve Bank of St. Louis, June/July. https://files.stlouisfed.org/files/htdocs/publications/review/87/06/Growing_Jun_Jul1987.pdf (accessed on 18 June 2020).

Our World in Data, https://ourworldindata.org/grapher/total-daily-covid-deaths-per-million (accessed on 6 August 2020).

Pant, S. (2020). 'Industries look at January to return to full production', *The Times of India,* 24 June.

Pramanik, A. (2020). '8 out of 10 workers lost jobs in urban India during lockdown: Azim Premji University survey', *The Economic Times,* 12 May, https://economictimes.indiatimes.com/jobs/8-out-of-10-workers-lost-jobs-in-urban-india-during-lockdown-azim-premji-university-survey/articleshow/75701810.cms#:~:text=BENGALURU%3A%20Eight%20out%20of%2010,Azim%20Premji%20University%20(APU).&text=It%20covered%20self%2Demployed%2C%20casual%2C,and%20regular%20wage%2Fsalaried%20workers (accessed on 4 June 2020).

PTI (2020a). 'Post-Covid, India will have V-shaped recovery: Subbarao', *BusinessLine,* 26 April, https://www.thehindubusinessline.com/economy/post-covid-india-will-have-v-shaped-recovery-subbarao/article31437294.ece (accessed on 5 June 2020).

PTI. (2020b). 'Coronavirus Outbreak: Leather goods exporters stare at 40-50% dip in shipments in FY21; govt yet to give any major relief measures', *Firstpost,* 14 May, https://www.firstpost.com/business/coronavirus-outbreak-leather-goods-exporters-stare-at-40-50-dip-in-shipments-in-fy21-govt-yet-to-give-any-major-relief-measures-8369191.html (accessed on 30 July 2020).

PTI. (2020c). '"Can't Monitor" Movement of Migrant Workers, States Should Take Action: Supreme Court', *The Wire,* 15 May, https://thewire.in/law/migrant-workers-movement-supreme-court (accessed on 1 August 2020).

PTI. (2020d). 'Donald Trump to charge tax on companies manufacturing outside US', *The Economic Times,* 15 May, https://economictimes.indiatimes.com/news/international/business/donald-trump-to-charge-tax-on-companies-manufacturing-outside-us/articleshow/75753601.cms (accessed on 1 August 2020).

Reed, J.R. (2019). 'President Trump ordered US firms to ditch China, but many already have and more are on the way', CNBC, 1 September, https://www.cnbc.com/2019/09/01/trump-ordered-us-firms-to-ditch-china-but-many-already-have.html (accessed on 1 August 2020).

RBI. (2019). *Monetary Policy Report,* Various Issues.

RBI. (2020). *Financial Stability Report,* Issue No. 21. July.

Saini, M. (2020). 'Haryana's industrial power consumption decreases by 55%', *The Times of India*, 24 June, https://timesofindia.indiatimes. com/city/chandigarh/haryana-industrial-power-use-falls-55/ articleshow/76540039.cms (accessed on 11 November 2020).

Saluja, N. (2020). 'Over one-third MSMEs start shutting shop as recovery amid Covid-19 looks unlikely: AIMO survey', *The Economic Times*. 2 June, https://economictimes.indiatimes.com/small-biz/sme-sector/ over-one-third-msmes-start-shutting-shop-as-recovery-amid-covid-19- looks-unlikely-aimo-survey/articleshow/76141969.cms (accessed on 8 June 2020).

Scroll Staff. (2020).'Coronavirus lockdown: Here is a list of firms that have laid off employees or enforced pay cuts', *Scroll.in*, 20 May, https:// scroll.in/latest/962452/coronavirus-lockdown-ola-to-layoff-1400- employees-says-ceo (accessed on 25 June 2020).

Segal, S. and Dylan, G. (2020). Breaking down the G20 Covid-19 Fiscal Response', Centre for Strategic & International Studies, 30 April, https://www.csis.org/analysis/breaking-down-g20-covid-19-fiscal- response (accessed on 4 July 2020).

Shinde, R and S. Kadam. (2020). 'Consumer and services sectors cushion Q1 show, analysts expect a revival in the second half of the fiscal', *The Economic Times*, 27 July, https://economictimes.indiatimes.com/ industry/banking/finance/banking/consumer-and-services-sectors- cushion-q1-show/articleshow/77188366.cms?from=mdr (accessed on 11 November 2020).

Singh, B.K. (2020). 'As States Race to Woo MNCs Shifting Out of China With Labour Reforms, Will Bureaucracy Rise to Occasion?', *News18*, 10 May, https://www.news18.com/news/india/as-states-race-to-woo- mncs-shifting-out-of-china-with-labour-reforms-will-beaureacuracy- rise-to-the-occasion-2613531.html (accessed on 1 August 2020).

Statista. (2020). 'Distribution of gross domestic product (GDP) across economic sectors in the United States from 2000 to 2017', https://www. statista.com/statistics/270001/distribution-of-gross-domestic-product- gdp-across-economic-sectors-in-the-us/ (accessed on 18 June 2020).

Sundaram, A. (2020). 'Yelp data shows 60% of business closures due to the coronavirus pandemic are now permanent', *CNBC*, 16 September, https://www.cnbc.com/2020/09/16/yelp-data-shows-60percent- of-business-closures-due-to-the-coronavirus-pandemic-are-now-permanent.html?__source=sharebar|email&par=sharebar (accessed on 28 October 2020).

Tax Haven Team. (2014). 'Swiss Bank/Offshore Banks, Tax Havens, Hawala: Answers to Some Common Questions', Centre for Economic Studies and Planning, School of Social Sciences, Jawaharlal Nehru University, http://www.issin.org/pdf/swissbanking.pdf (accessed on 27 June 2020).

Tiwari, S. (2020). 'Gurugram: Ridership just 10%, Roadways battles Rs 200cr loss in lockdown', *The Times of India*, 25 July, https://timesofindia.indiatimes.com/city/gurgaon/ridership-just-10-roadways-battles-rs-200cr-loss-in-lockdown/articleshow/77044950.cms (accessed on 11 November 2020).

The Hindu Data Team. (2020). 'An estimated 12.2 crore Indians lost their jobs during the coronavirus lockdown in April: CMIE', *The Hindu*, 7 May, https://www.thehindu.com/data/data-over-12-crore-indians-lost-their-jobs-during-the-coronavirus-lockdown-in-april/article31520715.ece (accessed on 28 June 2020).

The Hindu Special Correspondent. (2020). 'Travel demand muted, some airlines may go under: CAPA', *The Hindu*, 4 July, https://www.thehindu.com/business/travel-demand-muted-some-airlines-may-go-under-capa/article31983849.ece (accessed on 11 November 2020).

The Hindu. (2020). 'Residential deals dip 54% in H1: report', 17 July, https://www.thehindu.com/business/residential-deals-dip-54-in-h1-report/article32106458.ece#:~:text=Home%20sales%20in%20eight%20cities,quarter%20of%20the%20calendar%20year. (accessed on 11 November 2020).

TNN. (2020a). 'These diseases kill many more than coronavirus', *The Times of India*, 17 March, https://timesofindia.indiatimes.com/india/these-diseases-kill-many-more-than-coronavirus/articleshow/74670863.cms (accessed on 15 June 2020).

TNN. (2020b). 'Factory output sees the sharpest contraction of 55.5% in April', *The Times of India*, 13 June, https://timesofindia.indiatimes.com/business/india-business/factory-output-sees-sharpest-contraction-of-55-5-in-april/articleshow/76351000.cms#:~:text=NEW%20DELHI%3A%20The%20country's%20industrial,deadly%20coronavirus%20halted%20economic%20activity (accessed on 11 November 2020).

TNN. (2020c). 'Factory output shrinks 35% but pace of decline narrows', *The Times of India*, 11 July, https://timesofindia.indiatimes.com/business/india-business/factory-output-shrinks-35-but-pace-of-decline-narrows/articleshow/76903073.cms (accessed on 11 November 2020).

TNN. (2020d). 'Average daily positivity rate now at 4-month low'. *The Times of India*. 14 October. https://timesofindia.indiatimes.com/india/covid-19-average-daily-positivity-rate-now-at-4-month-low/articleshow/78651067.cms (accessed on 15 October 2020).

Valinsky, J. (2020). 'Big chains filed for bankruptcy every week in May. Here are 6 of them', CNN Business, 29 May, https://edition.cnn.com/2020/05/29/business/may-bankruptcies-coronavirus/index.html (accessed on 25 June 2020).

Voytko, L. (2020). 'Coronavirus Layoffs: Boeing Lays Off 6,770 Workers Amid Pandemic', *Forbes*, 27 May, https://www.forbes.com/sites/lisettevoytko/2020/05/27/coronavirus-layoffs-boeing-lays-off-6770-workers-amid-pandemic/#3191f64145bd (accessed on 25 June 2020).

WHO. (2020a). 'Ebola virus disease', https://www.who.int/health-topics/ebola/#tab=tab_1 (accessed on 2 August 2020).

WHO. (2020b). 'WHO Director-General's opening remarks at the media briefing on COVID-19 - 16 March 2020', 16 March, https://www.who.int/dg/speeches/detail/who-director-general-s-opening-remarks-at-the-media-briefing-on-covid-19---16-march-2020 (accessed on 2 August 2020).

WHO. World Health Statistics 2015, Table 6, and World Health Statistics 2019.

Wikipedia. (2020a). 'Timeline of the COVID-19 pandemic in India', https://en.wikipedia.org/wiki/Timeline_of_the_COVID-19_pandemic_in_India (accessed on 27 June 2020).

Wikipedia. (2020b). 'List of countries by hospital beds', https://en.wikipedia.org/wiki/List_of_countries_by_hospital_beds (accessed on 27 June 2020).

Wikipedia. (2020c). 'List of countries and dependencies by number of physicians', https://en.wikipedia.org/wiki/List_of_countries_and_dependencies_by_number_of_physicians (accessed on 27 June 2020).

Williamson, J. (1989). 'What Washington Means by Policy Reform', in *Latin American Adjustment: How Much has Happened*, ed. J. Williamson (Washington: Institute for International Economics).

World Bank Data. (2020). https://data.worlddbank.org/indicator/ SH.MED.PHYS.ZS (accessed on 26 July 2020).

WTO. (2020). 'Trade in Services in the Context of Covid-19: Information Note', World Trade Organization, 28 May, https://www.wto.org/ english/tratop_e/covid19_e/services_report_e.pdf (accessed on 3 June 2020).